Concise Guide to Paralegal Ethics

ASPEN PUBLISHERS

Concise Guide to Paralegal Ethics

Therese A. Cannon
Executive Associate Director
Accrediting Commission for Senior Colleges
and Universities
Western Association of Schools and Colleges

Wolters Kluwer
Law & Business

AUSTIN   BOSTON   CHICAGO   NEW YORK   THE NETHERLANDS

Aspen Publishers
Attn: Permissions Department
76 Ninth Avenue, 7th Floor
New York, NY 10011-5201

To contact Customer Care, e-mail customer.care@aspenpublishers.com, call 1-800-234-1660, fax 1-800-901-9075, or mail correspondence to:

Aspen Publishers
Attn: Order Department
PO Box 990
Frederick, MD 21705

Printed in the United States of America.

3 4 5 6 7 8 9 0

ISBN 978-0-7355-7867-8

Library of Congress Cataloging-in-Publication Data

Cannon, Therese, A.
   Concise guide to paralegal ethics / Therese A. Cannon. — 3rd ed.
     p. cm.
   Includes bibliographical references and index.
   ISBN 978-0-7355-7867-8
   1. Legal ethics — United States.   2. Legal assistants — United States.   I. Title.
   KF320.L4C365 2010
   174'.30973 — dc22

                                      2009022998

About Wolters Kluwer Law & Business

Wolters Kluwer Law & Business is a leading provider of research information and workflow solutions in key specialty areas. The strengths of the individual brands of Aspen Publishers, CCH, Kluwer Law International and Loislaw are aligned within Wolters Kluwer Law & Business to provide comprehensive, in-depth solutions and expert-authored content for the legal, professional and education markets.

CCH was founded in 1913 and has served more than four generations of business professionals and their clients. The CCH products in the Wolters Kluwer Law & Business group are highly regarded electronic and print resources for legal, securities, antitrust and trade regulation, government contracting, banking, pension, payroll, employment and labor, and healthcare reimbursement and compliance professionals.

Aspen Publishers is a leading information provider for attorneys, business professionals and law students. Written by preeminent authorities, Aspen products offer analytical and practical information in a range of specialty practice areas from securities law and intellectual property to mergers and acquisitions and pension/benefits. Aspen's trusted legal education resources provide professors and students with high-quality, up-to-date and effective resources for successful instruction and study in all areas of the law.

Kluwer Law International supplies the global business community with comprehensive English-language international legal information. Legal practitioners, corporate counsel and business executives around the world rely on the Kluwer Law International journals, loose-leafs, books and electronic products for authoritative information in many areas of international legal practice.

Loislaw is a premier provider of digitized legal content to small law firm practitioners of various specializations. Loislaw provides attorneys with the ability to quickly and efficiently find the necessary legal information they need, when and where they need it, by facilitating access to primary law as well as state-specific law, records, forms and treatises.

Wolters Kluwer Law & Business, a unit of Wolters Kluwer, is head-quartered in New York and Riverwoods, Illinois. Wolters Kluwer is a leading multinational publisher and information services company.

This book is dedicated to the thousands of paralegals who work tirelessly to provide quality legal services to clients and who strive to make legal services more accessible.

Summary of Contents

Contents   **xi**
Preface   **xix**

1. Regulation of Lawyers and Paralegals   1
2. Unauthorized Practice of Law   17
3. Confidentiality   43
4. Conflicts of Interest   63
5. Advertising and Solicitation   89
6. Fees and Client Funds   105
7. Competence   133
8. Special Issues in Advocacy   153
9. Professionalism and Special Issues for Paralegals   177

Appendices
A. NALA Code of Ethics and Professional Responsibility   195
B. NFPA Model Code of Ethics and Professional
   Responsibility and Guidelines for Enforcement   199

Glossary   **211**
Index   **217**

Contents

Preface   *xix*

1. Regulation of Lawyers and Paralegals   1

A. Regulation of Lawyers   2
    1. State Courts and Bar Associations   2
    2. American Bar Association   2
    3. State Statutes, Ethics Opinions, and Case Law   3
    4. Sanctions and Remedies   4
B. Regulation of Paralegals   5
    1. A Brief History of the Paralegal Profession   5
    2. Direct Regulation of Paralegals: Certification
        and Licensing   7
        Definitions of Terms   7
        Regulation of Supervised Paralegals   8
        The Regulation Debate   9
        Nonlawyer Legal Service Providers   10
    3. State Guidelines for the Utilization of Paralegal Services   11
    4. Paralegal Association Codes of Ethics and Guidelines   12
    5. Responsibility of Lawyers and Paralegals for
        Paralegal Conduct   12
        Review Questions   13
        Hypotheticals   14
        Discussion Questions and Projects   15

	Selected Cases	15
	Selected References	16

2. Unauthorized Practice of Law   17

A.	A Brief History of the Unauthorized Practice of Law	18
B.	Trends in the Unauthorized Practice of Law	19
	1. Nonlawyer Legal Service Providers and Related Trends	19
	2. Multijurisdictional Practice Issues	21
C.	The Practice of Law Defined	21
D.	The Attorney's Responsibility to Prevent the Unauthorized Practice of Law	23
E.	What Constitutes the Unauthorized Practice of Law	24
	1. Making Court Appearances	24
	Depositions	24
	Pleadings	25
	Exceptions	26
	Administrative Agencies	26
	2. Establishing the Attorney-Client Relationship	28
	3. Giving Legal Advice	29
	A Few Examples	30
	Exceptions	31
	Nonlawyer Legal Service Providers and Related Trends	32
F.	Disclosure of Status as Paralegal and Job Titles	33
G.	A Word About Paralegals as Independent Contractors	35
	Review Questions	36
	Hypotheticals	37
	Discussion Questions and Projects	39
	Selected Cases	41
	Selected References	41

3. Confidentiality   43

A.	The Principle of Confidentiality	44
B.	Attorney-Client Privilege	44
	1. Defined Generally	44
	2. Disclosure of Privileged Information	45
	3. Matters Not Covered by the Privilege	45

	4.	Inadvertent Disclosure of Privileged Material	46
	5.	Exceptions to and Waivers of the Privilege	48
	6.	The Privilege in the Corporate Setting	49
	7.	Court-Ordered Disclosure	50
C.		The Work Product Rule	50
D.		Ethics Rules of Confidentiality	51
E.		Confidentiality and the Paralegal	52
	1.	Application of the Rule to Paralegals	52
	2.	Protecting Confidentiality in Daily Practice	53
	3.	Special Issues Relating to Technology	55
		Review Questions	58
		Hypotheticals	59
		Discussion Questions and Projects	60
		Selected Cases	61
		Selected References	62

4. Conflicts of Interest 63

A.		Introduction	64
B.		Conflicts Involving Representation of Clients	65
	1.	Concurrent Representation	65
		General Rules	65
		Consents	66
		Withdrawal to Avoid Conflicts	67
		Imputed Disqualification in Concurrent Conflicts	67
		Issue Conflicts and Other Indirect Concurrent Conflicts	67
		Examples of Conflicts in Litigated Matters	68
		Examples of Conflicts in Nonlitigated Matters	68
	2.	Successive Representation	70
		General Rules	70
		Defining "Substantial Relationship"	71
C.		Other Conflicts Rules	72
	1.	Business Transactions with Clients	72
	2.	Publication, Literary, and Media Rights	73
	3.	Financial Assistance to Clients	73
	4.	A Lawyer's Interest in Litigation	73
	5.	Gifts from Clients	74
	6.	Agreements with Clients Limiting Malpractice Liability	75
	7.	Payment of Attorney's Fees by a Third Party	76
	8.	Relatives of Lawyers	76
	9.	Sexual Relations with Clients	77

D. Imputed Conflicts and Disqualification   78
    1. General Rules   78
    2. Use of Screens   79
E. Conflicts Checks   82
        Review Questions   83
        Hypotheticals   85
        Discussion Questions and Projects   87
        Selected Cases   88
        Selected References   88

5. Advertising and Solicitation   89

A. Advertising   90
    1. The Advent and Evolution of Lawyer Advertising   90
    2. The Current Ethics Rules   92
    3. Current Issues and Trends in Lawyer Advertising   94
B. Solicitation   98
        Review Questions   100
        Hypotheticals   101
        Discussion Questions and Projects   102
        Selected Cases   103
        Selected References   104

6. Fees and Client Funds   105

A. Fee Arrangements with Clients   106
    1. Fixed Fees   106
    2. Contingency Fees   106
    3. Hourly Fees   107
B. Ethics Rules About Fees   109
C. Terms and Communication of Fee Arrangements
    with Clients   112
D. Statutory and Other Court-Awarded Fees   115
E. Fee Splitting and Referral Fees   118
F. Partnerships Between Lawyers and Nonlawyers   119
G. Client Funds and Property   120

	1. Client Trust Accounts	120
	Interest on Lawyers' Trust Accounts and Client Security Funds	121
	2. Other Client Property and Files	122
	Review Questions	124
	Hypotheticals	125
	Discussion Questions and Projects	127
	Selected Cases	130
	Selected References	131

7. Competence 133

A.	Introduction	134
B.	Legal Education	134
C.	Paralegal Education	135
D.	A Definition of Competence	137
	1. Knowledge	137
	2. Skills	138
	3. Thoroughness and Preparation	139
	4. Diligence and Promptness	139
	5. Communication with Clients	139
E.	Sanctions for Incompetence	140
F.	Trends in Legal Malpractice	141
G.	Factors Affecting Paralegal Competence	144
	Review Questions	147
	Hypotheticals	148
	Discussion Questions and Projects	149
	Selected Cases	151
	Selected References	152

8. Special Issues in Advocacy 153

A.	Introduction	154
B.	Unmeritorious Claims, Delay, and Discovery Abuse	155
C.	Disruption in the Courtroom and Disobeying Court Orders	158
D.	Candor and Honesty	159
E.	Relationships and Communications with Judges	161

F. Contact with Jurors   162
G. Contact with Parties and Represented Persons   163
H. Contact with Unrepresented Persons   164
I. Contact with Witnesses   164
J. Trial Publicity   166
K. Special Rules for Prosecutors   167
        Review Questions   168
        Hypotheticals   170
        Discussion Questions and Projects   172
        Selected Cases   174
        Selected References   175

9. Professionalism and Special Issues for Paralegals 177

A. The State of Professionalism in the Legal Field   178
B. Professionalization of the Paralegal Occupation   181
    1. Commitment to Public Service   183
    2. Commitment to Education   183
    3. Commitment to the Highest Standards of
        Ethical Conduct   184
    4. Commitment to Excellence   184
    5. Commitment to the Paralegal Profession   184
    6. Commitment to a Strong Work Ethic   184
    7. Commitment to Acting with Integrity and Honor   185
    8. Commitment to the Development of the Whole Person   185
    9. Commitment to Exercising Good Judgment, Common
        Sense, and Communication Skills   185
C. Current Issues in Professionalism   185
    1. Regulation   185
    2. Education   186
    3. Utilization and Treatment   186
    4. Exempt Status   187
    5. Gender, Race, and Related Issues   188
D. Pro Bono Work   189
        Review Questions   190
        Hypotheticals   191
        Discussion Questions   192
        Selected References   193

Appendices

A.   NALA Code of Ethics and Professional Responsibility   195
B.   NFPA Model Code of Ethics and Professional
     Responsibility and Guidelines for Enforcement   199

Glossary   **211**
Index   **217**

Preface

Approach

This book is written for paralegal students, working paralegals, and lawyers who employ paralegals. It is intended for use primarily as a text, but can be used as a reference manual by teachers and those in practice.

In the past 40 years, the paralegal occupation has truly come into its own. Its growth in numbers, its expansion into all areas of law practice and all sectors of the legal services industry, and its general acceptance by the legal community and the public are impressive. The occupation continues to evolve into a true profession. One of the most critical aspects of any profession is its adherence to an accepted code of ethics. Legal ethics is now taught in virtually every paralegal program in the country. Because of the diversity in paralegal education programs in terms of content, length, and format, ethics is treated in a wide variety of ways in the curriculum. A growing proportion of programs has a separate course on ethics, and many programs include ethics as a short segment in another required course, teach ethics across the curriculum, or do both.

This text is a concise version of *Ethics and Professional Responsibility for Paralegals*. This concise version covers all the same subject matter as the full version, but in an abbreviated format that can be adapted to short courses and to use in several different courses.

Organization and Coverage of the Concise Edition

The content of this book is comprehensive. It covers all the major areas of legal ethics, placing special emphasis on how the rules affect paralegals. It begins with a chapter on the regulation of lawyers and paralegals, covering ethics codes, disciplinary processes for lawyers, and the variety of ways in which paralegals are regulated both directly and indirectly. Unauthorized practice of law is covered in Chapter 2, including the definitions of the practice of law, detailed descriptions of functions that only lawyers are permitted to perform, and information on how UPL is evolving in view of the growing role of paralegals and nonlawyer legal service providers. Chapter 3 covers the duty of confidentiality and the attorney-client privilege, including common issues that arise in these areas and ways to prevent disclosure of confidential information, including recent developments related to the use of technology.

Chapter 4 covers conflicts of interest, demonstrating how conflicts rules apply to paralegals, including the use of screens and conflicts checks. Rules regarding legal advertising and solicitation are covered in Chapter 5. Chapter 6 is devoted to financial matters, including billing and fees, fee agreements, statutory fee awards that include compensation for paralegal work, fee splitting, referral fees, partnerships between attorneys and nonlawyers, and handling client funds. Chapter 7 defines the concept of competence specifically in relation to paralegals and includes a discussion of malpractice. Special issues confronted by litigation paralegals are covered in Chapter 8. Finally, Chapter 9 examines professionalism, issues facing paralegals in today's law firm environment, and pro bono work.

Key Features

Each chapter begins with an overview that lists the topics covered in the chapter. The text of each chapter is divided topically. Key terms are spelled out in italics when first introduced and key concepts are noted in bold. At the end of each chapter are a few hypothetical fact situations that require the students to apply the rules and concepts covered in the chapter. These may be used in class discussion or for assignments. Review questions that test each student's memory and understanding of the material and discussion questions that call for in-depth analysis, legal research, or factual investigation are also included. Selected references, including cases and ethics rules, are found at the very end of each chapter.

Recognizing that every paralegal program teaches ethics in its own way, the concise version has been designed for use in short ethics courses or short segments of courses where there is not enough time to use case analysis as a teaching methodology or to pursue in-depth analysis of the ethics rules, including the history and evolution of those rules. Hypotheticals were added in place of actual cases to provide a method for students to test their understanding of the material by synthesizing it and applying it in a new factual context. Discussion of specific sections of the ABA Model Code and Rules has been abbreviated, as has coverage of trends.

Acknowledgments

Many people must be thanked for their support and assistance: the American Association for Paralegal Education, National Association of Legal Assistants, National Federation of Paralegal Associations, International Paralegal Management Association, and the American Bar Association Standing Committee on Paralegals. Special thanks go to the many students I have had the pleasure of teaching and the paralegals who have shared their experiences with me. My deepest appreciation must be extended to the wonderful people at Aspen, especially Betsy Kenny, whose patience, warmth, intelligence, and talents made this book possible.

I would like to thank the following copyright holders who kindly granted their permission to reprint from the following materials.

National Association of Legal Assistants, Code of Ethics and Professional Responsibility. Copyright © 1975, Revised 1979, 1988, 1995, 2007. Reprinted by permission of the National Association of Legal Assistants, 1516 S. Boston #200, Tulsa, OK 74119.

National Federation of Paralegal Associations, Model Code of Ethics and Professional Responsibility. Copyright © 1993 by the National Federation of Paralegal Associations, Inc. All rights reserved. Reprinted by permission of the National Federation of Paralegal Associations, Inc.

Therese A. Cannon
June 2009

Concise Guide to Paralegal Ethics

Regulation of Lawyers and Paralegals

This chapter provides basic background on the regulation of lawyers and paralegals. Paralegals or legal assistants, who work under the supervision of lawyers, need to understand the rules governing lawyer conduct and how those rules affect them. Also covered is a brief history of the paralegal profession and an explanation of how paralegals are regulated directly and indirectly by the states in which they work. Included is an overview of voluntary professional associations for paralegals and certification programs. Chapter 1 covers:

- the inherent power of the courts over the practice of law
- the organized bar's participation in lawyer regulation
- the role of the legislature and state statutes in governing the conduct of lawyers
- the American Bar Association and its influence on legal ethics
- the evolution of the paralegal profession
- professional associations for paralegals
- the status of paralegal regulation
- the distinctions among certification, licensing, and limited licensing
- the liability of paralegals and the lawyers who supervise them
- guidelines for the utilization of paralegal services
- ethics guidelines promulgated by paralegal associations

A. Regulation of Lawyers

1. State Courts and Bar Associations

Like other professions that affect the public interest, the legal profession is subject to regulation by the states. Unlike other regulated professions, however, the regulation of the legal profession falls mainly to the judiciary rather than the legislature. Because of the separation of powers and the role of lawyers in the court system, the judiciary has historically asserted inherent authority over the practice of law.

The highest court in each state and in the District of Columbia is responsible for making rules related to admission to the practice of law and to lawyers' ethical conduct. The states' highest courts also create and oversee mechanisms for disciplining lawyers who violate ethics codes. Most state legislatures have also passed statutes that supplement the ethics rules adopted by the courts. Some states consider legislative authority over the practice of law to be concurrent with the judicial authority; others consider legislative action to be only in aid of judicial action. In a few states, such as California and New York, substantial authority over the practice of law rests with the legislature. Sometimes the judiciary and the legislature have conflicting ideas about matters affecting the practice of law, and a court will be called on to strike down legislation that attempts to govern lawyer conduct in some way. Several state supreme courts have held unconstitutional legislation that would have authorized nonlawyers to engage in conduct that the court considered to be the practice of law. Local court rules also govern attorneys' conduct in matters before the courts.

In practice, many state supreme courts rely heavily on state bar associations to carry out their responsibilities for regulating the practice of law. These courts have delegated authority to the bar as a way to relieve the burden of overseeing lawyer conduct, updating the ethics rules, and disciplining lawyers.

Some state bar associations are **integrated** or unified, which means that membership is compulsory. In a state with an integrated bar, annual dues to renew the practitioner's law license carry automatic membership in the state bar. Some states have purely voluntary state bar associations; funds to operate the admissions and disciplinary functions in the state are derived from annual licensing or registration fees. Integrated bars generally play a more active role in the admissions and disciplinary functions of the court and in other matters relating to the legal profession.

2. American Bar Association

Most states have patterned their codes of ethics on the models of the American Bar Association (ABA). The ABA is a national voluntary professional association of lawyers. The ABA has more than 400,000 members — nearly half of the lawyers in the country. Over 100 years old, the ABA is the chief national professional association for lawyers. The ABA carries a strong voice in matters affecting substantive law, the judiciary, and the administration of justice. Among the ABA's many contributions to the profession is the promulgation of model codes of ethics.

The ABA first published the **Canons of Professional Ethics** in 1908. These Canons were patterned after the first code of ethics for lawyers adopted in 1887 by the Alabama State Bar Association. Prior to the adoption of state codes, lawyer conduct was governed largely by common law and some statutes. The 1908 Canons consisted of 32 statements of very general principles about attorney conduct, mainly conduct in the courtroom. Many states adopted these ABA Canons through court rule or statute.

In 1969, the ABA published a new code, called the ***Model Code of Professional Responsibility,*** designed as a prototype for states to use in developing their own codes. The Model Code was adopted in whole or in part by every state and is still followed in a few states. After six years of study, debate, drafting, and redrafting, a new code, called the ***Model Rules of Professional Conduct,*** was adopted by the ABA in 1983.

In August 1997, the American Bar Association launched a new review of the Model Rules, designated **Ethics 2000**. As a result of this review, several changes to the Model Rules were adopted in 2001 and 2003. The current versions of the Model Code and Model Rules are cited throughout this book. The relevant ethics rules in your jurisdiction should always be consulted for the current and accurate rules governing lawyer and paralegal conduct.

As of this writing, only California and Maine have not adopted the Model Rules. California has its own code, which is based on neither the Model Code nor the Model Rules. States generally make some modifications of the ABA Rules when they adopt the rules, so it is important for paralegals to consult the specific state rules that are applicable where they are working and not to rely on the ABA Model Rules.

Model Code of Professional Responsibility
ABA's code of ethics, designed as a prototype for states to use in developing their own codes, adopted in 1969

Model Rules of Professional Conduct
ABA's revised prototype code of ethics, adopted by the ABA in 1983

3. State Statutes, Ethics Opinions, and Case Law

Although the state codes of ethics contain most of the rules with which we are concerned in this text, statutes also govern attorney conduct. For example, some states have statutes that prohibit attorneys from engaging in certain conduct in their professional capacity as lawyers and provide for criminal and civil penalties. As we will see in Chapter 2, most states have laws that make the unauthorized practice of law a crime, usually a misdemeanor.

Ethics advisory opinions
Written opinions from a bar association interpreting relevant ethical precedents and applying them to an ethical issue

Not binding on attorneys but often consulted when ethical issues arise are *ethics advisory opinions* issued by state and local bar associations and the ABA. Bar associations have ethics committees that consider ethical dilemmas posed to them by attorney-members. The committees write opinions that are published in bar journals and manuals to give additional guidance to other attorneys facing similar dilemmas. Courts sometimes cite advisory opinions as persuasive authority. Some state and ABA advisory opinions that are important to paralegals are cited in this text.

Of course, **disciplinary cases** and **court decisions** involving lawyer malpractice, disqualification, and breach of lawyers' duties also contribute to the body of law that governs lawyer conduct.

4. Sanctions and Remedies

Disbarment
Rescinding of a lawyer's license to practice

Four main formal sanctions imposed on lawyers for ethical misconduct can be imposed by the state's highest court or other disciplinary body. The most severe sanction is *disbarment*, in which a lawyer's license to practice law is revoked. Disbarment is only imposed for the most egregious violations or when there is a long-term pattern of serious unethical conduct. Although disbarment is in theory "permanent," most admitting authorities do occasionally re-admit a disbarred lawyer after some period of time if the lawyer can demonstrate complete rehabilitation.

Suspension
Attorney is deprived of the right to practice law for a specified period of time

Probation
Attorney can practice, but certain requirements must be met

The second most severe sanction is *suspension*, under which the attorney is deprived of the right to practice law for a specified period of time. Some disciplinary authorities also have the option of imposing *probation*, under which the disciplined attorney may continue to practice on the condition that certain requirements are met, such as restitution to injured clients, passing an ethics examination, attending ethics "school," or participating in counseling. Sometimes a suspension is stayed but the attorney remains on probation for some period, during which the disciplinary body may reinstitute the suspension if further ethical violations come to light.

Reprimand
Warning that ethical violations have occurred and will not be tolerated

The mildest sanction is a *reprimand*, sometimes called a *reproval*. This action represents a slap on the hand, a warning that the conduct at issue will not be tolerated. Reprimands may be made public (placed in the public record and published in a bar journal or legal newspaper) or private (confidentially communicated in writing to the attorney). In either case, the reprimand becomes part of the attorney's record. A reprimand is considered further in determining the appropriate sanction if other violations occur.

In deciding the appropriate sanction, the disciplinary body considers the nature and severity of the offense and whether the attorney has a record of prior misconduct. Other **aggravating and mitigating**

factors may be taken into account, such as the extent to which the attorney cooperated in the investigation and appreciates the seriousness of the matter, the attorney's reputation and contributions to the community through public service and professional activities, the circumstances surrounding the offense and the extent to which these make the attorney more or less culpable for the conduct, and whether the offense was a one-time incident and is unlikely to be repeated or was a pattern of misconduct over time. Whether the lawyer shows remorse and willingness to remedy the problems that may have led to the conduct is critical in determining the sanction.

In addition to direct discipline by the court or state bar, an attorney may be **prosecuted criminally** for violations of statutes governing attorney conduct or conduct that may relate to an attorney's practice, such as laws prohibiting solicitation of clients in hospitals and jails and laws limiting the methods that can be used to collect debts. Civil *legal malpractice* lawsuits brought by former clients also constitute a major incentive for conforming to ethical requirements and standards of practice. (See Chapter 7 for more on legal malpractice.) The courts also exercise **contempt power** to sanction lawyers appearing before them who engage in improper conduct that affects the administration of justice and the smooth functioning of the courts. (See Chapter 8, Special Issues in Advocacy.) The courts also play a major role in deciding on matters in the area of conflicts of interest because they rule on **motions to disqualify counsel**, which are usually brought by the opposing counsel who claims that a lawyer or law firm has a conflict of interest that jeopardizes client confidentiality. (See Chapter 4, Conflicts of Interest.) It should be noted that disciplinary action may be taken not only against lawyers who are directly involved with the conduct of paralegals, but also against those who have supervisory or managerial authority or are partners in a law firm. Under recent changes to the rules in most states, a law firm may also be held responsible for ethical misconduct, depending on the nature of the violation and the surrounding circumstances and actions by the firm. (See ABA Model Rule 5.3, discussed below.)

B.   Regulation of Paralegals

1.   A Brief History of the Paralegal Profession

The use of specially educated and trained nonlawyers to assist lawyers in the delivery of legal services is a relatively new phenomenon in the history of American law. The concept is only about 40 years old.

The paralegal field's **beginnings** can be traced directly back to the late 1960s, when the rapidly rising cost of legal services, combined with the lack of access to legal services for low- and middle-income Americans, caused the federal government, consumer groups, and the organized bar to take a close look at the way legal services were being delivered. Many innovations were instituted, including legal aid clinics, storefront law offices, and prepaid legal plans. Private law firms became aware of the need to manage their operations more efficiently. The concept of using the services of trained nonlawyers to perform certain legal functions was introduced. In 1967, the ABA endorsed the concept of the paralegal and in 1968 established its first committee on paralegals, which has since become the **Standing Committee on Paralegals**.

During the late 1960s and early 1970s, the ABA and several state and local bar associations conducted studies on the use of paralegals. Although many studies showed initial attorney resistance to the idea of paralegals, the actual use of paralegals rose. The first **formal paralegal training** programs were established in the early 1970s. Only 11 paralegal education programs were offered in 1971, and there are more than 1,000 today. In 1974, the ABA adopted guidelines for the paralegal curriculum, and in 1975 began to approve paralegal programs under those guidelines. There were nine paralegal programs approved that year, and there are now more than 250 approved programs.

NFPA
National Federation of Paralegal Associations

NALA
National Association of Legal Assistants

AAfPE
American Association for Paralegal Education

IPMA
International Paralegal Management Association

NALS
An Association for Legal Professionals

AAPI
American Alliance of Paralegals, Inc.

In the mid-1970s, the first professional paralegal associations were formed. Dozens of groups cropped up locally. The **National Federation of Paralegal Associations** (NFPA) and **National Association of Legal Assistants** (NALA) were established. Paralegal educators formed their own organization, the **American Association for Paralegal Education** (AAfPE). In the 1980s, a group of paralegal supervisors and managers started the **Legal Assistant Management Association,** which has since changed its name to the **International Paralegal Management Association** (IPMA). *NALS,* which was an association for legal secretaries formed in 1929, seeks to serve all legal professionals, including paralegals. Finally, the American Alliance of Paralegals, Inc. (AAPI) is the newest national group for paralegals.

In 1976, the first voluntary **certification** program was established by NALA, called the **Certified Legal Assistant** (CLA) program. It was also at about this time that the U.S. Bureau of Labor Statistics predicted that a paralegal career would be one of the fastest-growing occupations. Job opportunities expanded dramatically in the 1980s, especially in large private law firms, and paralegals started to work as independent contractors.

In the 1990s, NALA developed advanced specialist examinations in a variety of areas, which are taken by paralegals who have already earned the CLA designation. Since then, NALA adopted the designation **Certified Paralegal (CP),** which CLAs can use instead of CLA if they prefer, in recognition of the trend toward greater use of this title.

In 1996, NFPA developed a certification examination called the **Parale-gal Advanced Competency Examination** (PACE). This program is designed for experienced paralegals who may use the designation **Registered Paralegal** upon passing the examination. In 2004, **NALS, the Association for Legal Professionals** (formerly the National Asso-ciation of Legal Secretaries) launched the **Professional Paralegal (PP)** certification examination program. AAPI, although smaller than the other national groups, also has a Certified Paralegal program.

NFPA and NALA each represent about 10,000 paralegals who are either members or are affiliated through membership in a local association. NALA's certification is the largest, with more than 14,000 paralegals certified by NALA and another 1,100 with advanced specialty certification.

IPMA, representing supervisors of paralegals mainly in large law firms and corporate law departments, has about 500 members and has local chapters in major cities across the United States and in Canada. AAfPE now has more than 300 institutional members.

2.   Direct Regulation of Paralegals: Certification and Licensing

Definitions of Terms

Certification of an occupation is usually a form of voluntary recog-nition of an individual who has met specifications of the granting agency or organization. NALA's CLA program and the NFPA's PACE are forms of certification. *Licensing* is a mandatory form of regulation in which a government agency grants permission to an individual to engage in an occupation and to use a particular title. Only a person who is so licensed may engage in this occupation. There is no licensing of paralegals at the present time in the United States. Attorneys are "licensed" by the state in which they practice. Typically, both licensing and certification require applicants to pass an examination and meet specified requirements regard-ing education and moral character.

The terms *paralegal* and *legal assistant* are used interchangeably in this book; however, there is a nationwide trend toward using the title "para-legal." In recent years, all of the professional entities involved in the paralegal profession have recognized paralegal as the favored term, and many, including the ABA Standing Committee on Paralegals and the IPMA, have changed their own names to reflect the common usage. In part, the change has come about because lawyers in many firms started to give the title "legal assistant" to their legal secretaries. The movement away from the title "secretary" complicates the matter, as no new title has emerged that fits this role in the legal services delivery team.

Certification
Voluntary recognition of an occupation based on a person's having met specified qualifications

Licensing
Mandatory form of regulation in which a government agency grants permission to engage in an occupation and use a title

The ABA adopted a **definition** of *paralegal/legal assistant* in 1997, which reads: "A legal assistant or paralegal is a person, qualified by education, training or work experience, who is employed or retained by a lawyer, law office, corporation, governmental agency or other entity and who performs specifically delegated substantive legal work for which a lawyer is responsible." Although states, bar associations, and paralegal organizations deviate slightly from the ABA definition, they generally subscribe to the basic ideas set forth in this definition: (1) paralegals meet certain qualifications, (2) paralegals work for lawyers who delegate work to them, (3) paralegals do substantive legal work, and (4) the lawyer is responsible for their work.

Regulation of Supervised Paralegals

Throughout the history of the paralegal profession, the need for certification or licensing has been raised and debated. Gradually, some minimal forms of regulation have been adopted.

Early in the profession's development, Oregon had a **voluntary certification** program for legal assistants, which was abolished after a few years because of low participation. Texas adopted a voluntary certification program for paralegals in 1994. Texas administers its program through its Board of Legal Specialization. Certification examinations are given in a number of areas, including family law, civil trial practice, criminal law, and personal injury practice. Certification, valid for five years, is renewable upon demonstrated participation in continuing education, employment by a Texas attorney, and substantial involvement in a specialty area. Nearly 1,000 paralegals have been certified since the program began. Since 2004, the North Carolina State Bar and the Ohio State Bar have established certification programs for paralegals, and the Florida Supreme Court has adopted rules for a Registered Paralegal Program, which is based on a paralegal's having specified educational credentials or work experience and passing the PACE or CLA.

The national paralegal associations continue to promote voluntary certification — NALA through its CLA/CP and CLA Specialist program, NFPA through its PACE, NALS through its PP designation, and now AAPI. On a national level, these organizations want to be poised for regulation if and when it comes by having proven examinations in place that can be adopted by states.

A few states have taken steps toward the **regulation** of paralegals. In 1999, Maine adopted a statute that defines "paralegal" and "legal assistant" and restricts the use of the title to those persons. Anyone who does not fit the definition, which requires the person to work under lawyer supervision, may be fined. A South Dakota statute defines *legal assistant/paralegal,* sets up minimum qualifications, and delineates ethical guidelines for attorneys to follow in working with paralegals. The law subjects the supervising attorney to sanctions for failing to meet the ethical standards. Both Florida and Arizona limit the use of the title "paralegal" and similar titles by Supreme Court Rule to persons working under lawyer supervision.

In 2000, California enacted a statute that defines who may use the title "paralegal" (and comparable titles) and sets qualifications and continuing education requirements. The statute requires paralegals to be supervised by lawyers and distinguishes them from "legal document assistants," a title used in other state legislation for nonlawyer legal service providers. This statute is not enforceable through any particular state agency and no registration or licensing is involved. Criminal penalties are available, however, for anyone using the title while providing legal services directly to the public.

The ABA has issued policy statements that reject the notion that paralegals should be licensed, indicating that the public is protected by the extensive ethical and disciplinary requirements to which lawyers are subject. IPMA also adheres to the position that licensing of paralegals who work under lawyer supervision is unnecessary for the protection of the public and would unduly interfere with a lawyer's prerogative to hire the best-qualified person for the job. NALA is also against mandatory licensing, mainly on the basis that there is no need for it to protect the public. NFPA has historically promoted regulation as a means to enhance and expand the role of the paralegal.

The Regulation Debate

Arguments **favoring licensing** of paralegals who work under lawyer supervision center mainly on the benefits to the paralegal occupation, in terms of establishing it as a separate and autonomous but allied legal career, one with its own identity and a concomitant increase in societal status and rewards.

Proponents believe regulation would:

- provide appropriate public recognition for paralegals as important members of the legal services delivery team
- ensure high standards and quality of work by paralegals
- expand the use of paralegals, thereby expanding access to legal services and lowering costs
- provide assurance to clients and employers of paralegals of their qualifications
- encourage needed standardization in paralegal education

Some proponents favor regulation only if it permits paralegals to expand their role by permitting them to engage in work that they are not currently permitted to do under state statutes and case law.

The primary arguments **against licensing** of traditional paralegals are that licensing would:

- not benefit the public because attorney-employers are already fully accountable to clients
- increase the cost of employing paralegals and therefore increase the cost of legal services
- stifle the development of the profession
- inappropriately limit entry into the profession
- unnecessarily standardize paralegal education
- restrict the movement of paralegals into new areas of practice or duties

One important concern cited by opponents is the practical difficulty of determining exactly what legal tasks and functions could be assigned exclusively to paralegals through this *regulatory* process.

Nonlawyer Legal Service Providers

The need to reform the legal services delivery system to provide **access to legal services** for low- and middle-income Americans is perhaps the biggest challenge facing the practice of law today. Study after study has indicated that most Americans do not have access to legal services, cannot afford an attorney when they need one, and do not know how to go about finding an attorney. Low- and middle-income persons who need legal services are more frequently than ever representing themselves, with or without the assistance of self-help manuals and nonlawyers. It is not unusual in many parts of the country for the majority of marital dissolutions to be handled in *propria persona*.

The ABA and some state supreme courts and bars have researched and studied access issues extensively, with an eye toward increased use of nonlawyers as one method of addressing the unmet need for legal services. Most studies find some form of nonlawyer practice in virtually every jurisdiction; many states have considered proposals related to the regulation of nonlawyer practice. Recommendations usually include expanding the role of supervised paralegals and granting limited authority to nonlawyers to provide legal services, with appropriate oversight and regulation to protect consumers.

In some states, court rules and legislation have authorized nonlawyers to perform certain tasks that might otherwise be reserved exclusively to lawyers. For example, some courts have **court facilitators** who assist persons who are representing themselves in completing forms to be filed with the court, a function that might require the facilitator to give legal advice. Court facilitators have been widely used in family law courts. California has legislation that regulates nonlawyer legal services providers, called *legal document assistants* and *unlawful detainer assistants*, by requiring them to register in the county in which they work. This statute does not, however, expand their role; in fact, it specifically prohibits them from providing legal advice. Similarly, Arizona has court rules much like California's statutes, which authorize *legal document preparers* to assist the public (without providing legal advice, of course).

Although not much progress has been made officially in expanding the role of nonlawyers in the delivery of legal services, nonlawyer practitioners continue to provide assistance to people who need legal help — and the debate continues. In the state of Washington, the Supreme Court some years ago created the Practice of Law Board with the purpose of increasing access to legal services. This Board has considered rules that would establish a system for limited nonlawyer practice in designated areas of need. This Washington program, if it is implemented, would be the most progressive plan anywhere for increasing access to legal services through the use of nonlawyers. (For more on nonlawyer practitioners see Chapter 2, Unauthorized Practice of Law.)

> **Legal document assistants/legal document preparers** Nonlawyers who are authorized to assist members of the public in representing themselves, but who are not permitted to give legal advice or represent clients in court

3. State Guidelines for the Utilization of Paralegal Services

In an effort to promote the effective and ethical use of paralegals, some states have adopted guidelines to assist attorneys in working with paralegals. These guidelines, directed specifically to attorneys, highlight the key ethical matters that come into play when a nonlawyer is involved in the delivery of legal services, such as unauthorized practice of law, confidentiality, conflicts, and fee splitting.

At the time of this writing, about 30 states have some kind of guidelines. In a handful of states, the guidelines have been adopted by the highest court of the state. In a few states, the legislature has acted. In most states, the guidelines have been approved by the state bar association, a state bar committee on paralegals, or both. Some of the states that have adopted guidelines have also prepared accompanying statements on the effective use of paralegals.

In 1991, the ABA adopted **Model Guidelines for the Utilization of Legal Assistant Services**, which were revised and renamed as the **Model Guidelines for the Utilization of Paralegal Services** in 2004. These guidelines were written to provide a model for states that want to adopt such guidelines and to encourage attorneys to use paralegals effectively and appropriately. Several jurisdictions have either adopted the ABA guidelines or amended their existing guidelines in response to the ABA model.

4. Paralegal Association Codes of Ethics and Guidelines

The two major national paralegal professional associations both have codes of ethics to guide the conduct of their members. NALA calls its code the **Code of Ethics and Professional Responsibility**, included in Appendix A at page 195. NFPA has a **Model Code of Ethics and Professional Responsibility**, which it encourages its affiliated local associations to adopt (included in Appendix B at page 199). It also has Model Disciplinary Rules to establish mechanisms for enforcing the rules. These rules are not included in the appendices but are available on the NFPA Web site.

NALA has both individual members and affiliated local chapters. Members sign a statement of commitment to NALA's code on their membership application, and a mechanism is in place at the national level to investigate allegations of code violations and to remove from membership or to remove the CLA/CP designation from any member who has violated the code.

NFPA issues ethics opinions on current concerns of interest to practicing paralegals. These opinions have addressed such matters as communications over the Internet and the role of paralegals who work in the corporate setting.

Both organizations make literature on ethics available. Their addresses, phone numbers, and Web sites are:

- The National Association of Legal Assistants 1516 S. Boston, Suite 200 Tulsa, Oklahoma 74119 918-587-6828 www.nala.org
- The National Federation of Paralegal Associations P.O. Box 2016, Edmonds, Washington 98020 425-967-0045 www.paralegals.org

5. Responsibility of Lawyers and Paralegals for Paralegal Conduct

Because paralegals are not lawyers, they are neither directly bound by state codes of ethics for lawyers nor subject to direct sanctions for breaches of those codes. Without certification, licensing, or some other form of direct regulation of the paralegal occupation, paralegals are bound to comply with high standards of professional behavior primarily because the attorneys for whom they work are responsible for any lapses in their behavior. Lawyers therefore have a strong incentive to ensure that the paralegals they employ are familiar with the state's ethics code and comply with it. Some states specifically require lawyers to take affirmative steps to educate the paralegals they employ about ethical obligations and to ensure their compliance.

The ABA Model Rules of Professional Conduct contain an important provision on supervision, Model Rule 5.3, which requires partners, supervising lawyers, and lawyers with managerial authority to "make reasonable efforts" to ensure that nonlawyer conduct is compatible with the lawyer's ethical obligations. Further, a lawyer is responsible for a paralegal's unethical conduct if the lawyer ordered it or ratified it, or if the lawyer is a partner in the firm, has managerial authority, or is the paralegal's supervisor and fails to take remedial action. Most states follow the principles of this rule and hold lawyers responsible for the unethical conduct of paralegals and other nonlawyers who work for them. As a result, lawyers may be disciplined for the unethical conduct of their paralegals.

Lawyers are also liable in civil suits for the negligent conduct of paralegals who they employ or retain. Paralegals themselves are potential defendants in civil legal malpractice suits brought by clients who believe paralegals in their attorney's employment may have acted negligently. Paralegals are subject to the same general tort principles that apply to lawyers and other professionals; that is, they are liable for negligent or intentional misconduct that injures a client.

Because clients always name their attorney and rarely name paralegals as defendants in malpractice cases, there is little case law available defining the standards of conduct to which paralegals are held. However, it is generally accepted that a paralegal is held to the same standard of care, skill, and knowledge as other paralegals, so long as the paralegal does not hold himself or herself out as a lawyer and performs typical paralegal tasks. Most lawyers carry insurance that provides coverage in the event that a client names a paralegal in a malpractice action. This coverage ordinarily extends to all the nonlawyer personnel who are employed by the lawyer.

REVIEW QUESTIONS

1. When and why did the paralegal profession begin?
2. What are the two main professional associations for paralegals?
3. What is certification? What is licensing?
4. What state(s) have some form of voluntary certification of paralegals?
5. What are the national associations' programs for paralegal certification called? How do they differ?
6. What is limited licensure? How do nonlawyer legal service providers differ from traditional paralegals who work under the supervision of attorneys?

7. What are the arguments in favor of the licensing of traditional paralegals? The arguments against?

8. To what extent are paralegals directly regulated at the present time?

9. How many states have guidelines for the utilization of paralegals? What is the purpose of these guidelines?

10. What are the ABA Model Guidelines for the Utilization of Paralegal Services?

11. Do NALA and NFPA have rules on the conduct of paralegals? If so, how are these rules enforced?

12. May a paralegal who is negligent while working on a client's case be held liable for malpractice? May this paralegal's attorney-employer also be held liable? If so, on what grounds?

13. Is an attorney responsible for a paralegal's breaches of conduct such that the appropriate state entity may discipline the attorney? Can the same state body discipline the paralegal?

HYPOTHETICALS

1. Lawyer Ann Adams and paralegal Ben Burns have been hired by client Carl Carlson to sue a grocery store where Carl, who is 85, fell down when he slipped in a puddle of water in the produce aisle. Ann delegates the task of preparing the complaint to Ben. Ben mis-calendars the date that the answer must be filed and the statute of limitations passes. What are Carl's remedies? Can he name Ben as a defendant if he brings a lawsuit? What kind of lawsuit can he bring? What will happen if he reports the matter to the proper disciplinary authorities? Is the failure to file the complaint on time an ethical breach? Can Ann and/or Ben be disciplined for this conduct by the state supreme court or another disciplinary authority? What if Ann already has a private reproval on her record for a similar violation? What if three other clients have reported Ann for failing to return calls and show up for court dates?

2. The state of Aurora is determined to regulate paralegals. A group of paralegals is lobbying hard for regulation so that the paralegals can be distinguished from nonlawyer legal service providers who often use the title "paralegal." Two years earlier, the Aurora supreme court struck down legislation that would have allowed nonlawyers to represent clients in workers' compensation cases. The proposed legislation regulating paralegals is passed and signed into law. A group of lawyers files suit, requesting that the court declare the legislation invalid. Under what theory might the court strike down the legislation? Would the same result be likely in all jurisdictions? If the legislation is found unconstitutional and struck down, what should the paralegals do to get the regulation they want?

DISCUSSION QUESTIONS AND PROJECTS

1. Find out where you can locate the recent decisions of disciplinary cases in your jurisdiction. What are the usual reasons for discipline? Do any of these cases involve paralegals?
2. Research your state statutes to find where paralegals are mentioned.
3. Obtain the position papers on regulation of all the paralegal-related groups mentioned in this chapter and compare their views. Have a debate in class. Bring in representatives of the local paralegal associations to discuss their views.
4. Research in phone books and other resources to see if nonlawyer legal service providers are working in your area. How many are there? Who uses their services? What titles do they use? In what areas of law practice do they work?
5. Does your state or local bar association allow paralegals to join as associate members? Does your state or local bar have a committee that concerns itself with paralegals? Does your state or local bar have guidelines for attorneys who work with paralegals? Has it considered licensing of traditional paralegals or independent paralegals who provide services directly to the public? If you are in a state with a certification or registration program (Ohio, North Carolina, or Florida), how many paralegals are now certified or registered?
6. Who is covered and not covered by the ABA definition of *paralegal/ legal assistant*? Do you like this definition? Why or why not? How would you change it?
7. Is voluntary certification through NALA or NFPA popular in your state or local area? Why or why not?

SELECTED CASES

Bennion, VanCamp, Hagen & Ruhl v. Kassler Escrow, Inc., 96 Wash. 2d 443, 635 P.2d 730 (1981) (case in which state supreme court struck down legislation relating to the practice of law).

Florida Bar v. Lawless, 640 So. 2d 1098 (Fla. 1994) (freelance paralegal whose mistakes resulted in lawyer discipline).

Musselman v. Willoughby Corp., 230 Va. 337, 337 S.E.2d 724 (1985) (paralegal involved in malpractice).

Supreme Court of Arizona v. Struthers, 179 Ariz. 216, 877 P.2d 789 (1994) (lawyer allows untrained "paralegals" to run his law practice and share fees).

Unauthorized Practice of Law Committee v. State Department of Workers' Compensation, 543 A.2d 662 (R.I. 1998) (case in which state supreme court upheld legislation relating to the practice of law).

| SELECTED REFERENCES |

- ABA Model Rules of Professional Conduct, Rule 5.3
- Also see your jurisdiction's rules of professional conduct and court rules and guidelines for paralegals, if any.

Unauthorized Practice of Law

This chapter defines the practice of law and describes the functions that fall within this definition. Special emphasis is placed on how these limitations affect paralegals. Chapter 2 covers:

- a brief history of unauthorized practice of law from the colonial era to the present
- definitions of the practice of law
- the attorney's ethical responsibility to prevent the unauthorized practice of law and to supervise paralegals
- key areas of special importance to paralegals, including:

  - court appearances, depositions, pleadings, and giving legal advice
  - establishing the attorney-client relationship and setting fees
  - job functions that may constitute the unauthorized practice of law
  - nonlawyer practice before administrative agencies
  - disclosure of status as a paralegal

A. A Brief History of the Unauthorized Practice of Law

Limitations on who can practice law in the United States can be traced back to the **colonial era**. At that time a proliferation of untrained practitioners caused local courts to adopt rules requiring attorneys who appeared before them to have a license granted by the court. Additional rules adopted during this period limited the amount of fees that could be charged and dictated that an attorney could not refuse to take a case. The stated purposes of these rules were to prevent stirring up of litigation by unscrupulous "pettifoggers" and "mercenary" attorneys, to stop incompetence that harmed not only the clients but the administration of justice and dignity of the courts, and to prevent exploitive, excessive fees.

The rules establishing entry to the practice of law evolved slowly and unevenly through American history. In the **mid- to late 1800s**, state and local bar associations began to gain strength, and the first ***unauthorized practice of law*** (UPL) statutes were passed. These laws prohibited court appearances by anyone not licensed as an attorney, prohibited the practice of law by court personnel such as bailiffs, and made it illegal for an unlicensed person to hold himself or herself out as an attorney and for a nonlawyer to form a partnership with a lawyer.

UPL
Unauthorized practice of law

The definition of *practice of law* being formulated in these cases was gradually broadened to cover activities beyond court appearances. Most early cases defined the term as the preparation of documents by which legal rights are secured. New justifications for restricting the right to practice law to licensed attorneys emerged, including the lawyer's professional independence, moral character, and special training, as well as the fact that, unlike unlicensed practitioners, lawyers are subject to sanctions for breaches of duty or competence.

Some legal historians and commentators believe that the height of unauthorized practice restrictions came during the **Depression**, when lawyers needed most to protect their economic interests from competition. Bar associations became especially powerful trade organizations during this era. Passed in virtually all states, unauthorized practice statutes made it a crime to practice law without a license. The definition of *practice of law* was further expanded to include "all services customarily rendered by lawyers." In the **1930s**, the ABA and state bars entered into agreements with accountants, collection agencies, insurance adjusters, life insurance underwriters, publishers, realtors, and other professionals that delineated the law-related activities that nonlawyers could perform without moving into the practice of law. These agreements were rescinded in the 1970s when it became apparent that they would be found illegal under the Sherman Antitrust Act.

Criminal prosecutions and civil suits to restrain unauthorized practice slowed during the 1960s and 1970s. Courts in several states found that the sale of legal self-help kits and books did not constitute UPL. And the movement to expand access to legal services by alternative means started to take hold.

The **1980s and 1990s** saw a resurgence of unauthorized practice prosecutions because of the increased number of independent "paralegals" providing low-cost legal services directly to the public. Studies since 2000 show that about half the states actively enforce the UPL rules although several states do little or no enforcement.

B.   Trends in the Unauthorized Practice of Law

1.   Nonlawyer Legal Service Providers and Related Trends

Many factors together have created the need for ***nonlawyer legal services providers***: the decrease in federal funding for the legal services corporation, which in turn funds organizations that provide legal services to persons of low and moderate incomes; the increase in the need for legal services because of the proliferation and complexity of laws; and the rising cost of legal services provided by lawyers, which makes it difficult or even impossible for most Americans to employ a lawyer when they need one.

Most nonlawyer legal service providers work in the **areas of practice** in which low- and moderate-income people need assistance, such as in landlord/tenant matters, divorce, child support, bankruptcy, and immigration. Some run "typing services" that assist persons only by typing documents, usually to be filed with the court, after the "customer" fills in the blanks. Others provide more complete information and assistance, helping the customer decide what forms to use, what information to include on the forms, and where to file them. Nonlawyer legal service providers use a variety of titles, including "independent paralegal," "legal technician," or "document preparer." As noted in Chapter 1, California uses the titles "***legal document assistant***" and "unlawful detainer assistant" in statutes that require such persons to register with the county in which they work. Similarly, Arizona uses "***legal document preparer***" as the designation for its nonlawyer legal service providers.

> **Legal document preparer/assistant**
> A nonlawyer legal service provider who is authorized by court rule or statute to assist persons in representing themselves, without being authorized to give legal advice or appear in court

Although the unmet need for legal services is well documented, lawyers are largely **opposed** to giving up any of their traditional functions to nonlawyers. Clearly, lawyers have both monopolistic and economic reasons for this stance and legitimate concerns about the quality of legal services that someone not trained as a lawyer can provide.

Defendants in widely publicized **prosecutions** in several states have argued unsuccessfully that they are not giving legal advice but are simply assisting laypersons in the preparation of legal documents. Defendants in unauthorized practice prosecutions have argued unsuccessfully that a statutory power of attorney from a client gives a nonlawyer the authority to represent the client in litigation. Some defendants have argued, to no avail, that they have a public necessity defense based on the lack of availability of legal services for their clients.

Meanwhile, several states have seen proposed **legislation** that would define the practice of law more expansively or would institute harsher penalties for UPL, or have stepped up their efforts to prosecute unauthorized practice cases. Bankruptcy reform legislation adopted in the 1990s contains provisions that limit the role of nonlawyer practitioners in Chapter 7 filings, including barring the use of the terms "legal" or "paralegal" in business names. Several states have taken action to regulate nonlawyers who assist persons with immigration matters. Although federal statutes establish nationwide standards for accredited visa consultants, some immigration "consultants" do not fall within the reach of these federal laws, and widespread abuses of clients have been documented.

Several states have determined that the **preparation of living trust documents** constitutes the practice of law, thus paving the way for the prosecution of companies that market living trust plans. Most decisions hold that the client's decision on whether a living trust is appropriate, the attendant preparation and execution of documents, and the funding of the trust are functions that require an attorney's judgment and involvement. Lawyers in several jurisdictions have been disciplined for aiding in UPL where they have participated in businesses that promote and sell living trusts. Most courts find that these lawyers have abdicated their responsibility to advise clients about the ramifications of such an important legal decision as making a living trust. The lawyers in these cases either failed to supervise the work of their employees in counseling clients and preparing the documents for them or were asked to review documents by the nonlawyer operators who had already advised the clients and prepared documents for them with no attorney involvement whatsoever.

Finally, there is a growing trend toward the **discipline of lawyers** who are running large-volume practices and inadequately supervising their paralegals and other employees. In most of these cases, the paralegals are accepting clients, having them sign retainer agreements, preparing and filing legal documents, and counseling clients about their legal rights with little or no lawyer involvement and no direct relationship between the lawyer and the client. In some cases, there has also been unlawful solicitation of clients by the nonlawyers, coupled with compensation arrangements that violate rules against fee splitting and/or with partnerships between lawyers and nonlawyers to engage in the practice of law. These fee-related and solicitation issues are covered in Chapters 5 and 6.

2. Multijurisdictional Practice Issues

The legal community has become concerned about **lawyers who are providing legal services across state lines** — that is, engaged, sometimes unethically, in **multijurisdictional practice**. Under longstanding traditions and rules, lawyers may be admitted *pro hac vice* by courts to represent clients in a litigated matter in a state in which they are not licensed to practice. This special court permission to practice in the state applies only to the one specific case in which the lawyer is acting. In other situations, the out-of-state lawyer employs co-counsel who is licensed in the state where the matter is being worked on. However, more complicated cases are arising all the time because of the global nature of the economy and the mobility of lawyers and clients.

> **pro hac vice**
> Special rules that allow a lawyer to represent a client in a state court in a state where the lawyer is not licensed to practice

For example, a lawyer who represents a corporation may have to handle litigation and transactional work that is done partially or wholly in another state or relates to an incident or transaction in another state. Is the lawyer who does this engaging in UPL? The ABA Model Rules (Model Rule 5.5) now provide **"safe harbors"** for lawyers who are in these situations. In addition to these traditional exceptions, lawyers may participate in alternative dispute resolution in one state if related to work in the state where they are licensed, may do other work reasonably related to work where they are licensed, and may advise corporate clients in a state where they are not licensed, unless it would require pro hac vice admission.

C.   The Practice of Law Defined

No one definitive list of activities constitutes the practice of law. As you can see from the foregoing history, the concept is somewhat flexible and has changed over time by the push and pull of economics, political and professional activity, public pressure and consumerism, and the complexity of laws. The oft-quoted ABA Model Code of Professional Responsibility (ABA Model Code) EC 3-5 states: "It is neither necessary nor desirable to attempt the formulation of a single, specific definition of what constitutes the practice of law." Court rules, court decisions, statutes, and advisory opinions have produced several tests for determining what defines the practice of law. A few unauthorized practice statutes attempt to define the practice of law; most do not. Several states have a definition in a court rule. The ABA established a task force in 2002 to create a model definition of the practice of law and found the task fraught with so many differences of opinion that it eventually gave up, and recommended that each state adopt its own definition. The cases interpreting the unauthorized practice of law statutes analyze the facts in determining if specific conduct constitutes the practice of law. In doing so, they may consider:

- Whether the services required the skills and knowledge of an attorney
- Whether the activity is one that is traditionally performed by a lawyer
- Whether the services are essentially legal or are "incidental" to some other transaction

Most comprehensive **definitions** of the practice of law contain some of the foregoing language, and some specifically prohibit anyone but a lawyer from doing the following:

- Preparing pleadings and legal instruments, such as wills, contracts, deeds, leases, and trusts
- Preparing any document by which legal rights are secured
- Preparing documents for or making statements to a client that contain legal opinions, arguments, or interpretations of the law
- Appearing in court on behalf of clients or acting as an advocate in a representative capacity
- Giving legal advice — that is, applying knowledge and judgment to a client's particular situation and advising of rights and responsibilities and possible courses of action

Injunctive relief
A court order to stop someone from engaging in certain conduct; in this chapter, the unauthorized practice of law

The unauthorized practice of law is a **misdemeanor** in more than 30 states and subjects a person to civil contempt proceedings in more than 25 states. A common remedy is *injunctive relief,* which may be requested by prosecutors, bar associations, or courts to stop someone from engaging in activities believed to be the practice of law. This remedy is available in most jurisdictions. Other consequences of UPL include liability for negligent performance, unenforceability of the contract for legal services, court dismissal of an action filed by someone engaging in UPL, and voiding of a judgment in which a nonlawyer represented the prevailing party.

D.   The Attorney's Responsibility to Prevent the Unauthorized Practice of Law

Rules that prohibit the unauthorized practice of law affect both paralegals who work under lawyer supervision and nonlawyer legal service providers who deal directly with the public. Ample opportunity exists in a traditional legal setting for a nonlawyer — especially a paralegal — employed by a lawyer to overstep the accepted boundaries into the practice of law.

Lawyers are obligated by various rules not to **aid the unauthorized practice of law**. In many states, a statute prohibits a lawyer from aiding unauthorized practice and, in most states, the ethics code contains such a restriction. This prohibition makes attorneys responsible for the training, supervision, and delegation of legal work to the nonlawyers they employ. The obligation of adequate supervision applies to all areas of ethics — such as confidentiality, conflicts, and competence — but carries special force in the area of unauthorized practice. Allowing a nonlawyer under a lawyer's supervision to engage in the practice of law is considered an abdication of the lawyer's fundamental obligation to "exercise independent professional judgment" on behalf of the client. Forming a partnership and dividing legal fees with a nonlawyer are also forbidden under this principle. Chapter 6 discusses these topics in more depth.

As noted in Chapter 1, ABA **Model Rule 5.3**, adopted in most states, establishes the duty of a partner, lawyer with managerial authority, and supervising lawyer to make "reasonable efforts to ensure that the firm has in effect measures giving reasonable assurance that the [nonlawyer assistant's] conduct is compatible with the professional obligations of the lawyer." Lawyers with managerial authority and the law firm as a whole were added to the list of lawyers who are ethically responsible for paralegal conduct in the most recent revisions to this rule. The rule also makes any lawyer who employs or directly retains the nonlawyer responsible for the nonlawyer's ethical breaches if the lawyer orders, knows of, or ratifies the conduct. Partners and supervising and managing lawyers are also responsible if they learn of the conduct and do not take remedial action. The comment to Rule 5.3 speaks to the lawyer's duty to instruct and supervise assistants, especially with regard to confidentiality.

Guideline 1 of the **ABA Model Guidelines** for the Utilization of Paralegal Services phrases this responsibility a bit differently, stating that a lawyer is "responsible for all of the professional actions of a paralegal performing services at the lawyer's direction. . . ." The comment to Guideline 1 emphasizes the lawyer's duty to provide instruction to paralegals concerning ethics and to supervise paralegals.

Guideline 2 provides an expansive definition of the permissible functions of a paralegal by allowing lawyers to delegate any task except "those tasks proscribed to a nonlawyer by statute, administrative rule or regulation, controlling authority," or the relevant ethics rules.

E. What Constitutes the Unauthorized Practice of Law

1. Making Court Appearances

The one lawyering function that is universally considered to be the exclusive province of licensed attorneys is the representation of a client in court proceedings. You will recall from the history of unauthorized practice at the beginning of this chapter that this was the first kind of restriction placed on nonlawyer practitioners in the early days of the United States.

The rationale for this rule is strongly supported by the avowed purposes of unauthorized practice rules generally. Presumably, a court appearance, especially an adversarial one such as a pretrial motion or a trial, requires **knowledge and skills** that only a lawyer possesses by virtue of long and specialized education, training, and experience. In addition to benefiting from an attorney's special competence, the client is protected by evidentiary rules relating to *attorney-client privilege.* A court appearance is the legal event that decides a client's rights and responsibilities; therefore, the client deserves the best protection and most highly **qualified representation** at this critical moment. Further, incompetent representation in court harms not only the client but also the administration of justice.

Attorney-client privilege
Rule of evidence that protects confidential communications between a lawyer and client during their professional relationship

Deposition
Method of discovery in which a witness or party makes statements under oath in question-and-answer form

Depositions

The rationale for prohibiting nonlawyer representation in court appearances extends to another aspect of the litigation process: the taking of depositions. In a *deposition*, one of the key discovery tools, the attorney asks questions, usually in a face-to-face setting, of an opposing or a third party. The responses are given orally under oath and are recorded by a court reporter or stenographer, who then produces a verbatim transcript of the questions and answers.

A deposition may be **introduced in court** as evidence. It carries the same weight as testimony given under oath in court. This testimony may be used at trial to impeach the credibility of the deponent, or may be admitted in place of direct testimony if the person deposed is no longer available.

The attorney's role in representing a client being deposed includes **making objections** to questions on evidentiary grounds and preserving these objections for the record. Typically, objections are based on relevancy or privilege. The attorney who is deposing a party or witness is performing a task similar to that of direct examination in a trial and therefore must be familiar with the complex rules of evidence.

During a deposition, the attorney asking the questions wants to learn as much as possible about the facts of the case from the witness's perspective, especially if there is information that weakens the opponent's case. This function requires not only a full understanding of the factual and legal issues, but also highly developed skills in phrasing **questions** so as to elicit candid and thorough responses.

Nonlawyers, including paralegals, may not conduct a deposition. State ethics opinions have advised that a lawyer may not allow a paralegal to conduct a deposition even where the paralegal has a written list of attorney-approved questions. The basis for this opinion is that the paralegal would not be qualified to answer any questions that might arise and may be called on to give legal advice.

Paralegals nonetheless play an active role in the discovery and trial phases of the litigation process. They are often the **factual experts** in cases and, as such, work with attorneys in preparing for depositions by assisting in identifying areas of questioning. Many paralegals help to **prepare clients** for the experience of being deposed or testifying at trial. Some accompany clients to independent medical examinations. It is common for paralegals to attend depositions and trials, where they take notes, assist with the introduction of evidence, and otherwise handle last-minute details or unanticipated matters that arise during trial. One open question is whether paralegals can **attend the deposition** of a witness without a supervising lawyer present for the sole purpose of observing the witness. Most ethics experts believe that this is acceptable, but a few do not on the basis that the paralegal must state for the record the party he or she is "representing."

Pleadings

In addition to being restricted from representing clients in court and taking depositions, paralegals cannot **sign pleadings** or other documents filed with the court on behalf of a client. A *pleading* constitutes a written **"appearance"** in court that only a licensed attorney can undertake. Paralegals often prepare pleadings and other documents that are filed with courts. Lawyers must review these documents so that, in essence, the lawyer adopts the paralegal's work and it merges into the lawyer's.

Pleading
A written document filed with a court that sets forth the facts of a party's case or the defendant's grounds for defense

Exceptions

Despite the clear rules and strong rationale for these prohibitions on the nonlawyer's role in court-related matters, a few notable exceptions do exist. Perhaps most important is the general rule of *self-representation.* The right of self-representation in federal courts is guaranteed by statute (28 U.S.C. § 1654) and upheld in court cases such as *Faretta v. California,* 422 U.S. 806 (1975). However, cases in federal and several state courts have determined that the right to self-representation does not encompass a right to be represented by a nonlawyer.

Some states have carved out narrow exceptions for the **marital relationship**. A California statute, for instance, permits one nonlawyer spouse to represent the other if both are joined as defendants in the same case and are appearing in **propria persona** (sometimes called *pro per* or *pro se*). However, parents cannot generally represent their children in actions before the courts, nor can a nonlawyer plaintiff represent other nonlawyer co-plaintiffs. A California court has held that a nonlawyer representing an estate in pro per may not act for the estate in a nonprobate matter.

All jurisdictions have rules permitting **law students** to engage in limited practice under a lawyer's supervision, and nearly all allow law students to represent clients in court. This exception has been created for the dual purposes of providing practical training for law students and increasing the availability of legal services. Rules governing law student practice vary from jurisdiction to jurisdiction. Most states' rules identify specific qualifications that the law student must meet, require certification of the student by the law school dean and attorney-sponsor, and impose strict limitations on the kind of court appearances that the law student may make without being accompanied by the supervising attorney.

In some local courts, paralegals are allowed to make appearances for their attorney-employers in uncontested matters under **local court rules**. These rules usually permit paralegals who are registered with the local bar or court to present stipulated, ex parte, and uncontested orders in court when such orders are based solely on the documents in the record. Paralegals must meet specified educational and work experience requirements and must be sponsored by the employing lawyer.

Administrative Agencies

An *administrative agency* is created by a state or federal legislature to provide for the regulation of a highly specialized area. A few examples of administrative agencies are the Patent Office and Social Security Administration (at the federal level) and workers' compensation, unemployment insurance, public utility, and disability boards (at the state level). Many administrative agencies handle an extremely large volume of cases that do

---

pro per/pro se
A nonlawyer representing himself or herself in a legal matter

Administrative agency
A government body responsible for control and oversight of a particular activity, usually in a highly specialized field

not require much more than a mechanical application of rules. The volume of cases and the specialized nonlegal subject matter involved make it impractical and inefficient to adjudicate disputes in these fields through regular court procedures.

Administrative agencies are **quasi-judicial** in nature, which means that disputes before these agencies are resolved through a hearing similar to although usually less formal than a trial court. Proceedings are conducted before an administrative law judge or hearing officer or examiner, with advocates representing the parties. Procedures include the issuance of subpoenas, testimony under oath, admission of evidence, and oral and written arguments.

It should be fairly clear why practice before administrative agencies constitutes the practice of law without some specific **exception** carved out for it. Someone representing a client before an administrative agency needs similar advocacy skills to those required of an attorney representing a client in a trial. The representative must have knowledge of the law and of the procedures used by the agency; must be able to apply this knowledge to the specific facts and context of the case, using the proper analytical and judgmental abilities in doing so; and must be able to advocate the client's case competently in an adversarial setting. Although the area of law might be narrower and the rules of evidence and procedure more informal than in a court, the functions of the advocate-representative and the skills necessary for success in this setting are similar to a trial lawyer's.

Despite these similarities, many administrative agencies do not require persons appearing before them to be attorneys. And lawyers and the organized bar have not fought very hard to keep administrative agencies within the exclusive domain of the practice of law. Many administrative cases involve low-income individuals and small amounts of money. The fees paid or awarded by the agencies are also relatively small and provide little economic incentive for a turf battle over unauthorized practice.

The **federal government** has long permitted nonlawyer practice before many of its administrative agencies. The purpose of doing so is twofold: to allow easy access to these agencies and to make the process as informal, efficient, and inexpensive as possible. The Administrative Procedure Act, 5 U.S.C. § 555(b) (1994), specifically authorizes individual federal administrative agencies to permit nonlawyer practice. It states that persons compelled to appear before an agency may be "accompanied, represented, and advised by counsel or, if permitted by the agency, by other qualified representative." This provision leaves the decision about nonlawyer practice to the agency itself. Some agencies have set very specific criteria (for example, a degree such as a JD or a license as a lawyer or certified public accountant, the recommendation of others admitted to practice, or an exam that must be passed) for nonlawyers to practice before the agencies. A few such federal agencies are the U.S. Patent Office, Internal Revenue Service, and Interstate Commerce Commission.

Other agencies allow all nonlawyer representatives without requiring them to meet any specific standards. Examples of these agencies include the National Labor Relations Board, Small Business Administration, Social Security Administration, and Bureau of Indian Affairs.

There is no consistency among the **states** about nonlawyer practice before administrative agencies. Some state statutes authorize representation by nonlawyers before the state's agencies, and some do not. In states that have a strong judicial history supporting the inherent power of the court to oversee the practice of law, legislation authorizing nonlawyer practice before state administrative agencies has been struck down. Most states that have considered the matter endorse a lawyer's use of a paralegal employee to represent a client before an administrative agency if a nonlawyer is otherwise allowed to make such appearances, with the proviso that the paralegal be adequately supervised.

2. Establishing the Attorney-Client Relationship

The lawyer-client relationship is a **fiduciary relationship** that is held sacrosanct under ethics rules and statutes that relate to lawyers. Lawyers are held to a high standard of care in serving clients and are bound by duties of loyalty and confidentiality. Lawyers' communications with clients are protected by the attorney-client privilege, discussed in Chapter 3. The privilege and the duties of the lawyer generally begin with the formation of the relationship.

Only the lawyer should agree to represent a client. A paralegal should not state orally or in writing to a prospective client that the lawyer will represent the client and should not sign a retainer or other agreement on behalf of the lawyer. The lawyer must be directly involved in making the decision to undertake the representation and in making the arrangements with the client concerning the **scope of the representation** and the **fees** to be paid for the work. Chapter 6 includes a comprehensive discussion of what should be contained in the agreement between the lawyer and the client.

The prohibition on a paralegal establishing the lawyer-client relationship is sometimes stated in terms of the paralegal not **"setting fees"** or **"accepting cases."** One distinction that needs to be made is between "setting" fees and "quoting" fees. The prohibition on "setting fees" does not preclude a paralegal from quoting standard fees to a prospective client or a client with the lawyer's permission and with the proviso that only the lawyer can actually contract with the client for legal services and determine the fee that will be charged to handle the client's case.

The ethical violation of setting fees or accepting cases usually arises in combination with other **unauthorized practice** matters. For example, there have been many disciplinary cases in which a lawyer is operating a law firm with many nonlawyer employees who handle the cases completely on their own up until the time the case goes to a hearing or to court. Typically, these firms operate in the bankruptcy field. In some of these cases, the nonlawyers (called "paralegals" whether trained as such or not) interview the prospective clients and have them sign a standard retainer agreement without the lawyer's involvement. The nonlawyers usually prepare and file all the documents with little or no lawyer review. The clients do not meet the lawyer until they have to go to court.

Bear in mind that this ethical prohibition on forming the lawyer-client relationship does not protect the lawyer if the client later claims that no relationship was formed. Courts have found that the lawyer-client relationship was formed because of the **apparent authority** of the nonlawyer employee to establish that relationship.

Finally, paralegals should be aware that lawyers have **duties to prospective clients**, including the duty not to reveal information learned in a consultation and not to agree to represent a client if there is a conflict. (See Chapters 3 and 4.)

3. Giving Legal Advice

The prohibition against nonlawyers giving legal advice has its foundation in the same precepts as the prohibition against court appearances by nonlawyers. Formulating a **substantive legal opinion** that will guide a client's conduct is one of the most important and critical functions an attorney undertakes. Formulating legal advice requires the application of the attorney's knowledge of law gained through extensive formal education and experience, judgmental and analytical abilities, and an understanding of the client's situation, context, and goals.

Defining the parameters of "giving legal advice" is complex and contains a lot of gray. In general, giving legal advice may be any of the following:

1. **directing or recommending** a course of action to a client about how to proceed in a matter that may have legal consequences;
2. **explaining** to a client his or her legal rights and responsibilities;
3. **evaluating** the probable outcome of a matter, including litigation; or
4. **interpreting** statutes, decisions, or legal documents to a client.

In practice, many paralegals and other nonlawyers in legal settings have frequent contact with clients, which may open the door to potential problems. Paralegals often cite **client contact** as an area of their work that affords considerable job satisfaction. Paralegals are often easier to reach by telephone than attorneys, who are frequently unavailable because they are in court or at meetings. Because most paralegals enjoy client contact, they may be more patient with clients than attorneys are, especially with clients who need a lot of attention. Paralegals may use less legal jargon than lawyers and may be able to explain matters in simple language. Finally, it is more cost-efficient for the client and the firm to have the client speak with a paralegal rather than a lawyer.

It is not uncommon for a client to develop an especially strong rapport with a paralegal who works with that client over time, and for the client to **ask questions** that would require the paralegal to give legal advice in response. That the paralegal may know the answer to the question further exacerbates this dilemma. To avoid engaging in unauthorized practice, the paralegal must first consult with the attorney before relaying advice to the client. The paralegal may communicate such advice so long as it is the advice of the attorney. It must be the exact legal opinion of the attorney, however, without expansion or interpretation by the paralegal.

An attorney cannot avoid all client contact by delegating to the paralegal responsibility for all fact gathering and drafting. Attorneys must maintain a **"direct" relationship** with clients and must exercise independent professional judgment. Overdelegation creates great potential for ethical problems to arise, especially if a client becomes dissatisfied.

A Few Examples

There is general agreement that most common paralegal functions can be performed within the bounds of ethics so long as the functions are performed with appropriate supervision and a lawyer reviews the work. However, there are a few matters that not everyone agrees about. One of these is *will executions*, a relatively simple but critical step in the process of estate planning. Whether by case law or statute, very specific rules exist in every state about the signing and witnessing of wills, including the number of witnesses, their relationship to the person(s) making the will, and their presence during the signing. In early ethics opinions, some state bars took the position that delegating the task of supervising a will execution is tantamount to having the paralegal counsel the client, and therefore constitutes the practice of law. The weight of opinions is now to the contrary, and most states that have addressed the matter say that a paralegal may oversee a will execution or serve as a witness to a will so long as he or she does not give legal advice.

Likewise, a few states prohibit attorneys from allowing a paralegal to appear at *real estate closings* without the supervising lawyer present, based on the rationale that the client is likely to ask the paralegal for legal advice, particularly for an explanation of the meaning and legal consequences of the various legal documents that must be signed. In addition, there is always the potential for last-minute disputes to arise over terms, disputes

Will execution
The formal process of signing and witnessing a will

Real estate closing
The consummation of the sale of real estate by payment of the purchase price, delivery of the deed, and finalizing collateral matters

that require the services of the attorneys to resolve. A paralegal who gives legal advice by explaining the legal consequences of documents or by attempting to resolve a dispute over terms would likely be engaging in UPL.

These concerns are addressed by bar association opinions that endorse the use of paralegals to attend real estate closings unaccompanied by a lawyer by placing certain conditions on the paralegal and lawyer. These conditions include attorney supervision and review up to the time of the closing; attorney availability to give advice during the closing if needed; client consent; a determination that the closing will be purely ministerial and that the client understands the documents in advance; and a prohibition against the paralegal giving legal advice or making legal decisions during the closing. Most ethics opinions now support this role for the paralegal.

Finally, paralegals sometimes are involved in **negotiating settlements**. Paralegals in personal injury firms frequently handle all the documentation for "working up" the case, such as collecting medical bills, assisting the client with medical insurance claims, and discussing the case with insurance claims adjusters. The paralegal often has extensive contact with adjusters and provides information on the nature of the client's injuries, treatment, and property damage. The adjuster makes offers to settle to the paralegal. The paralegal must pass these offers on to the attorney, who discusses with the client whether or not to accept an offer. The paralegal may in turn communicate the decision to accept or reject to the adjuster and handle follow-up negotiations or settlement paperwork. The paralegal may not accept a settlement offer on behalf of a client, however, even if the paralegal knows that it is an offer the client should or will accept.

Exceptions

One major exception to the prohibition against nonattorneys giving legal advice has been created in the criminal area for so-called *jailhouse lawyers*. In *Johnson v. Avery,* 393 U.S. 484 (1969), the Supreme Court held that a state may not bar inmates from helping one another to prepare postconviction writs unless the state provides a reasonable alternative. However, it should be remembered that communications between persons and their nonlawyer advisors are not protected by the attorney-client privilege. This important proviso applies to all nonlawyer representatives. Courts have consistently refused to extend the privilege to communications between nonlawyers of all kinds and their "clients" or "customers."

The prohibition against nonlawyers giving legal advice has also been the basis for challenges to **do-it-yourself and self-help legal kits**, which now include books, forms, CD-ROMs and online instructions and forms. After years of state litigation over whether the sale of kits (such

Jailhouse lawyers
Inmates who help other inmates prepare postconviction writs

as divorce kits or books and forms to assist in preparing one's own will) is unauthorized practice, a few general rules have emerged. Distributing self-help materials does *not* constitute the unauthorized practice of law as long as the materials are not distributed in conjunction with direct personalized assistance in completing the forms or procedures by nonlawyers. The cases about self-help legal materials make an important distinction between providing "legal information" that helps people bhandle their own legal affairs, and providing "legal advice," that is the application of legal knowledge and skills to a specific situation and client.

Nonlawyer Legal Service Providers and Related Trends

Typing services that type legal documents for laypersons are not engaging in unauthorized practice unless they select forms for the customer or assist the customer in deciding how and what to fill in on the forms. The line here is not always clear in practice and in the future may change with the growth of nonlawyer legal service providers.

There is a clear nationwide trend toward **expanding the role of nonlawyers** in providing legal advice to pro se litigants despite the unauthorized practice prohibitions. Most of the progress in this area has come about as the result of legislation that narrowly circumscribes the role of the nonlawyer to a particular area of law in which there is a great need for access to the legal system by persons who cannot afford attorneys and who therefore seek to represent themselves. For example, in some states, government-employed small claims advisers are authorized by statute to assist persons in filling out and filing forms and preparing for appearances. Legislation in several states permits private nonlawyer practitioners to assist litigants in unlawful detainer/summary ejection proceedings. In several states, court facilitators assist pro se litigants in divorce, restraining order, and child support proceedings. In at least one state, paralegals have been hired to assist prisoners in preparing their habeas corpus writs because it is less expensive than providing a full law library to serve the prisons.

Finally, **technological advances** that are being used to increase access to legal information are posing new challenges to the traditional notions of what it means to give legal advice. User-friendly computer programs have been set up in kiosks in courthouses in several states, enabling users to prepare court-approved forms in domestic relations, small claims, and landlord-tenant matters. Users answer a series of questions, and forms and instructions are printed out. The individualized nature of this service raises new issues about the distinction between legal information and legal advice. Although most courts have found that such programs are comparable to self-help books and are therefore not UPL, a few courts have found that the programs crossed the line into the practice of law.

A related issue is giving out legal **information or advice over the Internet**. Giving out general legal information, such as that given in a newspaper column on law, not only is considered ethical, but is also encouraged by ethics codes. However, answering questions in a way that "customizes" the information to the specific person converts the legal information to "legal advice" and raises questions about whether a lawyer-client relationship has been formed. Before a lawyer-client relationship is formed, the lawyer must determine where the matter will be undertaken and whether this is a jursidiction in which he or she is admitted. The lawyer must also check for conflicts of interest. Once a lawyer-client relationship is formed, the lawyer owes duties to the client and is liable for negligence. If the advice concerns a person or matter in a jurisdiction where the lawyer is not licensed, the lawyer may be committing UPL in that state. Although most Web sites that give legal information have disclaimers about these matters, the issues about online legal advice have yet to be fully addressed by bar associations and the courts.

F.   Disclosure of Status as Paralegal and Job Titles

One of the main functions of many paralegals is acting as liaison to persons outside the law firm — clients, witnesses, opposing law firms, courts, and so forth. This contact may take the form of telephone conversations, correspondence, or meetings in person. A key ethical aspect of the liaison role is ensuring that the person with whom the paralegal is dealing is fully aware that the paralegal is not a lawyer.

A discussion of **disclosure** of one's status as a paralegal is appropriate in this chapter on UPL for two reasons. First, a nonlawyer may appear to be engaging in unauthorized practice if he or she seems to others to be an attorney. Not clearly identifying one's status as a paralegal may mislead the other party into believing that the paralegal is a lawyer. Others may misconstrue the status of a paralegal if the paralegal "sounds" like an attorney. To the other person, a paralegal's inadvertent lack of disclosure may appear to be intentional. If this conduct by the paralegal creates problems later, the paralegal could be charged with "holding himself or herself out as an attorney." This claim may give rise to a charge of UPL against the paralegal, against the paralegal's attorney-employer, or both. (In many jurisdictions, misrepresenting oneself as an attorney is itself a misdemeanor.) Disciplinary action may be taken against the attorney for aiding in UPL.

The second reason that disclosure of the paralegal's status relates to UPL is that a paralegal who is mistaken for an attorney may be called on to perform functions that constitute UPL. If a client mistakenly believes that a paralegal is an attorney, the client may ask for legal advice. This places the paralegal in the uncomfortable position of having to backtrack in the conversation to explain his or her status and how that status makes giving a legal opinion unethical.

Guideline 4 of the ABA Model Guidelines holds lawyers responsible for taking measures to ensure that clients and others are aware that the paralegal is not licensed to practice law. The comment to this guideline mentions several means by which this may be accomplished, including the attorney's oral and written communication to clients and third parties. Most state guidelines on paralegal utilization cover disclosure and many call for **"routine, early disclosure"** or **disclosure at the "outset"** of the communications with the third party. Many ethics guidelines explain that this rule is intended to avoid confusion or misleading of clients or the public.

Some advisory opinions and state guidelines have addressed the **titles** that paralegals may use. One specifically prohibits the use of the title "*associate*" for a paralegal because law firms commonly use this title to identify their attorneys. "Paralegal" and "legal assistant" are the most commonly used titles, although their use and shades of meaning vary across the country. "Lawyer's assistant," "nonlawyer assistant," and "attorney assistant" are also used. Although the titles "paralegal" and "legal assistant" usually are used interchangeably, they carry different connotations in some regions of the country, and one or the other appellation may be preferred within the local legal community. Frequently, a legal specialty is attached to one of these titles to indicate more specifically the area of practice in which the paralegal works — for instance, "probate paralegal" or "litigation paralegal." As paralegals have become more specialized and firms have developed career paths for them, new titles have been created, such as "senior paralegal" and "litigation support specialist." As a general rule, any title that does not potentially mislead a third party into believing that the paralegal is an attorney is permissible.

One early ethics opinion (in Iowa) disallowed the use of the designation "Certified Legal Assistant" on the grounds that it may mislead the public into thinking the paralegal is state certified, but this opinion was reversed in 2003 and other state ethics opinions endorse the use of this designation. New York endorses the titles "paralegal" and "senior paralegal" but finds unacceptable and ambiguous the terms "paralegal coordinator," "legal associate," "public benefits advocate," "family law advocate," "housing law advocate," "disability benefits advocate," and "public benefit specialist."

As a general rule, paralegals may sign **correspondence**, be listed on **firm letterhead**, and have their own **business cards**, so long as an appropriate and clear title is used. The ABA long ago issued ethics opinions endorsing these practices. In the major lawyer advertising case, *Bates v. State Bar of Arizona,* 430 U.S. 350 (1977), the Supreme Court held that the state could not impose blanket restrictions on lawyer advertising. In its opinion, the court emphasized that consumers need information about legal services to make them more accessible and to help consumers select a lawyer. After this decision, ethics rules and opinions were revised to allow nonlawyers' names on letterheads and business cards.

In general, most law firms who have paralegals on staff do provide them with business cards but do not list them on the firm letterhead. Practice regarding paralegal listings on letterhead varies with the locale, the size of the firm, and the nature of its practice. Small and midsized firms are more likely to list paralegals than are large firms for both practical and firm-culture reasons. Some midsized and small law firms list paralegals on their letterhead, and many firms have individualized letterhead for each attorney and paralegal.

The NFPA Model Code addresses the issue of disclosure in DR 1.7, which requires that titles be fully disclosed. The ethical considerations that follow spell out the details, including the use of titles on business cards, letterhead, brochures, and directories, and in advertisements. Canon 5 of the NALA Code also requires disclosure "at the outset of any professional relationship. . . ."

G.   A Word About Paralegals as Independent Contractors

Paralegals now commonly offer their services as *independent contractors,* handling projects for attorneys on an as-needed basis. Early on, most of these *freelance paralegals* worked in the probate area, which lends itself well to the effective use of paralegals because the probate process is highly structured and procedural. In addition, many firms handle only a small amount of probate work — not enough to warrant having a full-time staff paralegal to perform the paralegal functions in this specialized area of practice.

Gradually, freelance paralegals began to offer their services in other areas of practice, especially litigation. Most **freelance litigation** paralegals are litigation support specialists who focus on trial preparation, usually in large civil lawsuits. Freelance litigation paralegals assist law firms in organizing, usually electronically, the sometimes massive numbers of documents in a case. The use of independent contractors has

Independent contractor paralegals
Paralegals who handle projects for attorneys on an as-needed basis (Also **freelance paralegals**)

become well accepted in the legal field, especially in large metropolitan areas. Many employment agencies place temporary or contract lawyers and paralegals in firms, as the growing use of part-time and freelance workers has become an essential feature of the economy.

Working as a freelance paralegal has ethical ramifications in many areas — such as confidentiality and conflicts of interest. One concern has been clarifying the difference between an independent contractor paralegal who provides legal services to an attorney, and a nonattorney who provides legal services directly to the public. The latter often call themselves **"independent paralegals,"** exacerbating the confusion between themselves and the paralegals who are acting under the supervision of lawyers.

A related concern involves the degree of **supervision** to which independent paralegals are subjected. Some state courts have expressed concern that a lawyer may not be properly reviewing the work performed by a freelance paralegal, especially if the lawyer is not conversant with the area of law in which the paralegal does the work. All courts and bars agree that lawyers who use the services of independent paralegals must exercise the same degree of supervision they would for an employed paralegal and are equally responsible for an independent paralegal's work.

REVIEW QUESTIONS

1. What were the purposes of the early unauthorized practice rules?
2. What was the role of bar associations in limiting the practice of law to licensed attorneys?
3. What kinds of legal functions do most nonlawyer legal service providers perform? Whom do they serve? In what areas of law do they work?
4. Give a complete and accurate definition of *practice of law*.
5. What are all the potential consequences of engaging in the unauthorized practice of law? Do most states address violations of UPL rules or statutes?
6. What are an attorney's responsibilities to prevent UPL? What might happen to an attorney whose paralegal engages in the practice of law?
7. Make a list of the specific functions that constitute the practice of law and are prohibited to paralegals. What rationale lies behind each prohibition?
8. What are the exceptions to the general rule against a nonlawyer appearing in court on behalf of a client?
9. What is the difference between setting fees and quoting fees? Which is prohibited as UPL?
10. Give your best definition of what constitutes giving legal advice.

11. What are the exceptions to the general prohibition against giving legal advice?

12. Does selling a self-help divorce kit constitute giving legal advice? What about a software program or online service that helps a person fill out and file forms with the court? What about answering legal questions on the Internet? Why or why not?

13. What kinds of work can legal typing services perform without engaging in the unauthorized practice of law?

14. Why are paralegals prohibited from setting legal fees? From accepting cases?

15. May a paralegal supervise a will execution without an attorney present? Why or why not?

16. May a paralegal handle a real estate closing without the supervising attorney present? Why or why not?

17. Why are nonlawyers allowed to practice before some administrative agencies?

18. Why must a paralegal be careful to disclose his or her status?

19. Name some job titles that are appropriate for paralegals to use in identifying their status. Name some titles that are not appropriate and explain why.

20. May paralegals sign correspondence on firm letterhead? May paralegals have business cards? May their names be listed on law firm letterhead?

21. Is it ethical for paralegals to work as independent contractors for lawyers? What are the ethical concerns in working this way?

HYPOTHETICALS

1. Dean Downs has been working as a personal injury paralegal for a small law firm for six months. He specialized in litigation in paralegal school and has never worked in another law firm or done any other kind of legal work. One of the lawyers in the firm, Enid East, is handling an appeal of a criminal case pro bono. Enid asks Dean to prepare the appellate brief in the case. Dean does not know where to begin. What should he do? Dean finishes the draft brief and gives it to Enid to review. Enid does not have any experience in criminal work either and gives the brief a cursory look before she approves it for filing with the court. What should Dean do now? Has Enid breached any ethical duties? What if the brief is terrible and the client loses because they missed a key case? Does it matter that the client was not paying a fee?

2. Fran Francis has just gone to work for a sole practitioner who is very disorganized. The lawyer, George Graham, has hired Fran in part to get him organized. Fran finds a file in the bottom drawer of a desk that

relates to a case in which the statute of limitations is about to run. George is out of the country until next week, by which time the statute will have run. Fran knows how to prepare the standard form complaint for this kind of case and also realizes that if she makes any minor mistakes in the complaint, they can be remedied by amending the complaint later on. What should she do? Can she prepare the complaint? Sign it? File it? What are her other options?

3. Hanna is a family law paralegal with ten years of experience. She works very independently and really knows the process well. Her friend, Isabel, wants to file for divorce. She and her husband, Jim, do not have any children, both work and have good benefits, and together they own a couple of pieces of property. Isabel asks Hanna to help her do the divorce papers because Isabel and Jim don't want to pay a lawyer to do it. It seems like the situation is not contentious and that the couple will be able to end the relationship without a fight. What should Hanna do? To what extent, if any, can she help Isabel and Jim? Can she advise them how to proceed? Can she help them fill out the paperwork? Fill it out for them? Can she draft a settlement agreement for them? If she helps them and the court finds an error in her work, what are the consequences? If she helps them and the situation becomes contentious between them, what happens? Can Hanna be called to testify about what she knows about them if they end up in court?

4. Joan Johnson is a paralegal for a large law firm that handles corporate and securities work. The lawyer for whom Joan works always introduces her to clients and encourages clients to call her for updates on matters. Joan enjoys this work and is good at it. One day a client, Ken Kaplan, calls her about a new corporate entity he is forming. He explains what the corporation will do and asks whether it would be better to incorporate in New York or in Delaware. Can Joan answer? What should she do? What are the consequences of the different actions she might take?

5. Laura Lane is a business litigation paralegal for a firm that handles construction litigation. A prospective client comes in to see an attorney, Mary Moore, who is tied up in court and asks Laura to interview the client. The client, Nathan North, tells a story about the faulty construction done on the remodeling of his kitchen. He asks Laura, "Do I have a good case?" What should she say? He also asks: "Can I handle this myself, or do I need an attorney?" Laura is certain that Mary will want to take the case and that Nathan will get some compensation for damages. How should Laura answer each of Nathan's questions? Can Laura get Nathan to sign an agreement for Mary to represent him? Can Laura tell Nathan what kind of fee agreement Mary would normally make with a client in a case like this? What ethics rules are

implicated? Does it make any difference if Laura and Nathan are friends?

6. Owen Olson, a paralegal in a personal injury firm, handles a lot of negotiations on cases. One day, an insurance adjuster, Peter Paul, calls to discuss a new case. After a few minutes, the adjuster says, "What if we just settle this for $20,000 right now?" What should Owen do? After more discussion, Owen realizes that Peter believes that Owen is a lawyer. Should Owen do anything about this? If so, what?

DISCUSSION QUESTIONS AND PROJECTS

1. Does your state have a definition of the practice of law? Where is it — in a statute, court rule, or case? Does your state or local bar association have a UPL committee? Who prosecutes UPL in your state?
2. Do you think that a sole practitioner lawyer who has ten paralegals working in her or his office can adequately supervise these paralegals? What office procedures and policies might ensure adequate supervision? What if the lawyer is in court every day and only spends a few hours a week in the office?
3. Do you think that an attorney who hires a paralegal without any formal paralegal training is violating his or her duty to supervise? Why, or why not? Could this situation be appropriate or inappropriate depending on the circumstances? What factors would you consider in deciding?
4. Which of the following acts by a paralegal would be permissible and which would be prohibited under the definitions of *legal advice* given in this chapter?

   a. interviewing a client to obtain the facts relating to an automobile accident;
   b. telling the client that the firm probably would be able to get a recovery;
   c. telling the client that the firm will probably be able to get $10,000 plus expenses;
   d. explaining to the client what happens at a deposition;
   e. explaining to the client the meaning of an affidavit given to the client for signature;
   f. telling a client that his or her case is likely to settle;
   g. telling a client that he or she would be best off to file a small claims action;
   h. answering a client's questions about the meaning of terms in a contract;
   i. giving a client the legal opinion that she or he knows the attorney would give;

    j. relaying a message from the attorney to the client that tells the client that it is okay to sign a contract.

5. In a personal injury law firm that takes every case that comes to it and charges the same contingency fee, why should it be necessary for the lawyer to set the fee and establish the relationship with the client? Should this be an ethical rule, or is it really a matter of good practice? Suppose the initial contact between the attorney and client is a five-minute meeting to formalize the relationship and the client never speaks to the attorney again because the paralegal "works up" the case, negotiates the settlement, and has all the client contact. Is the attorney maintaining a direct relationship with the client?

6. What are the rules governing will executions in your state? Does the state or local bar association have an advisory opinion about paralegals supervising will executions without the presence of an attorney?

7. Do parties to residential real estate transactions in your state usually use the services of lawyers? If not, who does this work? If so, are paralegals who work for real estate lawyers permitted to handle closings without an attorney present? Is it common practice? Does the state or local bar have an opinion about it?

8. Has your state bar or supreme court studied the issue of providing access to legal services? If so, do any of its findings or recommendations relate to nonlawyer legal service providers or paralegals?

9. How can the prohibition against nonlawyers representing clients in court be reconciled with nonlawyer representation of clients before administrative agencies? Do you think that the differences in these two settings are substantial enough to warrant differences in practice?

10. Are there any administrative agencies in your state that permit nonlawyer practice? Do nonlawyers appear before these agencies frequently or infrequently? What about paralegals working under the supervision of lawyers? Are there any state or local bar ethics opinions on this matter? Do any statutes in your state disallow fees for nonlawyer representatives in administrative agencies?

11. How can independent paralegals who work under the supervision of lawyers distinguish themselves from those who serve the public directly? Would different job titles make a difference? For example, nonlawyer direct service providers have sometimes been called "legal technicians" and are called "legal document assistants" in California. Can a title be "forced" on the public and the occupation? Would it make a difference if the state regulated the occupation?

12. Are lawyers who use the services of independent contractors more likely to fail in their responsibility to select, train, supervise, and review the work of these paralegals than paralegals who are employed? How would this happen? Are these risks significant enough to warrant a complete ban on independent contractor paralegals? What about other independent contractors who serve

lawyers — for example, process servers, investigators, accountants, and experts?

SELECTED CASES

In re Anderson, 79 B.R. 482 (Bankr. S.D. Cal. 1987) (nonlawyer legal service provider and UPL).

Board of Commissioners of the Utah State Bar v. Petersen, 937 P.2d 1263 (Utah 1997) (nonlawyer legal service provider who had been to "paralegal school" and was "registered" as a paralegal is prosecuted for UPL).

Davies v. Unauthorized Practice Committee of State Bar of Texas, 431 S.W.2d 590, at 593 (Tex. Civ. App. 1968) (definition of the practice of law).

Drake v. Superior Court of San Diego County, 21 Cal. App. 4th 1826, 26 Cal. Rptr. 2d 829 (1994) (power of attorney).

Florida Bar v. Beach, 675 So. 2d 106 (Fla. 1996) (discipline of lawyer for relationship with nonlawyer legal service provider).

Florida Bar v. Brumbaugh, 355 So. 2d 1186 (Fla. 1978) (nonlawyer legal service provider and UPL).

Florida Bar v. Furman, 376 So. 2d 378 (Fla. 1979) (nonlawyer legal service provider and UPL).

People v. Landlords Professional Services, 215 Cal. App. 3d 1599, 264 Cal. Rptr. 548 (1989) (nonlawyer legal service provider and UPL).

In re Moffett, 263 B.R. 805 (Bankr. W.D. Ky. 2001) (nonlawyer bankruptcy preparer sanctioned by bankruptcy court for UPL and other statutory offenses).

In re Morin, 319 Or. 547, 878 P.2d 393 (1994) (supervised paralegals in estate planning practice and UPL).

In re Reynoso, 477 F.2d 117 (9th Cir. 2007) (operation of online bankruptcy software program found to constitute UPL).

State v. Foster, 674 So. 2d 747 (Fla. 1996) (UPL conviction of nonlawyer legal service provider who was taking depositions on behalf of a client).

UPL Committee v. State Department of Workers' Compensation, 543 A.2d 662 (R.I. 1998) (nonlawyer assistants in administrative agency proceedings).

In re Welch, 185 A.2d 458, 459 (Vt. 1962) (definition of practice of law).

SELECTED REFERENCES

ABA Model Rules of Professional Conduct, Rule 5.1 [lawyer responsibility for other lawyers]

ABA Model Rules of Professional Conduct, Rule 5.3 [lawyer responsibility for nonlawyers]

ABA Model Rules of Professional Conduct, Rule 5.5 [aiding in the unauthorized practice of law; multijurisdictional practice and safe harbors]

ABA Model Code DR 3-101(A) [aiding in the unauthorized practice of law]

NALA Code of Ethics and Professional Responsibility, Canons 1 through 5 [unauthorized practice of law, supervision, and disclosure of status]

NFPA Model Code of Ethics and Professional Responsibility, DR 1.7 and 1.8 [unauthorized practice and disclosure of status]

ABA Committee on Ethics and Professional Responsibility, Informal Opinion 1185 (1971) [business cards]

ABA Committee on Ethics and Professional Responsibility, Informal Opinion 1367 (1976) [signing correspondence] ABA Committee on Ethics and Professional Responsibility, Informal Opinion 1527 (1989) [letterheads and advertisements]

NFPA Informal Ethics Opinion 95-2 [letterhead]

3

Confidentiality

This chapter covers the rules relating to confidentiality, one of the most critical elements of legal ethics, and teaches how to identify and resolve issues related to confidentiality. Chapter 3 covers:

- basic principles of confidentiality
- the attorney-client privilege and the difference between the privilege and the ethics rules on confidentiality
- what information is privileged or protected by the rule of confidentiality
- how and when the privilege and the duty of confidentiality may be broken or waived
- the work product rule
- how the principles and rules of confidentiality come into play for paralegals in practice
- how to protect confidentiality of information and records
- special problems in maintaining confidentiality with technology

A. The Principle of Confidentiality

Confidentiality is one of the oldest precepts of legal ethics and is fundamental to the lawyer-client relationship. The principle of confidentiality is based on the notion that lawyers must know all the facts if they are to to best serve the client and that clients will not fully disclose the facts unless they are assured that information will not be revealed to others. The principle of confidentiality is also based on agency law. Lawyers are in a fiduciary relationship with their clients, which requires the lawyer's highest trust, including confidence, loyalty, and good faith.

The general duty of confidentiality encompasses both ethics rules and evidentiary rules relating to **attorney–client privilege** and **work product**. The attorney-client privilege is a rule of evidence that relates to what confidential information is protected in litigation from discovery or testimony. The ethics rules covering confidentiality are much broader than the attorney-client privilege, as they cover a lawyer's duty not to divulge information about a client in any context. The ethics rules also encompass information that may not qualify to be covered by the privilege.

B. Attorney-Client Privilege

1. Defined Generally

All jurisdictions make provision for the attorney-client privilege by statute, court rule, or common law. The **general rule** is that a client who seeks a lawyer's advice or assistance may invoke an unqualified privilege not to testify and to prevent the lawyer from testifying as to communications made by the client in confidence to the lawyer. The privilege lasts indefinitely. The client is the holder of the privilege, and only the client may waive it by way of consenting to the disclosure of the privileged communication. Although the client is the holder of the privilege, the attorney must advise the client of the privilege. It should be noted that the privilege only extends to the attorney-client relationship and does not cover nonlawyer legal service providers, like legal documents assistants and jailhouse lawyers.

Case law has **clarified the meaning** of the attorney-client privilege: The privilege covers confidential communications between lawyer and client — whether oral or written — so long as the advice sought by the client is legal; other kinds of advice — personal or business, for instance — are not covered. It also covers initial consultations even if the lawyer does not undertake representation, and it includes attorney-client communications whether or not the attorney charges a fee.

The privilege does not cover material or information that is not classified as a communication. The privilege lasts after the representation of the client ends and even after the death of the client. There are very limited reasons for which the privilege will be waived, as noted below.

2. Disclosure of Privileged Information

One of the key aspects of the privilege for paralegals is that it extends to communications made directly to or in the presence of the ***attorney's agents***, a category that includes colleagues and employees in the law firm who are working or may be working on the client matter. This principle also covers consultants, investigators, and outside agencies working with counsel on a case. For example, the privilege extends to an outside vendor, such as a data processing firm that stores confidential information for a law firm.

Attorney's agents
Colleagues, vendors, and employees working at the behest or under the supervision of a lawyer to effectuate the representation of clients

Some state statutes on the privilege specifically extend its scope to employees of attorneys. Even without such statutory language, the privilege does cover employees, including paralegals. The privilege would have no practical value if it were not extended to persons who work on clients' matters as members of the legal services delivery team. Cases have confirmed that the communications between clients and paralegals are covered by the privilege.

Communications must be made in a **confidential setting** to merit the protection of the privilege. This means that the setting must be private — that is, one in which others cannot overhear — and there should not be any other persons present who would not otherwise be covered by the privilege — a friend of the client, for example. Under contemporary rules, an eavesdropper who listens in on a confidential communication will not destroy the privilege.

The **client can waive** the privilege by repeating the communication to nonconfidential third parties or expressing an intention to make the confidential information public. For example, if a client makes public disclosures of otherwise protected communications, the privilege is considered to be waived. However, the waiver applies only to the communications revealed, not to other related protected communications. It should be noted also that some disclosures are themselves protected and therefore do not result in a waiver of the privilege. For example, disclosures made during plea bargaining or settlement negotiations cannot later be admitted at trial to prove guilt or liability.

3. Matters not Covered by the Privilege

The privilege usually does not extend to **the identity of a client** or to **a client's whereabouts**. However, the Supreme Court has held that the identity of a client is privileged when a lawyer sends a payment to the Internal Revenue Service anonymously on the client's behalf for underpayment of federal taxes. Because revealing the identity of the client could have led to conviction of a federal crime, the client's identity was protected. However, only a few cases have followed this reasoning and then only when revealing the client's identity would lead to a criminal prosecution.

The **fee arrangement** between a lawyer and client historically has not been privileged although some states now have statutes making fee agreements privileged. The only exception to this rule is triggered when details of the fee arrangement would reveal the identity of a client and the identity itself is privileged. This exception has been used by government prosecutors, grand juries, and the Internal Revenue Service to identify and then seize legal fees paid to attorneys with money or assets obtained through illegal activity, such as the drug trade. Criminal defense attorneys object to the exception and have challenged the government on the basis of the privilege. They contend that fee arrangements, payment records, and client names are privileged and that the government's actions constitute harassment and interference with the right to counsel. There is a split of authority in the courts that have decided cases on this issue.

Protection of confidential communications about a client's whereabouts is almost never extended. In such cases, the client is usually a fugitive, so the attorney's nondisclosure of the client's location would amount to assisting the client in committing a future crime, one of the traditional bases for an exception to the privilege.

A client cannot bring a **preexisting document** within the protection of the privilege simply by giving it to his or her attorney. However, if a preexisting document is covered by another privilege, such as the spousal privilege, it will continue to be privileged while in the attorney's possession. **Physical evidence** of a client's crime is not protected by the privilege, and an attorney who comes into possession of such evidence is usually required to turn it over to the prosecutor. The attorney may or may not be compelled to testify about the source of the evidence, depending on the attorney's role in obtaining the evidence and the state's precedents. If the lawyer obtained the evidence illegally, a court would be more inclined to force such testimony.

4. Inadvertent Disclosure of Privileged Material

In addition to actual client consent to waiver of the privilege and consent implied from the actions of the client, inadvertent disclosure might destroy the privilege. For example, if a protected document is accidentally given to opposing counsel in a ***document production***, this document may be deemed by the court to lose its privileged status.

Document production
A form of discovery under which one party must provide copies of specified documents to the other side

The cases across the country about this kind of "waiver" are not uniform but the trend is against an automatic waiver. A few states consistently hold that inadvertent disclosure constitutes a **waiver of the privilege**, with the majority of courts holding that inadvertent disclosure does not necessarily constitute a waiver. Most cases find that the disclosure is not tantamount to a waiver so long as the lawyer took reasonable good-faith measures to prevent disclosure. Some courts also look at the extent of the disclosure, the timeliness of attempts to rectify it, and the issue of fairness.

Many courts hold that inadvertent disclosure should not result in waiver of the privilege because the client is the holder of the privilege and would not consent to the revelation of damaging protected information. However, obvious practical difficulties arise with continuing protection of information once such information is revealed; even if not admissible at trial, opposing counsel will have the benefit of the knowledge and may seek evidence about the facts at issue through other means.

Incidents of inadvertent disclosure are not uncommon, in large part because of the increase in multiparty litigation, the large scale of discovery, and the use of electronic records and means of communication. Some compelling examples of damaging inadvertent disclosure do exist: For example, a lawyer in a large law firm accidentally released sealed documents to a magazine; a firm inadvertently placed sealed records in an appellate court file only to find them later published in a magazine; privileged documents were produced to opposing counsel when sticky notes marking them as privileged fell off the papers; and a lawyer's assistant accidentally sent a memorandum outlining legal strategy to the opposing lawyer. In yet another case, a trial judge dismissed a panel of prospective jurors when the defense firm inadvertently faxed a secret document on jury selection strategy to the plaintiff's firm. To avoid loss of the privilege in cases of inadvertent disclosure, many law firms have agreements with opposing counsel under which both sides agree not to use and to return inadvertently disclosed documents.

Paralegals often have extensive responsibility for discovery, including responding to *subpoenas duces tecum* and handling document productions. When hundreds of documents are requested by opposing counsel, the paralegal is often the one to review, organize, and examine these documents to see that they are purged of privileged material before they are copied and provided to the opposing counsel. In addition to needing guidance from the supervising attorney as to what documents to look for, paralegals need a clear understanding of the privilege so that they can identify and flag documents that may need to be protected for review by a lawyer.

Another important issue is what paralegals should do if they **receive privileged documents** that were inadvertently sent. The ABA recently withdrew two earlier ethics opinions on the matter that have been followed in many jurisdictions. Although the ABA no longer supports the view expressed in these opinions, many state bars and courts continue to follow the general rules established in those opinions:

1. to **refrain from reviewing** such materials as soon as it is evident that they are privileged
2. to **notify the sender** (often the opposing counsel) about the materials
3. either to **follow instructions** of the sender, which will likely be to return the material immediately, or to **seek a resolution** of the disposition of the materials from a court

Some jurisdictions have not addressed this issue and do not have a provision in their ethics rules or advisory opinions to cover this situation. Some states, such as California, have case law that requires the lawyer to follow all three steps or risk being sanctioned by the court. In two recent California cases, lawyers and their experts were disqualified from a case after it was discovered that they had acquired privileged defense documents and attempted to use the information from those documents to impeach the defense experts.

5. Exceptions to and Waivers of the Privilege

An exception to or waiver of the privilege may occur when the client calls into question the **attorney's professional competence** through criminal charges, a malpractice suit, a disciplinary action, or a contention of ineffective counsel on appeal from a criminal conviction.

When an **attorney represents two clients** who later become adversaries, otherwise privileged communications relating to the joint matter are not protected. However, pooled information shared by counsel who represent different clients with common interests generally is protected although it may be used by the parties in later litigation in which the interests of the parties are adverse.

Also, confidential communications about a **future crime or fraud** that a client is planning are not protected. Under the important crime-fraud exception, privileged communications can be disclosed if they were made in furtherance of a crime or fraud. What communications fall into this exception varies from jurisdiction to jurisdiction, but the trend allows more court-ordered disclosure. For example, in major tobacco litigation, the crime-fraud exception was used successfully in several cases to gain access to incriminating documents between the companies and their lawyers.

6.   The Privilege in the Corporate Setting

Special problems in applying the attorney-client privilege exist in the representation of corporations. Questions sometimes arise as to **who the "client" is** and, flowing from that, what communications are protected. Different jurisdictions use different tests to determine the application of the privilege. On one end of the spectrum is the ***control group test***, which limits the privilege to confidential communications between the lawyer and the management personnel responsible for acting in the legal matter. The broader ***subject matter test*** is followed in other jurisdictions. Under that test, a corporation's employees are covered if they communicate in confidence with the corporation's lawyers or paralegals for the purpose of enabling them to render legal services to the corporation.

Another issue that arises in corporate representation relates to the **holder of the privilege**. The corporation, not the employee, is the client and thus the holder of the privilege; only the corporation may waive it. The employee who communicates the information may not object to the corporation's waiver of the privilege. The board of directors controls the exercise of the privilege. Therefore, the corporation can reveal statements made by the employee, even if the employee wants to keep information confidential because it is incriminating or embarrassing.

Finally, another issue that arises in the corporate setting is whether an **internal audit or investigation** conducted by a corporation's attorneys is protected under the attorney-client privilege. Whether or not a court will extend the protection of the privilege to such audits varies from state to state and depends to a large extent on how carefully the lawyers and their client constructed the audit to preserve the privilege.

Paralegals who work in-house are covered by the privilege in the same way they would be if they worked in a private law firm; in essence the in-house counsel's office functions as a law firm with one client. However, paralegals in this setting must take care to ensure that they are fully and properly supervised by a lawyer, or a court may find that they are simply lay employees to whom the privilege is not extended. This scenario arose in a recent patent case in California, and although its reasoning has not been followed in other cases, it serves as a warning to paralegals who work in house.

Finally, the Sarbanes-Oxley Act resulted in the adoption of a new code of conduct for lawyers working with corporate securities. This federal law created new duties concerning responsibility of lawyers for reporting of wrongdoing in ways that are not always in alignment with the privilege or ethics codes in the controlling jurisdiction.

Control group test
Limits attorney-client privilege to confidential communications between the attorney and top management personnel

Subject matter test
Applies attorney-client privilege to all corporate employees who communicate in confidence with the attorney for the purpose of enabling the attorney to render legal services

7. Court-Ordered Disclosure

If protected communications are sought, the lawyer must respond to the court and invoke the privilege. If the court orders the lawyer to testify or to produce documents, the lawyer may do so or may refuse and appeal the ruling. Sometimes a court will order an ***in camera*** examination to determine whether to order disclosure in open court. If a lawyer breaks the privilege without a client's consent or a court order, the client may seek to enjoin or suppress the lawyer's testimony or seek dismissal of the case before the court. The client, of course, may sue the lawyer for legal malpractice and file a complaint with the appropriate disciplinary authorities.

in camera
Proceedings held in the judge's chambers without the jury or public present

C. The Work Product Rule

Federal and state rules of evidence and discovery provide for the protection of materials prepared by lawyers in anticipation of litigation. This *work product doctrine* derives from the 1947 case of *Hickman v. Taylor,* 329 U.S. 495, in which the Court created a qualified immunity from discovery for a lawyer's trial preparation. The purpose of this rule is to allow each side to prepare fully and in private. This doctrine has been codified in the Federal Rules of Civil Procedure and in state statutes.

The work product rule covers two kinds of trial preparation material: informational and mental impression. ***Mental impressions***, which are covered by an unqualified privilege, are the lawyer's ideas on how to conduct the case—that is, his or her strategies, theories, and related legal research. Because the privilege covering mental impressions is unqualified, this kind of material is completely protected. ***Informational material***, which is protected by a qualified privilege, covers factual research material such as witness statements. When an opposing party finds that such informational material is critical to its case and can show that there is no effective substitute, it may convince a court to break the privilege and obtain access to the material.

Mental impressions
Lawyer's ideas on how to conduct the case

Informational material
Factual research material, such as witness interviews

Because only material prepared in anticipation of litigation is protected under the work product doctrine, some material, such as an investigator's report prepared before there has been a clear indication that a lawsuit would be filed, may be discoverable. Cases in this area vary widely, with some lending protection whenever an insurance company investigation is made, but others only after an attorney becomes involved and orders the investigation or report.

The work product doctrine has become increasingly critical with the advent of **electronic database management** systems. Discovery under the information prong of the rule is generally permitted if documents are input verbatim. However, paraphrased or summarized documents, selectively input documents, and documents sorted topically by means of an index of issues prepared by a lawyer generally are protected because such information relates to strategy and legal theories that the lawyer is developing.

The life of the work product protection varies with the jurisdiction. Some states hold that the protection terminates with the end of the litigation; others continue it indefinitely; still others terminate it with the end of the litigation except as to future related litigation. As with the attorney-client privilege, work product protection can be waived by actual or implied consent of the client.

D. Ethics Rules of Confidentiality

Broad protection for client confidentiality was included in the earliest codes governing attorney conduct and is included in the ethics rules in every state. In addition to requiring lawyers to protect client confidences, these rules also provide part of the foundation for conflict of interest rules, discussed in Chapter 4.

Canon 4 of the ABA Model Code of Professional Responsibility provides that "[a] lawyer should preserve the confidences and secrets of a client." The related Disciplinary Rule (DR 4-101) spells out the specifics of this requirement, including exceptions. A few states still follow this rule, which distinguishes between **confidences**, defined as information protected by the attorney-client privilege, and **secrets**, which include "other information gained in the professional relationship that the client has requested to be held inviolate or the disclosure of which would be embarrassing or would likely to be detrimental to the client." Under this rule, lawyers must protect all confidential information from release, may not use the information to the disadvantage of the client, and may not use the information to the advantage of the attorney or a third person without client consent after full disclosure. Confidentiality may be broken only (1) with client consent; (2) when required by ethics rules, law, or court order; (3) to prevent the commission of a crime; and (4) to establish or collect a fee or to defend against an accusation of wrongful conduct. The rule also requires a lawyer to exercise reasonable care to ensure that employees and others involved in client matters do not disclose or use client confidences or secrets.

The ABA Model Rules, adopted in most jurisdictions, eliminate the distinction between confidences and secrets and contain a **general prohibition** against revealing "information relating to representation of a client" (Model Rule 1.6). Setting the parameters of what is confidential in this way means that virtually all information is covered, regardless of when and how it was learned by the attorney. No private setting is required, the information need not have been communicated directly by the client, and information learned either before or after the representation is covered. Further, the client need not request confidentiality, and the attorney must abstain from revealing information, whether or not it has the potential to harm or embarrass the client. The Model Rules allow judicially ordered disclosure only in accordance with exceptions to the attorney-client privilege or work product rule, as noted above.

If confidential information becomes public, a paralegal is not relieved of responsibility to protect the confidentiality of the information under the ethics rules; however, under the evidentiary privilege, the duty to protect the confidentiality of this information lapses. The rule provides for disclosure only if the client gives informed consent, unless implied authorization exists because the disclosures are necessary to carry out representation.

The ABA Model Rules permit, but do not require, a lawyer to reveal confidential information to prevent **death or substantial bodily harm**; to prevent a **crime or fraud** likely to cause serious harm; and to **prevent, mitigate, or rectify** a substantial financial or other injury. When a lawyer may reveal confidential information to prevent a future crime is the most controversial aspect of the ethics rules on confidentiality. Many states have adopted their own versions of this rule: Some *require* an attorney to reveal information to prevent the commission of a crime likely to result in death or substantial bodily harm; others follow the ABA exception *permitting* revelation of information to prevent commission of a crime without provision that the crime be serious. Still others allow the attorney discretion to reveal confidential information to prevent future crimes, fraud, or acts only if they are likely to result in substantial injury to the financial or property interests of another. Other ethics rules that relate to this exception prohibit a lawyer from counseling a client to engage in criminal activity or from assisting a client in committing a crime. Lawyers may also reveal confidential information to **secure legal advice** about an ethical matter, **establish a claim or defense** in a controversy with the client, and comply with a **court order or law**.

E. Confidentiality and the Paralegal

1. Application of the Rule to Paralegals

Every state that has guidelines on the utilization of paralegals requires lawyers to ensure that paralegals preserve client confidences. The ABA Model Guidelines for the Utilization of Paralegal Services provide rules on confidentiality in Guideline 6: "A lawyer is responsible for taking **reasonable measures** to ensure that all client confidences are preserved by a paralegal." Most state guidelines speak in terms of the attorney "instructing" the paralegal to preserve client confidences or to "exercise care" to ensure that paralegals preserve client confidences. Some guidelines remind attorneys that the confidentiality duty covers everything from casual disclosure (for example, by common gossip) to intentional misuse (for example, insider trading).

NALA Model Guideline IV requires paralegals to preserve confidences and secrets using the terminology of the ABA Model Code. Canon 7 of the NALA Code calls for paralegals to protect client confidentiality and to uphold the laws on the attorney-client privilege. The NFPA Model Code requires paralegals to "preserve all confidential information provided by the client or acquired from other sources, before, during, and after the course of the professional relationship" (NFPA DR 1.5). The ethical considerations that accompany this rule set forth exceptions, cover the misuse of information, and establish a prohibition against "indiscreet" communications.

2. Protecting Confidentiality in Daily Practice

Law firms need well-established **policies and procedures** to help prevent inadvertent disclosure of confidential information. Some firms include these in their written manuals, orientation programs, and training videos.

Policies should be established to deny unauthorized personnel access to **files** and to the file room. Code numbers instead of names can be used on client files. Old files and papers (even scratch paper) concerning clients should be disposed of properly, preferably by shredding, so that no one outside the firm will have access to them. Electronic files should be purged so that they cannot be reconstructed. Computer screens should not be visible to those walking through the office. **Conversations** over intercoms and speakerphones should be limited to nonconfidential matters to prevent unauthorized personnel, clients, or others visiting the office from overhearing. Privileged documents should be labeled as such when they are created to lessen the risk that they will not be handled carefully. Privileged **documents** should also be segregated from nonconfidential documents in separate files whenever possible. Procedures should limit the personnel who have access to any privileged documents, whether in hard or electronic form.

The most common kind of disclosure of confidential information takes place in conversations about work outside the firm's offices. Casual conversations concerning clients that are held with coworkers and friends outside the firm are potentially serious breaches of ethics. Other participants in such conversations are not only receiving confidential information but may repeat these confidences to others, and conversations held in public places can be overheard. Although such improper disclosures take place often and rarely result in sanctions, the consequences — losing a client, having a court deny protection to the information, having a client bring a malpractice suit or initiate a disciplinary complaint — are serious and should provide a sufficient incentive to paralegals to exercise great discretion when discussing client matters.

Lawyers and paralegals should not have conversations with clients in the **presence of parties** who are not necessary to the representation. Confidential conversations should take place in the privacy of a closed office or conference room, not in the reception or secretarial area, lunchroom, hallway, or elevator. The presence of others should be limited to the lawyers and employees who are working on the client's case. Other law firm employees should not be present when a confidential conversation with a client is being held.

Paralegals should not take **calls** from a client while meeting with another client because the client that is present in the room might overhear the paralegal's half of a confidential conversation. Likewise, when seeing a client or anyone else from outside the firm, a paralegal should not have any other clients' files exposed or an active computer screen visible to the visitor.

The privilege and the work product rule protect information in **databases**, including those used for litigation support. To ensure that the database is protected, lawyers must be involved in the design and planning of the database. Head notes should include their legal theories, opinions, conclusions, and strategies. Clients, witnesses, and others should not have access to the database. Full-text databases are most likely to be found discoverable. To prevent this, only selected material should be included, and headings or annotations to assist with searches should be developed cooperatively by attorneys and paralegals.

Confidentiality
agreement
Agreement between a law firm and an employee or vendor in which the employee agrees to keep client information confidential

Confidentiality agreements are another means to protect against disclosures of confidential information. A confidentiality agreement should require the signer (such as an employee or vendor) not to disclose and to prevent any disclosure of confidential information. It should also require the signer to return all documents acquired or developed during the course of work and admonish the signer not to remove any documents from the workplace. Such agreements should be signed by all employees, independent contractors, and outside agencies with access to privileged information. Access to extremely sensitive confidential information should be limited to as few employees as possible, preferably permanent staff members.

In a law firm or corporate setting, paralegals and others often have access to confidential information that they could **misuse** for their own gain. For example, if a paralegal learns that a real estate development being handled by a firm will result in dramatic increases in property values in the surrounding areas, the paralegal should not misuse this information to buy property. Similarly, insider trading rules forbid using confidential information to benefit in stock trading. In addition to the individual's liability under securities law, the firm is also liable. Under the Insider Trading and Securities Fraud Enforcement Act of 1988, large fines may be levied against a law firm whose employee uses confidential or inside information to engage in unlawful securities transactions if the firm did not exercise appropriate supervision to prevent the unlawful trading. Many large firms that handle securities work screen paralegal employees very carefully and require them to sign agreements not to misuse confidential client information in trading.

3. Special Issues Relating to Technology

Technological advances that have changed the way law is practiced have also created new problems in protecting the confidentiality of information. **Electronic records** are more portable and accessible than paper; are easier to retrieve, copy, and transmit; are easier to alter and intercept; and are more difficult to delete. Firms must take special security measures to preserve confidentiality and to protect against potential claims that the privilege has been waived because communications were not treated as private and confidential.

Facsimile machines pose special risks to confidentiality if the law firm does not know who will pick up the fax at the other end of the line. Generally, faxing extremely sensitive confidential communications should be avoided and courier service should be used. If faxing is necessary, steps should be taken to ensure that the appropriate person is on the receiving end, to guard against third parties who are not covered by the privilege reading the communication. A notice of confidentiality should accompany the material on the cover sheet, and the word "confidential" or "privileged" should be stamped on every page. Some of these concerns are mitigated if the fax goes directly to the client's personal computer by way of e-mail.

Calls made on some **cellular and cordless telephones**, especially older analog versions, may be intercepted by special scanners, making them less secure for sensitive conversations than ordinary land-based telephone lines. Under the Federal Electronic Communications Privacy Act and some state statutes, an interception of any kind of communication made through these media does not destroy the privilege if the communication is otherwise protected by a privilege, such as the attorney–client privilege. Caution should be exercised when using cordless or cellular telephones for privileged communications. Although interception of cellular calls has been made more difficult by improvements in the technology, such communications are still not as secure as those made on land-based lines. A few state and local bar associations have issued opinions recommending that lawyers not use such telephones for confidential communications because of the risk of interception and the lowered expectation of privacy. These opinions also suggest that lawyers inform their clients of the risks involved and obtain their consent to use this means of communication to discuss confidential matters. The safest practice is obviously to limit conversations on such phones and to communicate about sensitive and privileged matters only on a secure land-based phone. Also, because cell phones can be used anywhere, some people do not take precautions when making calls in public settings. Making a confidential call in a public place may violate the duty of confidentiality and jeopardize the privilege.

Special protections must be in place to ensure that privileged material on **computers** is not vulnerable. Physical security of computers and network servers is essential. Servers should be in a locked room and should be secured to the furniture or floor. Access to these areas should be restricted to those who need it. Computers should have screensavers and should not be placed where a passerby can view the screen.

The system should be protected by requiring everyone to log in with **passwords**, which should be carefully chosen so that they are not obvious (avoiding passwords such as initials, birth dates, and the like). Passwords should also be changed periodically. Obviously, passwords should not be written down and left in an accessible place, and employees should be admonished not to reveal their passwords to anyone except their supervisor or another designated co-worker. Some firms use electronic identification cards (**smart cards**) in conjunction with passwords. Computers that are left unused for a designated period should be set to automatically log off the user and employees should be asked to log off when they leave their computers for extended periods.

Effective antivirus software must be used and backup tapes should be kept and stored in secure locations. Special software must be used to delete material; otherwise it may be subject to retrieval. The number of persons serving as **network administrators** should be small, and these persons should be specially screened and trained. The firm should establish policies that prohibit access to materials except to service the network. Laptop computers should have protective software so that if they are stolen, confidential information and the firm network cannot be accessed.

Care should be taken to "scrub" documents before transmitting them electronically to opposing counsel. If documents are not prepared as "read-only" PDF files or in some other protected format, prior versions of the documents, including comments and revisions, may be reconstructed. This hidden information, called metadata, may reveal information that is otherwise protected by the attorney-client privilege. Some recent advisory opinions hold metadata is not protected if it is inadvertently disclosed. The ABA and a few other bar associations have issued opinions that hold that a lawyer who receives embedded metadata does not have to disclose the receipt and may use such data. However, a few state bar associations hold otherwise and admonish lawyers not to use metadata that may be exposed in electronic documents.

Electronic mail has become the preferred method of communicating in law firms and businesses. Privileged e-mail communications are protected by the same federal and state laws as other forms of communication, as noted above. In the past, when e-mail was new, some commentators contended that using e-mail might be a breach of the duty of confidentiality because e-mail can be intercepted and is subject to being read as it passes through the system. Some early ethics opinions advised against using e-mail with clients; however, later ethics opinions, including a major opinion issued by the ABA, have endorsed the use of unencrypted e-mail with the advice to lawyers that they disclose the risks to clients and get their permission to use it and consider carefully whether to use it for especially sensitive communications.

Some firms have closed networks with clients to guard against inadvertent disclosure and some use encryption. Special protections for wireless networks are also needed to ensure that no one outside the law firm can access data through the "wireless cloud."

Firms should use the following procedures to protect confidentiality in addition to those noted above that apply to computers generally:

- Refrain from using e-mail for very **sensitive communications**.
- **Mark all confidential e-mails as privileged** and include a statement telling the reader what to do if the communication is misdirected (that is, not to read it and to contact the sender).
- **Limit the recipients** of a privileged e-mail to those who are absolutely essential to the privileged communication and warn recipients not to forward such communications on to other persons.
- Consider the use of **encryption** software that locks the message into unreadable form until it is unlocked by the intended recipient, who has the only "key" to decrypt the message.
- Consider **closed networks** using land-based lines with regular clients.

Firms should have internal policies that employees are required to follow. These policies should prohibit employees from misusing e-mail to send personal, sexually explicit, or harassing material; prohibit accessing another person's e-mail; stress the importance of sending confidential material only to those who need to have it; prohibit unauthorized downloading and excessive personal use, especially online; and remind employees not to leave their e-mail access open and unattended and not to share their passwords.

REVIEW QUESTIONS

1. What is the basis for the principle of confidentiality?
2. Define the attorney-client privilege.
3. A client seeks advice from an attorney but later decides not to hire that attorney. Is the conversation they had about the matter privileged?
4. Are conversations that take place in the presence of law firm employees covered by the privilege?
5. Are communications privileged that are relayed to outside vendors hired by a lawyer?
6. Does the privilege cover communications in cases in which the attorney does not charge a fee?
7. Are conversations protected by the privilege if they take place in the reception area? In the lobby? Elevator? A restaurant? A cocktail party?
8. What happens to the privilege if the client tells a friend everything that was said in the privileged conversation with the attorney?
9. Does the privilege cover information about a client's identity? A client's whereabouts? The fee arrangement made with the attorney? Are there any exceptions to these rules?
10. When are a client's written papers protected by the privilege? When are they not protected?
11. What does an attorney do when a court requests disclosure of information that the attorney believes to be privileged?
12. What happens when privileged information is inadvertently disclosed to opposing counsel?
13. What should you do if you receive a document that appears to be privileged and that has been sent to you by mistake by the opposing counsel?
14. When may an attorney disclose privileged information?
15. When the client is a corporation, what personnel are covered by the privilege? Describe the two approaches that states have taken.
16. Define the work product rule, including its two prongs. What is the reasoning behind this rule?
17. Is the database in a computerized litigation support program protected as work product? Explain why or why not.
18. What work product is discoverable and under what circumstances?
19. If a nonlawyer helps a friend prepare divorce papers, are their communications covered by the privilege?
20. Should you use a cell phone to communicate with a client?
21. Should you use e-mail to communicate with a client?
22. Is it acceptable to send to opposing counsel a document in regular text form? Why or why not?
23. What should you do if you get a document and can see previous versions of it through tracked changes?

24. What are some security measures that may protect against breaches of security in using computers?
25. What is a confidentiality agreement and when is it used?
26. Name some common law office procedures that should be used to protect confidentiality.

HYPOTHETICALS

1. Jan Jones works for a criminal defense attorney. One morning a man, Adam Anderson, comes into the office very distraught. He wants to see the lawyer, Bonnie Burns, who is not in the office. He starts talking very loudly in the reception area about an incident the night before in which someone has apparently been killed. What should Jan do? Assume that Adam continues to tell Jan the whole story, which includes his participation in an attempted burglary. Is this information privileged? Why, or why not? What if someone followed Adam and was listening outside the office in the hallway?

2. Bonnie Burns decides to represent Mr. Anderson, who has subsequently been charged with several crimes. Ms. Burns asks Jan to assist in preparing Mr. Anderson for the upcoming trial. During Jan's discussions with Mr. Anderson, he hints that he might have an alibi for the time at which the crime was committed, which Jan knows not to be true. What should Jan do? What should Bonnie Burns do if Mr. Anderson proceeds to tell this story while testifying at the trial?

3. Karen Kent is a paralegal working on a large document production. Karen has no idea what the case is about but is asked to review and stamp some documents that will be copied and produced for the opposing counsel. What kind of documents should Karen look for that might legitimately be withheld from discovery? What is the best way to "flag" these documents? Should she attach sticky notes to them? Mark them in pencil? Remove them? What should she do after she has identified and isolated them?

4. Leonard Lessing is working on a top-secret corporate securities matter. The matter involves a corporate merger that could cause the value of one of the corporation's stocks to rise. Leonard overhears another paralegal, Tom Thompson, telling one of his friends about the matter over the phone. What should Leonard do? Is it okay for Tom or Leonard or Tom's friend to buy the stock involved? What might the consequences be to Leonard and his law firm if any one of them buys the stock?

5. Natalie Neari is working on some business litigation. She gets an e-mail from Cathy Cramer, paralegal for the opposing counsel,

which is a letter to Dan Dinkel, who is "of counsel" to Ms. Cramer. Natalie is puzzled and starts reading the letter but quickly realizes it was sent by mistake, as it concerns the testimony of an expert witness in the case. What should Natalie do? Assume that she goes to the supervising lawyer in the case, Earl Everest, and he takes the letter and reads the whole thing. Has he done anything wrong? What should he have done? What should Natalie do now? What if the letter proposes that the expert be paid a bonus for a successful outcome in the case? (Also see Chapter 8 for a discussion about expert witnesses.)

6. Owen Oliphant is an in-house paralegal for Conklin Corporation. He has been with Conklin for 20 years and serves as a patent specialist. He confers with the research and development and marketing departments as they come up with new products and plans to market them. He commonly drafts memoranda to the department heads, explaining the results of research into the patents and providing information on how they can be marketed within the bounds of the law. Owen's supervisor, Pam Park, is general counsel for Conklin. She has been there about three years and knows little about patents. Pam meets with Owen monthly at staff meetings. Owen sends copies of all his memos to Pam. A lawsuit is filed against Conklin by Bizz, charging that Conklin has violated one of its patents. Bizz seeks to discover memoranda from Owen to the research and development department concerning this patent. Is this material discoverable? What might a court look at in deciding? What procedures should Owen and the legal department have in place to protect the privileged status of these materials? (See the *HPD v. Clorox* case cited below for some information.)

DISCUSSION QUESTIONS AND PROJECTS

1. Find the source of the attorney-client privilege in your state. Is it in the statutes? A case or series of cases? A court rule? How does it compare with the general definition of the privilege given in this chapter?
2. Are there any cases in your state relating to paralegals and the privilege?
3. Find the rule for the work product doctrine in your state. How does it compare with the provision in the Federal Rules of Civil Procedure?
4. You discover that opposing counsel has included clearly privileged documents in a document production. What would you do? What rule does your state follow in deciding whether an inadvertent disclosure destroys the privilege?
5. What would you suggest if a lawyer working on a civil lawsuit instructed you to have all the information your client had given

you on the matter input electronically into a database verbatim in full text?

6. What is the ethical rule on confidentiality in your state's rules of professional conduct for lawyers?

7. What would you do as a paralegal if an attorney at your firm during the company's Christmas party introduced you to a client, who then proceeded to tell you the whole sordid story that led to his being represented by the firm?

8. What would you do if while attending a local paralegal association meeting you overheard a group of paralegals talking about a case on which you worked for opposing counsel? Would your answer be any different if you weren't working on the opposite side of the case?

9. What would you do if you overheard a paralegal in your firm discussing confidential information about a client with a paralegal in another firm? Would your answer be different if an attorney were doing the talking?

10. You happen to know that on Tuesdays and Fridays the file room personnel always have their friends (who do not work at the firm) eat lunch with them in the file room. What should you do? Would your answer be different if the friends were employees of another firm?

11. What would you do if you caught a client going through other clients' files on your desk while you were momentarily out of the room?

12. What should you do with handwritten notes of a confidential conversation once they have been typed up and put into a client's file?

13. Have any cases on inadvertent disclosure been decided in your jurisdiction? What about ethics opinions issued by the bar?

14. Contact some large law firms and find out what policies and procedures they have in place to protect client confidentiality, including policies relating to confidentiality agreements, cell phones, and e-mail.

15. Does your jurisdiction have a case or ethics opinion about the lawyer's duties concerning metadata?

16. Contact a corporate law department and see what procedures they follow when dealing with confidential legal matters in which the paralegals may have to talk with an employee.

SELECTED CASES

Baird v. Koerner, 279 F.2d 623 (9th Cir. 1960) (identity of client is privileged).

Berg Electronic, Inc. v. Molex, Inc., 875 F. Supp. 261 (D. Del. 1995) (inadvertently disclosed documents in document production).

Bloss v. Ford Motor Co., 126 A.D.2d 804, 510 N.Y.S.2d 304 (1987) (work product rule applicable to document indexes).

In re Cendant Corp. Securities Litigation, 343 F.3d 658 (2003) (trial strategy consultant's advice to corporate auditor communicated during confidential consultation with counsel is protected as work product).

In re Grand Jury Investigation of Ocean Transportation, 604 F.2d 672 (D.C. Cir. 1979) (inadvertently disclosed documents in document production).

HPD Laboratories, Inc. v. Clorox Co., 202 F.R.D. 410 (Cal. 2001) (communications of in-house paralegal not protected by the privilege).

People v. Mitchell, 86 A.D.2d 976, 448 N.Y.S.2d 332 (1982) (setting and presence of persons as factors in determining if communication is privileged).

Richards v. Jain, F. Supp. 1195 (USDC WD Wash. 2001) (firm disqualified when paralegal viewed and passed on privileged e-mail communciations that he was not authorized to have).

Rico v. Mitsubishi Motors Corp., 42 Cal. 4th 807 (2007) (lawyer disqualified after he used confidential notes of opposing lawyers' conversations with experts to impeach experts).

Samaritan Foundation v. Superior Court, 844 P.2d 593 (Ariz. App. Div. 1 1992) (extension of privilege to paralegals).

Upjohn Co. v. United States, 449 U.S. 383 (1981) (control group and subject matter tests for determining client/privilege).

SELECTED REFERENCES

ABA Model Code of Professional Responsibility, Canon 4
ABA Model Code of Professional Responsibility, DR 4-101
ABA Model Code of Professional Responsibility, EC 4-2
ABA Model Rules of Professional Conduct, Rules 1.2 and 1.6
ABA Guidelines for the Utilization of Paralegal Services, Guideline 6
ABA Formal Ethics Opinion 88-356 [duty of confidentiality extends to freelance lawyers]
ABA Formal Ethics Opinion 99-413 [use of unencrypted e-mail to communicate with clients]
ABA Formal Ethics Opinion 06-440 withdrawing Ethics Opinions 92-368 and 94-382 [receipt of inadvertently disclosed privileged documents]
ABA Formal Ethics Opinion 06-442 [duty to remove metadata before sending electronic document and use of metadata by recipient]
NALA Code of Ethics and Professional Responsibility, Canon 7
NFPA Model Code of Ethics and Professional Responsibility, DR 1.5

4

Conflicts of Interest

This chapter covers the rules and cases governing conflicts of interest and their application to paralegals, including the procedures that paralegals should follow to avoid conflicts and to handle conflicts that arise. Covered are:

- rules governing conflicts involving clients, including concurrent and successive representation
- rules governing personal and business conflicts, including:
  - business transactions with clients
  - publication rights
  - financial assistance to clients
  - lawyer's interest in litigation
  - gifts from clients
  - agreements with clients limiting malpractice liability
  - payment of attorney's fees by third persons
  - conflicts involving family members or relatives
  - sexual relations with clients
- disqualifications caused by individual conflicts of interest that are imputed to an individual's firm
- client consent to conflicts
- screens to protect against disqualification
- the use of conflicts checks and paralegals' responsibility to maintain records

A. Introduction

Conflicts of interest are one of the most troublesome areas of ethics for law firms and their clients. The growth in the size of law firms, the development of branch offices, the merger of firms, the increase in lawyers moving from firm to firm, and legal specialization make the potential for conflicts of interest a prominent concern. The traditional, strict, straightforward rules governing conflicts are increasingly difficult to apply in the complex legal environment and in some situations result in undue hardship on law firms, law firm employees, and clients.

The ethics rules governing conflicts of interest are based on the duties of **loyalty and confidentiality**. Both of these duties are threatened when a lawyer or paralegal has an interest that is adverse to a client's, whether the adverse interest is a personal or business one or relates to the current or past representation of the client. For example, a lawyer or paralegal who has received confidential information from one client that may help another client may feel compelled out of a sense of loyalty to use that information to help the second client. An attorney who represents two clients, even if in different matters, may not represent them both with equal zeal, especially if one is a favored client (perhaps because this client brings more business to the law firm).

Ethics rules governing conflicts of interest have existed since the first codes of lawyer conduct came into being, and conflicts are included in the ethics rules of every jurisdiction. These rules form the basis for attorney discipline and are supplemented by **court interpretations** in cases where a party has moved to disqualify a lawyer or a law firm because of a conflict of interest. The courts have seen many more conflict dilemmas than have disciplinary bodies and have applied the rules to growing numbers of complicated conflict situations.

The ethics rules cover:

- **concurrent representation** of adverse interests
- representation that is **adverse to a former client**
- **representation of clients whose interests are aligned**
- lawyer's **financial, personal, or business interests** that are or may be adverse to a client

Imputed/vicarious conflicts
The conflict of interest of one person in a law firm is imputed to everyone in the firm, causing the whole firm to be disqualified

Finally, the rules and cases cover *imputed* or *vicarious conflicts*, a principle under which the conflict of interest of one person in a firm is imputed to the entire firm and all its lawyers, causing the whole firm to be disqualified. Paralegals must pay special attention to this rule because it may apply to a paralegal's conflicts, subjecting the law firm to disqualification.

Guideline 7 of the ABA Model Guidelines for the Utilization of Paralegal Services advises attorneys to take reasonable measures to prevent conflicts resulting from a paralegal's other employment or interests.

Personal and business interests are covered, in addition to conflicts created by working on two or more different clients' matters. The ABA Guidelines and an important ABA ethics opinion endorse the use of screening of paralegals in cases in which a conflict exists. About half of the states that have guidelines on paralegals refer to paralegal conflicts of interests and call on the lawyer generally to ensure against conflicts impinging on the services rendered to a client. Most states endorse screening of paralegals.

The NFPA Model Code includes an extensive section on conflicts of interest (Disciplinary Rule 1.6). The NALA Code of Ethics and Professional Responsibility does not refer directly to conflicts of interest, although general language about confidentiality and adherence to ethics codes for lawyers covers conflict situations. (See Canon 3(c) and Canon 7.)

B. Conflicts Involving Representation of Clients

1. Concurrent Representation

General Rules

The most clear-cut case of a prohibited conflict of interest is a ***concurrent or simultaneous representation*** of two clients whose interests are adverse to one another. The most obvious and extreme example of this is an attorney attempting to represent both the plaintiff and the defendant in the same lawsuit. However, concurrent representation problems arise in other less blatant situations, such as in nonlitigated matters and when the adverse representation involves the same client or clients but in a different case.

Concurrent representation
Where an attorney represents two clients whose interests are adverse to one another

The ABA Model Code and Model Rules permit concurrent representation only if:

1. The lawyer can **adequately represent** the interests of each client (under Model Code) or the lawyer reasonably believes that he or she can provide **competence and diligent representation**, the dual representation is not prohibited by law, and the representation does not involve the same litigation (under Model Rules); and
2. Each client **consents after full disclosure** (under Model Code) or **informed written consent** (under Model Rules).

ABA Model Code 5-101(A) and ABA Model Rule 1.7.

Both configurations have a twofold test: first, an assurance of adequate representation of both clients, and second, client consent. The latest revisions to the Model Rules added the requirement that consent be in writing. Some states had already adopted that requirement for consents, and others have revised their rules to reflect this requirement.

The courts generally have treated simultaneous representation as improper on its face and start with the **presumption that disqualification is required**. The more remote the adverseness, however, the less stringently the rule is applied. It is not considered a direct conflict of interest per se for an attorney to represent business competitors simultaneously in unrelated matters.

Consents

Determining whether there has been client **consent** (called **"waiver"** by many firms) is critical. Whether a court honors a client's consent depends on a number of circumstances, including:

- the extent of the **disclosure** and discussions with the client about the implications of the dual representation
- whether the consent was truly **voluntary** and not given under pressure from the attorney or others
- **when** the attorney raised the issue with his or her client
- the **capacity** of the client to understand fully the implications of the dual representation and consent
- whether or not the client consulted with and relied on **independent counsel**
- whether the consent is **written and signed**

These factors suggest some guidelines that should be followed to ensure that consents will be upheld. Thorough written disclosures are highly recommended and are required in some states. The lawyer should provide in writing to the client information on the circumstances giving rise to the potential conflict and the actual and reasonably foreseeable consequences to the client if the lawyer undertakes or continues the representation. If independent counsel is consulted, the consulting counsel should not be from the same firm or be recommended by the firm. Consents should also include:

- **consideration** for the consent (that is, future or continued representation)
- procedures to **screen** appropriately to protect confidentiality
- procedures to follow if a client decides to **withdraw consent**

Finally, it should be kept in mind that courts sometimes will not uphold a consent if the two clients' interests are so clearly adverse that the court believes the attorney cannot adequately represent them.

Withdrawal to Avoid Conflicts

A lawyer may attempt to avoid the strict rule against concurrent representation by dropping one client in order to represent the other, more favored client. This may seem desirable for the attorney because the rules governing representation of interests that are adverse to former clients are not as strict (see Section B below). However, a court may not allow continued representation under these circumstances. The court will look to see if representation was concurrent at any time. Improper concurrent representation generally results in disqualification of the attorney from representing *either* client unless, of course, there is proper consent under the rules.

Imputed Disqualification in Concurrent Conflicts

Imputed disqualification rules are applied strictly in cases of concurrent representation. These rules apply to branch offices of the same firm. A screen to protect against improper access to confidential information will not overcome the rule, as it might in cases involving former clients. Fortunately for paralegals, the courts have been more lenient in applying these rules to situations in which the paralegal carries the concurrent conflict to a new firm. (See Section D in this chapter.)

Issue Conflicts and Other Indirect Concurrent Conflicts

Another kind of concurrent conflict that is not fully addressed in the ethics rules is *issue conflicts*. An issue conflict occurs when an attorney is representing two clients in unrelated cases and is urging a legal position in one case that, if the attorney prevails, will have negative consequences for the other client. In general, representation of both sides is permitted in different **trial courts**, but some commentators believe it is improper in cases pending at the same time in **appellate court**. The Comments to the ABA Model Rules indicate that withdrawal from one case should be undertaken if an action in one matter will "materially limit" the lawyer's effectiveness in the other. Some advisory opinions refuse to apply prohibitions against conflicts to an issue conflict situation even where the attorney would be arguing opposite positions before the same judge; however, others recommend against lawyers handling cases that present issue conflicts at the appellate level or allow only if there is consent after full disclosure. Related to issue conflicts is the representation of **competitors**. The ethics rules do not prohibit such representation, but some firms have internal policies that prohibit the same attorney from handling competitors to protect their relationships with valued clients.

> **Issue conflicts**
> Occur when an attorney argues opposing sides of a legal issue, the result of which may be that one client's interests are harmed

The Model Rules further prohibit concurrent representation when a lawyer's responsibilities to one client may materially limit the lawyer's ability to represent the other client. In this scenario, the interests of the two clients are not adverse, but the attorney's **loyalty or zeal may be impaired** because of the demands of a case. For example, an attorney representing two criminal defendants with conflicting trial dates will have to delay one trial, possibly to the detriment of that client.

Examples of Conflicts in Litigated Matters

Concurrent conflicts of interests may arise in litigation in various ways. One of the most common and controversial is dual representation of a husband and wife in a **marital dissolution**. Many dissolutions that begin amicably and seem to lend themselves to resolution by one attorney for reasons of cost and efficiency still end up in court. Many lawyers refuse to represent both parties to a dissolution.

Similar problems can arise in representation of **co-parties** in litigation. Although aligned initially, co-parties may become adversaries during the course of litigation if cross-claims are filed or another party seeks to realign the parties. For example, a passenger and driver who sue a third party may find themselves adversaries if the passenger also sues the driver. Some jurisdictions, such as California, have case law that prohibits any joint representation of a driver and a passenger as an inherent conflict of interest.

Both the ABA Model Code (DR 5-106) and ABA Model Rules (Rule 1.8) prohibit a lawyer who is representing multiple clients from making an **aggregate settlement** of civil claims or a collective plea in a criminal case unless all clients give informed written consent. Representing seemingly aligned defendants in criminal cases is especially dangerous because the interests of the defendants are often potentially adverse. In addition to the ethical concerns, multiple representation may deprive one or both of the defendants of effective assistance of counsel, which constitutes grounds to overturn a conviction.

Other less obvious conflict traps arise in litigation and can result in further litigation and serious sanctions, including disqualification. For example, a firm may be disqualified for retaining an **expert witness** who was previously interviewed by the opposing counsel if confidential information was disclosed to the expert during the interview. Representing both present and future claimants in **class action suits** may also result in an allegation of a conflict if a settlement seems to favor one group over another.

Examples of Conflicts in Nonlitigated Matters

Litigation is the most obvious setting for conflicts of interest, but many other kinds of cases can pose conflicts. An attorney may represent more than one party to a **negotiation** if the parties' interests seem aligned, but the attorney should be aware of the potential for adverse interests to arise if negotiations fail or the agreement becomes the subject of a dispute. If litigation is the result, the attorney may not represent either of the parties against the other and may be sued by a former client for malpractice because of the conflict. For example, entertainment law firms that represent producers, directors, writers, and actors have been accused of favoring wealthier and more prestigious clients in negotiations on film deals, resulting in less advantageous positions for other clients. Clients of these firms do sign consent forms to the multiple representation, but later, when deals fall apart, complain that there was not full disclosure or that they would have been frozen out of deals if they had not consented and had sought independent counsel.

Conflicts may arise in the **drafting of wills** for members of the same family if the family members are not in complete agreement about the disposition of the estate. Consents to such joint representation are essential. Similarly, conflicts between an estate and the heirs of the estate may prohibit representation of both parties. For other conflicts in a probate setting, see Section C.5, on gifts from clients.

An attorney who represents a **corporation** and serves on its board of directors may face conflicts if the corporation's and board's interests become adverse, such as in a derivative suit. The ABA Model Rules suggest that an attorney who is asked to serve on a corporate client's board should consider several factors, including the likelihood of a conflict arising, and should not serve as a director if there is a "material risk that the dual role will compromise the lawyer's independence of professional judgment." Serving on a corporate board increases an attorney's risk of being sued for malpractice and threatens the attorney–client privilege as well. Even without serving on a corporate client's board, a lawyer may find that the interests of the board, management, and shareholders often diverge. These interests become quite problematic in derivative suits, especially in cases of self-dealing, when there are allegations of fraud, and in hostile corporate takeovers. Although the attorney is bound to represent the corporate entity, identifying clearly who the attorney represents or how to act in the best interests of that entity is often complicated. Conflicts may also occur in the corporate setting if an attorney represents several entities within the corporate family (for example, parent, subsidiary, and "sister" companies) and these entities find themselves in an adversarial position.

A lawyer may be acting as an intermediary or representing multiple clients whenever he or she represents more than one party to a **transaction**, such as a real estate sale, a mortgage, a loan, or a contract. For example, a firm has been held to have acted improperly when it represented both a school district and the underwriters in a school bond issuance. Several states now have advisory opinions on the issue of representing both sides in a real estate transaction. Most opinions recommend against dual representation except in purely ministerial matters. As mentioned above, representing both spouses in a **divorce settlement** is generally not acceptable because the interests of the parties are inherently adverse, and the potential for a real dispute necessitating litigation is too great. It should be noted that this rule does not apply to situations in which an attorney is acting as a neutral **arbitrator or mediator** between or among parties who are not the attorney's clients, such as in a bar-sponsored divorce mediation program or in a court-appointed arbitration.

2. Successive Representation

General Rules

The rules governing the conduct of lawyers who desire to represent a client in a matter that may be adverse to a former client — called *successive representation* — take into account the ability of clients to be represented by the counsel of their choice and the increasing mobility of lawyers.

> **Successive representation**
> Conflict of interest situation involving a current matter and a former client

The general rule is that a lawyer will be disqualified from successive representation only if the interests of the former and current client are **truly adverse** and if the past and current matters are **substantially related**. This formulation presupposes an attorney-client relationship with the former client within which the lawyer would have learned confidential information. If the current representation relates to the same or a closely related matter, the lawyer would be in a position to breach his or her duty of confidentiality to the former client by revealing the confidential information to assist the current client. (Remember from Chapter 3 that the duty of confidentiality continues after the termination of the attorney-client relationship.)

The ABA Model Code did not have a specific provision covering conflicts of interest in successive representation, although it prohibited employment if it were likely to involve representing differing interests. As a result, some courts have relied on general language in Canon 9 of the ABA Model Code in deciding whether to disqualify an attorney or firm from successive representation. Canon 9 calls on lawyers to avoid even the **appearance of impropriety**. Most circuits and states, however, do not order disqualification solely on the basis of an appearance of impropriety; instead, they determine whether the former client's confidential information is threatened by the representation. Most commentators disfavor disqualification predicated solely on Canon 9 because an appearance of impropriety may be only that — an appearance. It does not mean that anything improper, such as revealing confidential information, has or will take place; it does not address directly the conflict problem; and disqualification can seriously harm the interests of the current client as well as the attorney.

The ABA Model Rules contain a clearer and more complete statement than the ABA Model Code. Rule 1.9 states the general rule that has been followed by most courts: A lawyer may not represent a person in a matter that is the **same or substantially related** to the representation of a former client in which the interests of the potential client are **materially adverse** to the former client. Such representation is permitted if the former client gives informed written consent.

A separate ABA Model Rule applies to **government lawyers**. Model Rule 1.11 allows a former government lawyer, with the government agency's informed written consent, to represent a private client in a matter in which the lawyer previously participated or obtained confidential information about while in government service. It further allows a screen to prevent firm disqualification in such a representation. A lawyer who moves to private practice from government service is prohibited from switching sides or from negotiating for private employment with a party or an attorney with whom the lawyer is dealing on a matter. The older ABA Model Code (DR 9-101) prohibited a former public employee from accepting "private employment in a matter in which he had substantial responsibility as a public employee." The more flexible approach for government lawyers is predicated on a public policy to encourage lawyers to enter government and civil service knowing that they will be able to move into private practice later in their careers.

Defining "Substantial Relationship"

Courts across the country have been somewhat inconsistent in deciding the question of whether a substantial relationship exists between the former and current client matters. Some courts have examined the **facts** of the two matters to see whether it is likely that the attorney would have learned confidential information that relates to both matters. Others look to the **legal issues** and require a clear or even identical congruence of the issues before ordering disqualification. If the court finds that the matters are not substantially related, the attorney and the attorney's firm will not be disqualified. If the matters are found to be substantially related, a presumption that confidential information was disclosed arises. Some courts have held that this presumption is irrebuttable and automatic, thereby precluding evidence that the attorney did not learn any confidential information on the prior matter or that the lawyer has been screened. Other courts have held that this presumption is rebuttable and that the lawyer may provide evidence to overcome the presumption that confidential information has been or will be revealed. This rebuttable presumption is the trend among the courts.

C. Other Conflicts Rules

1. Business Transactions with Clients

Business transactions between a lawyer and client contain great potential for a conflict of interest in which a lawyer's interests conflict with the client's and/or with the lawyer's role in representing the client. In addition to the inherent conflict in business dealings, clients rely on the lawyer's superior **legal knowledge** and are generally in a weaker **bargaining position**. The attorney's duties of loyalty, trust, and zealous representation are implicated whenever a lawyer enters into a business transaction with a client.

Both the ABA Model Code and Model Rules prohibit business transactions between lawyers and clients but provide for an exception with **client consent** (ABA Model Code DR 5-101 and ABA Model Rule 1.8(a)). The Model Rule affords protection for the client by requiring that (1) the transaction and terms must be fair and reasonable to the client; (2) the client is advised in writing of the desirability of seeking independent counsel and be given a reasonable amount of time to do that; and (3) the client must give informed written consent.

In practice, lawyers and clients have many opportunities to enter into business transactions, not all of which are prohibited. **Commercial transactions** that clients in their business capacities may provide to the public — as well as to law firms — such as banking, medical services, products, and utilities are not prohibited.

Some examples of business transactions with clients that lawyers are prohibited from entering into without proper client consent are: (1) purchasing real estate from a client while also drafting the documents relating to the sale; (2) advising clients to make investments in businesses in which the lawyer has an interest; (3) borrowing money from a client and advising the client how to perfect the client's security interest; (4) going into business with a client, forming the corporation for the business that gives the lawyer an ownership interest while continuing to represent the corporation as its attorney; and (5) taking as his or her fee an interest in a business entity that he or she has formed or is advising.

Conflicts based on business transactions may arise also for **paralegals**. For example, a paralegal may be invited to invest in a client's business or may own stock in a client's company. Such conflicts are easier for paralegals to cure than they are for an attorney. Because the client relies on the lawyer for legal advice, the lawyer is more likely than a paralegal to have an unfair advantage over the client. However, paralegals should be aware of the general prohibition on business transactions with clients and take care to avoid dual roles that might create a conflict. If such a conflict arises, the paralegal should consult with the supervising attorney about obtaining client consent under the relevant provisions of the state ethics rules.

2. Publication, Literary, and Media Rights

Both the ABA Model Code and Model Rules prohibit lawyers from entering into an agreement that grants the lawyer publication, literary, or media rights relating to the subject matter of the representation prior to the conclusion of the representation (ABA Model Rule 1.8(d); ABA Model Code DR 5-104(B)). This rule protects against conflicts that might arise during the representation about what is best for the client and what would enhance the value of the "story" — that is, the value of the lawyer's interests in the literary or media rights.

In addition to disciplinary action for violation of this rule (which is rare), this kind of conflict may be the basis of a motion to disqualify counsel or of an appeal in a criminal case based on ineffective counsel.

3. Financial Assistance to Clients

Whenever a lawyer lends funds to a client, a new dimension — that of **creditor and debtor** — is imposed on the attorney-client relationship. Because of the inherent conflict in representing the client while being the client's creditor, the ABA Model Code and Model Rules prohibit most kinds of financial assistance to clients.

In general, the rules prohibit a lawyer from giving a client financial assistance except for **advancing or guaranteeing expenses of litigation**. The ABA Model Rule is more liberal in that it allows repayment of the advanced costs of litigation to be contingent on the outcome of the litigation and allows an attorney to pay litigation costs outright for an indigent client. Several states adopted the ABA Model Rules without adopting these two notable exceptions.

It should be noted that advancing a client funds for living expenses is not covered by the rules allowing advances for "costs." Doing so is generally regarded as unethical conduct; however, a loan from attorney to client for living expenses may be evaluated separately under the rules relating to business transactions, rather than under the rules about advancing costs (Model Code DR 5-103(B) and Model Rule 1.8(e)).

4. A Lawyer's Interest in Litigation

Lawyers are prohibited from acquiring a proprietary interest in litigation in which they are involved (ABA Model Code DR 5-103(A) and ABA Model Rule 1.8(i)). **Contingency fees** in civil cases and **liens** to secure fees or expenses are excepted.

The rule prohibiting an attorney from obtaining an interest in litigation derives from the old prohibitions on maintenance, champerty, and **barratry**. Under English common law these were crimes concerned

Contingency fee
Fee depends on the successful outcome of a case and is based on a percentage of the recovery

with "stirring up litigation." **Champerty** meant obtaining a financial interest in the litigation. It was long felt that such conduct encouraged unmeritorious litigation and dishonesty in the courtroom.

Obviously, attitudes have changed dramatically. The widespread use of contingency fees and lawyer advertising have undercut these ideas about fees. The current rules against obtaining an interest in litigation are all that remain. The current rules are based on the conflict that arises when an attorney "owns" a lawsuit and may have a financial interest that conflicts with the best action for the client.

5. Gifts from Clients

Because of the inherent conflict in a lawyer's dual role of adviser to a client and recipient of a gift from a client, a long-standing rule strongly **disfavors such gifts** from clients to their lawyers. This rule is especially pertinent when a lawyer drafts a document under which he or she receives a gift, such as a will or trust. The courts have long held that this scenario is rife with potential for undue influence, fraud, and over-reaching, especially because the cases often involve elderly clients who are vulnerable to overreaching by their attorneys.

Inter vivos
During life

Testamentary
Takes place at the time
of death, such as
through a will

Courts frequently void both ***inter vivos*** and ***testamentary*** gifts in such cases, even without an affirmative showing of undue influence. Some courts allow the attorney-beneficiary to present evidence showing the legitimacy of the gift. To do so, the attorney usually must show that the gift was fair and fully intended by the client, who had the requisite capacity and was not subject to undue influence by the lawyer. One serious additional problem sometimes results from such a gift: It may raise the question of the client's testamentary capacity, potentially voiding the entire estate plan, including the gift to the attorney. A particularly egregious abuse of these rules led the California legislature to adopt a statute that invalidates instruments that purport to make such gifts except for gifts to blood relatives or when independent counsel certifies that there was no fraud or undue influence.

An attorney may also be subject to discipline for accepting such gifts (ABA Model Code EC 5-5 and Model Rule 1.8(c)). The rules prohibit a lawyer from **soliciting a gift** or **preparing a document** in which the lawyer or a close relative of the lawyer is given a gift. Family members named include parent, child, grandparent, grandchild, spouse, and other relatives or persons with whom the lawyer "maintains a close familial relationship." An exception is permitted if the client is also a relative of the attorney-donee or beneficiary. "Simple gifts," such as a holiday present or token of appreciation, are permitted. In cases that require the attorney-donee to draft a document, **independent counsel** should be consulted.

Two unresolved issues that are handled in a variety of ways by different jurisdictions are gifts that do not require a conveyance document and situations in which the attorney is nominated in the document he or she drafts to perform additional services, such as those of **executor or trustee**. This second practice is common and is rarely questioned; more questionable is when an attorney nominated to such a position in a document he or she drafts also acts as his or her own counsel or has another attorney in the same firm act as his or her counsel. Some states prohibit this arrangement unless the court approves it upon a finding that it is in the best interests of the estate.

A paralegal should also be aware of the potential conflict created when a client gives him or her a **gift**. As with business transactions, there is less risk of undue influence when a gift is bestowed on a paralegal than on a lawyer, but the appearance of impropriety may be present nonetheless. In the case of a substantial gift, especially by an elderly or otherwise vulnerable client, the paralegal should see that the supervising attorney recommends that the client seek the advice of independent counsel and refrains from working on the gift document.

6. Agreements with Clients Limiting Malpractice Liability

Both case law and the ethical rules prohibit attorneys from attempting to limit their liability for malpractice. The conflict in this situation is clear: The attorney is trying to protect his or her own interests at the expense of the client. A few cases deal with attorneys who attempt to limit their liability by asking their clients to sign a **disclaimer** before representation even begins; most cases deal with attorneys who exercise undue influence to pressure a client into signing a **release** after the alleged malpractice has taken place.

The ABA Model Code prohibits lawyers from attempting to exonerate themselves from or to limit their liability to clients for malpractice (Model Code DR 6-102). The ABA Model Rules prohibit a lawyer from attempting to limit liability up front unless the client is represented by independent counsel in making the agreement. The rules also prohibit a lawyer from settling a malpractice claim unless an unrepresented client is advised in writing to seek independent counsel and has a reasonable opportunity to do so (Model Rule 1.8(h)).

A lawyer may not circumvent the rule against limiting liability by including in a retainer agreement provisions that relieve the lawyer from responsibility if the client takes certain actions. One such provision, for example, might relieve the attorney from further responsibility if the client fails to inform the attorney of a new address or phone number. Both case law and bar ethics opinions have consistently disallowed such provisions. Equally unacceptable as a means to limit liability is endorsing a client's check for a fee with a release of liability.

It should be noted that lawyers can limit the **"scope" of representation** if the limitation is reasonable and the client gives informed written consent. Good engagement and retainer agreements state the exact nature and limits of representation for the protection of both the lawyer and the client (Model Rule 1.2(c)).

7. Payment of Attorney's Fees by a Third Party

If someone other than the client pays the attorney's fees, a conflict may arise over who is guiding the representation — the client or the payer. The attorney's loyalty and sense of responsibility may be divided and judgment clouded if the person paying the fee wants to be involved in making decisions about the case. The potential for harm to the client is greatest when the interests of the client and the one paying for the representation diverge. Some common instances of this kind of conflict occur when a parent pays the fee for a child, a spouse for the other spouse, a corporation for a director, and an employer for an employee.

There have also been instances in which the legal fees for the representation of **criminal defendants** in drug cases were paid by an unknown third party, very probably the operator of the criminal enterprise. It is likely that the unnamed third party sought to guide the defense by keeping the client quiet about matters that may have mitigated the defendant's guilt or lessened the sentence imposed while implicating the third party. This situation would not only result in an ethical breach, subjecting the attorney to a civil suit and disciplinary action, but also would constitute grounds for appeal based on ineffective assistance of counsel.

Generally, the ethics rules permit third-party payment of attorney's fees so long as the third party does not interfere with the exercise of the attorney's **independent professional judgment**, does not otherwise interfere with the attorney-client relationship, and the client gives informed **consent**. **Confidentiality** must be maintained as well; the one who pays the fee is not covered by the attorney-client privilege (Model Code DR 5-107(A) and ABA Model Rules 1.8(f) and 5.4(c)).

8. Relatives of Lawyers

When married or other closely related attorneys represent adverse interests, the possibility of a conflict that may harm a client clearly exists. Husbands and wives and other close family members naturally discuss their work with one another, giving rise to the **risk of disclosure** of confidential information, which is potentially quite harmful if the spouse who learns the information represents an adversary. Duties of **loyalty and zealous representation** are also implicated; an attorney-spouse may not fight as zealously for a client when the opposing counsel is his or her spouse. Last, because spouses have a financial interest in one another's income, the potential to increase the marital funds from a large fee may also influence an attorney-spouse's sense of loyalty or independent judgment.

Comment 11 to Model Rule 1.7 provides that lawyers should not represent clients in the same or a substantially related matter if they are "closely related by blood or marriage." An earlier version of this rule had references to other relatives: parents, children, siblings, and spouses. Each client must give informed consent; such conflicts are not imputed to the firm for which the lawyer works. Some jurisdictions have adopted a rule on familial conflicts rather than relying on a comment for guidance. For example, California has a separate rule and it expands the scope of coverage to **specified nonrelatives,** such as persons who live with or have an intimate personal relationship with the lawyer. Informed written consent is also required in California.

The ethics rules governing conflicts based on family relationships are also applicable to **paralegals.** The potential for conflicts and disclosure of protected information are great between married or related paralegals and paralegals married or related to lawyers or other law firm employees when they are working on opposite sides of a case. Law firms must check prospective employees for family conflicts, and paralegals and other affected persons covered by the rules should inform their firms fully of any situation that might give rise to such a conflict.

State ethics opinions that have addressed family conflicts involving paralegals advise that the firm does not have to withdraw as along as the paralegal in question does not work on the matter, no confidences are revealed, and the client is fully informed or consents with full disclosure.

9.   Sexual Relations with Clients

The 2001 revisions to the ABA Model Rules added a provision prohibiting lawyers from having sexual relations with clients unless a sexual relationship **predated** the representation (Model Rule 1.8(j)). The basis for this rule is twofold: (1) a sexual relationship between lawyer and client has the potential to involve **exploitation** of the client, who is sometimes in a vulnerable state; and (2) the emotional involvement of the lawyer with the client may prevent the lawyer from exercising **objective and rational judgment** on the client's behalf. Consent is not acceptable in such cases, and a lack of actual prejudice to the client does not mitigate the lawyer's actions.

There are no cases or ethics opinions on record that involve paralegals having sex with clients. The basis for the ethics rule is not as compelling for paralegals because the paralegal is not the one who is required to exercise independent professional judgment about the client's legal matter.

D. Imputed Conflicts and Disqualification

1. General Rules

As mentioned above, the disqualification of one lawyer in a firm may cause the entire firm to be disqualified from representing a client—that is, the lawyer's conflict is imputed to the other persons in the firm. The principle of imputed or vicarious conflicts is based on the idea that all the lawyers in a firm know everything about all the clients and cases being handled by the firm. Particularly, the partners in a firm (rather than other employees, whether lawyers or nonlawyers) are believed to **share confidential information** about clients. Although extensive sharing of information among all the partners in a firm does not take place in many law firms, especially large ones, **financial incentives** may create a conflict and support the application of imputed conflict rules in some situations. Although confidential information can be protected by careful screening, it is much more difficult to protect against the actual or perceived pressure to handle a case in a manner that will most benefit the firm and not necessarily be the most beneficial for the client.

It should be noted that when a firm is disqualified by a court, the firm may be required to **disgorge fees** paid for the legal services during the representation. This remedy is most often applied when the firm knew or should have known of the conflict and failed to disclose it to the client. A disqualification may also be the basis for a malpractice case against the lawyer and firm for breach of fiduciary duty.

The strict application of imputed conflict rules has created serious problems for law firms, individual lawyers, and clients, given lawyer mobility and clients' choosing representation on a matter-by-matter basis. Vicarious disqualification also poses special concerns for paralegals, whose job mobility is also threatened by an overly rigid application of the rules.

The ABA Model Code contains a strict rule that states if a lawyer cannot represent a client under the code because of a conflict or for any other reason, neither can any other lawyer affiliated with the tainted lawyer's firm, whether partner, associate, or of counsel. This sweeping rule does not allow screening or client consent to overcome the disqualification (Model Code DR 5-105). The ABA Model Rules, however, do not apply imputed disqualification equally to all kinds of conflicts situations. The disqualification is imputed in client-based concurrent and successive conflicts, but not those based on the lawyer's personal or business interests; i.e., the Rule excludes business transactions, familial relationships, gifts from clients, literary rights, sexual relationships, and more (Model Rule 1.10). Rule 1.10 prohibits representation in cases where a lawyer has changed firms only if the matter is the same or substantially related and the lawyer learned confidential information about the matter while with the previous firm. Clients may waive such conflicts with informed written consent. Comment 4 to Rule 1.10 states the ABA position that the conflicts of paralegals and other nonlawyer personnel are not imputed to the firm. (See discussion below under Use of Screens.)

Most court decisions on vicarious disqualification were made during the time that the ABA Model Code was followed by nearly all jurisdictions. As a result, the courts have frequently applied a per se rule of imputed disqualification. The trend, however, is toward a more flexible approach, under which the presumption of imputed disqualification may be rebutted by evidence that the person with the conflict did not have access to confidential information in working on the first matter, or that the affected person is being properly screened from any involvement in the matter. A few state courts have resisted this trend.

Disqualification motions are sometimes used as a **strategy to delay or harass the opposition**. Courts look askance at such motions, especially if they are not made as early as possible in the proceedings or are based more on appearance of impropriety than on any real danger of harm to a client or a likely breach of confidentiality or loyalty. Firms and clients have also been known to use the disqualification rules as a strategy to prevent another firm from being able to represent a specific client on a specific matter. For example, a large corporate client may give minor matters to competitor firms so that, in the event of litigation, there is no qualified attorney at another firrm that does not have a conflict — that is, all the firms are "conflicted out."

2. Use of Screens

The use of screening in the law firm to overcome imputed disqualification of the entire firm first arose in cases involving **former government lawyers**. Although the risk of conflicts involving such lawyers is especially high because of their perceived inside knowledge, connections, and influence, the legal community has been concerned primarily about the ability of government lawyers to move into private practice. If conflicts rules are strictly applied and screens are not allowed to overcome them, government lawyers' employment options are quite limited. Going into government service would become a "permanent" career choice — a significant deterrent to entering government service in which salaries are substantially lower than in private practice.

Screening in private law firms, in cases involving attorney and non-lawyer employees not previously in government service, has become common practice. A *screen* (formerly a *Chinese wall* and sometimes called *cone of silence*) isolates the disqualified attorney or paralegal by setting up office procedures to prevent the disqualified person from having access to information, including case files and other documents, and from communicating with anyone in the firm about the case.

These **procedures** should include:

- a **memorandum to all individuals in the firm** informing them of the conflict and screen and admonishing them not to discuss the matter with the disqualified person
- **indications on files and documents** that show the limitations on access
- programmed **computer warnings or blocks** to prevent a screened employee's access to documents on the firm's computer network

The screen must be erected at the **time** the disqualified person begins employment with the firm or when work on the new matter is commenced. **Physical separation** of the disqualified person from those working on the case is also advisable. The firm may also require the disqualified person to **sign an agreement** in which he or she vows not to disclose any confidential information about the matter and not to discuss the matter with anyone at the firm. An attorney who is disqualified is not permitted to **share in fees** generated by the matter. This part of the screen is designed to prevent the disqualified lawyer from having a financial stake in the case.

Proving the **effectiveness** of a screen can be problematic. For the most part, a court evaluating the procedures must accept what the firm says by way of affidavits and testimony about the thoroughness and care of the measures taken and the extent to which they have been observed. Screening procedures should be routine and careful records should be kept. A court will examine not only the specific procedures in place, but also the context of the situation. Is the firm large or small? Does the disqualified attorney or paralegal work in the same department or physical area of the office as the team representing the client in question? Where are the case files kept? Do the person with the conflict and the rest of the team working on the matter in question work together on other matters? Does the firm sanction employees for breaking the rules relating to a screen? How many other persons in the firm have access to the confidential information?

The extent to which conflict rules apply to paralegals and whether a screen will prevent a firm from being disqualified over a paralegal's conflict have been the subject of several cases and ethics opinions in the last decade. The ABA endorses **screening of paralegals** even in concurrent conflicts

Screen
Isolates a disqualified person by setting up procedures to prevent the affected person from any involvement with or communication about the matter

if the firm is strict in adhering to the screen, no confidential information is revealed, and the former employer admonishes the paralegal not to reveal any confidential information. This ethics opinion distinguishes between the application of a screen to an attorney's conflicts and those of a paralegal. When a lawyer moves to another firm, the new firm is ordinarily disqualified from representing an adverse interest of the attorney's former firm; a screen would not protect the firm from disqualification. However, a paralegal who previously worked on a matter adverse to his or her former firm may be screened effectively, thereby preventing the disqualification of the paralegal's new firm. The rationale for the more flexible application of screens in cases involving paralegal conflicts is based on protecting paralegals' employment mobility (ABA Ethics Opinion 88-1521).

The ABA Model Guidelines for the Utilization of Paralegal Services (Guideline 7) endorse the use of screens for conflicts involving paralegals, as do most state guidelines and the comments to the ABA Model Rules. Most of the cases that address paralegal conflicts support the use of screens. The only state that clearly does not yet endorse the use of screens in paralegal conflict situations is Kansas.

There are several important **cases on paralegal conflicts** and the use of screens. In *In re Complex Asbestos Litigation,* the plaintiff's attorney, a sole practitioner, was disqualified from a number of asbestos cases because his paralegal had previously worked for a firm representing several of the defendants in the case, and the attorney had made no attempt to screen the paralegal. The California Court of Appeals clearly endorsed the use of a screening procedure for paralegals to rebut the presumption that confidential information was shared (232 Cal. App. 3d 670 (1991)). The Texas Supreme Court endorsed the use of screens for paralegals in ongoing litigation in the case of *Phoenix Founders, Inc. v. Marshall,* 887 S.W.2d 831 (Tex. 1994). In other cases, the courts approved the use of screens but found the procedures employed by the firms to be inadequate (*Grant v. Thirteenth Court of Appeals,* 38 Tex. Sup. Ct. J. 12 (1994), and *Smart Industries Corp. v. Superior Court,* 876 P.2d 1176 (Ariz. App. Div. 1 1994)). In 1998, the Texas Supreme Court again addressed paralegal conflicts, finding in the case of *In re American Home Products,* 985 S.W.2d 68 (Tex. 1998) that conflicts rules apply to freelance paralegals who work on the opposite side of ongoing litigation. The Nevada Supreme Court overruled and clarified an earlier case disallowing screens in cases of paralegal conflicts in *Leibowitz v. Eighth Judicial District Court of the State of Nevada,* 78 P.3d 515 (Nev. 2003).

Several state and local **ethics opinions** have addressed the issue. Nearly all opinions endorse the use of screens and do not demand adherence to strict disqualification rules that would apply to lawyers in similar conflict situations. Courts will continue to apply the conflicts rules flexibly because they have shown sensitivity to the different roles of the lawyer and paralegal and to the problems of job changing in an increasingly mobile legal business. A comment to the revised ABA Model Rules may have some influence in encouraging the use of screens for paralegal conflicts in the few remaining states that are undecided or have found against screens.

E.   Conflicts Checks

Conducting a conflicts check when a firm is considering hiring a new employee or undertaking a new matter is critical to identify and address potential and real conflicts. The ethics rules necessitate that lawyers adopt reasonable procedures to determine in both litigation and nonlitigation matters the parties and issues involved, and whether there are actual or potential conflicts of interest.

When a **prospective client** seeks representation by a firm, the attorney or paralegal should obtain first all the information necessary to conduct the conflicts check before the prospective client reveals confidential information about the matter for which representation is sought.

This practice gives greater protection for the confidential information in the event that the firm does not undertake representation. The new client information obtained should relate to the client's activities and the nature of representation sought. If the client is a business client, such as a corporation or partnership, the information should include the names of subsidiaries and other related businesses as well as principal shareholders, officers, directors, partners, and the like. The lawyer and client should discuss the nature of the legal services sought — for instance, whether representation is needed for a single matter such as a lawsuit or negotiation of a business deal, or whether representation is needed for an array of ongoing legal matters. If a lawsuit is contemplated, the names of potential adversaries should be obtained. If the client has other legal matters pending, basic information about these matters (such as the names of adversaries) should also be obtained. When an existing client seeks representation on a new matter, information relating to the nature of this matter and potential adversaries should always be obtained. Firms should update client information on existing clients regularly — names of officers and directors and the nature of business activities, for instance — to ensure the accuracy and currency of all information.

Similarly, **prospective employees**, including both attorneys and nonattorneys, must provide the firm with basic information about matters on which they worked in previous employment, major business or financial interests that have the potential to create conflicts, and personal and family relationships that may give rise to conflicts.

The firm must process the information to determine if any conflicts or potential conflicts exist that would preclude representation or employment or require the erection of a screen to isolate the disqualified employee.

Many firms have **computer programs** that conduct searches quickly and thoroughly. Firms need an established procedure for evaluating conflicts that have been identified to decide how the firm should deal with them. Many firms have an **ethics or conflicts committee** or an ethics counsel to act on these matters. Prompt action on new clients and matters is essential to prevent a client or prospective client from delay in securing counsel. The firm's conflicts committee should evaluate each new client, new matter, and new prospective employee — along with any potential conflicts they carry with them — applying the relevant ethical rules, case law, and firm policies that may apply to the matter.

If a potential conflict exists, the firm examines the information relating to the new client, matter, or prospective employee to determine whether the conflict is one that could disqualify the firm. It may need to decide, for example, whether an apparent conflict with a former client concerns a "substantially related" matter. Once it is clear that a potential conflict of some type exists, the firm may recommend declining the representation, or it may accept the representation while seeking consent from the appropriate party or parties and/or creating a screen. Avoiding conflicts of interest is a critical matter for paralegals. They have an ethical responsibility to keep good **records** of the matters on which they work and to be forthcoming with this information when appropriate. Generally, this information becomes pertinent when the paralegal prepares to make a job change, begins work on a new matter, or engages in freelance work, which in essence is a job change with every new assignment. **Freelancing** greatly increases the potential for conflicts. Although it has become common practice for freelance paralegals and lawyers to handle assignments on a temporary, as-needed basis, this practice does necessitate careful monitoring. In providing prospective employers with information that enables them to conduct a conflicts check, paralegals must take care to protect client confidentiality as well. Information about matters on which the paralegal has worked should not be revealed until the firm is ready to make a firm job offer and should be limited to the minimum information necessary to conduct the check.

REVIEW QUESTIONS

1. On what principles are the conflicts of interest rules based?
2. Why are conflicts problems becoming more common?
3. What is the general rule about simultaneously representing two clients whose interests are adverse?
4. May clients consent to a concurrent conflict of interest? Under what circumstances may clients consent? Why might a court not honor this consent?
5. What are the requirements for a client's consent? What should be disclosed in a letter to a client regarding the potential conflict?

6. What do NALA and NFPA ethics rules say about conflicts?
7. What is an issue conflict? Are lawyers allowed to represent clients where these conflicts are present?
8. Would it be a conflict of interest for an attorney to represent two clients whose interests are not adverse but whose trial dates conflict? Would it be a conflict of interest if the attorney could obtain a postponement of one of the trials?
9. Is it ethical for a lawyer to represent both the husband and the wife in an uncontested divorce?
10. Is it ethical for an attorney to represent the passenger and the driver in a lawsuit against another driver?
11. Is it ethical for an attorney to represent codefendants in a criminal case?
12. May a firm represent more than one party to a business transaction?
13. Do the rules permit a firm to represent all the family members in creating an estate plan?
14. Can a lawyer with a conflict withdraw from representing one client and continue representing the other client?
15. What is the general rule about representing a client whose interests may be adverse to a former client?
16. How does a court decide if matters in successive representation are "substantially related"? If a court finds that matters are substantially related, is the attorney or firm automatically disqualified? In what two ways might the attorney or firm rebut a presumption that the confidentiality is at risk?
17. What is the general rule about business transactions between lawyers and clients? What are the conditions necessary for a business transaction to override the rule's prohibitions?
18. What is the general rule about an attorney being granted publication or media rights? What is the rationale behind it?
19. Are attorneys prohibited from paying clients' costs in a matter? From lending a client money? Why? Are there any circumstances under which a lawyer may cover a client's costs?
20. Why are lawyers prohibited from obtaining an ownership interest in a lawsuit they are handling? What are the exceptions?
21. Under what circumstances are gifts from clients prohibited? Explain the rationale. What steps should be taken to legitimize a gift to an attorney?
22. May an attorney attempt to limit his or her malpractice liability to a client in an engagement letter? To settle a malpractice claim with a client?
23. What potential conflicts arise when a third party pays a client's legal fees? How can an attorney ensure against such conflicts?
24. What family relationships give rise to conflicts of interest rules? How do these rules apply to paralegals? Do the rules cover relationships outside of blood or marriage?

25. What is imputed disqualification? What is the basis for this rule? What kinds of conflicts does it cover? How does the rule apply to paralegals?
26. Describe how to create an effective screen that will withstand judicial scrutiny.
27. What do the majority of jurisdictions and the ABA say about the use of screens in conflicts cases involving paralegals? What jurisdiction(s) do not follow this trend?
28. How should a conflicts check be conducted when a firm has a new client? A new matter or case? A new employee?
29. Do conflicts rules apply to freelance paralegals?

HYPOTHETICALS

1. Amy Anderson graduated from paralegal school in June and was immediately offered a position by one of the best firms in town, Xavier & Young. Her job is in the business litigation department.

    The firm asks Amy to complete a conflicts check form in which she has to state the names and affiliations of her relatives who work in the legal field, stock she owns, and client matters she has worked on. She completes the form, and in the third section indicates that she has not worked on any client matters. On her second day at the job, Amy is assigned to work on the Toxall pharmaceutical litigation. She remembers that she worked briefly on the opposite side of this litigation for her internship sponsor, another large law firm, Abernathy & Crum. What should Amy do? Is there a conflict? Was Amy wrong not to report her internship work on her conflicts check form? Does it matter that her internship was unpaid? Does it matter that Amy only worked on the matter briefly and doesn't remember anything about it?

2. Bill Brown is a paralegal who works for a large firm that is handling some major products liability litigation involving Ford Motors. He knows that his job is being phased out and starts looking for another job. He likes one of the lawyers he has met working on the case; the lawyer, May Meredith, is one of the opposing counsel in the case. May's firm, Meredith and Lansing, handles real estate transactions, and Bill is interested in doing more real estate work and less litigation. Is it ethical for Bill to approach May about working at her firm? Is it ethical for May to hire Bill? Does May need to screen Bill in any way? What about after the Ford litigation is over?

3. Danielle Durham, a paralegal, works for Nally & Overland, a small law firm that handles family law, bankruptcy, and other small business and personal legal matters. She works for all three lawyers in the firm, each of whom specializes in one or two areas of practice. The firm represented John and Katherine Jackson in a bankruptcy in 1997, and

Danielle worked on that matter. Now the Jacksons are getting divorced and John wants the firm to represent him. May Nally & Overland represent John Jackson? May Danielle work on the case? May the firm represent both the Jacksons? Is a consent or screen needed?

4. Evelyn Ellerbe is a paralegal who works for an estate-planning lawyer, Timothy Taft. An elderly client, Sam Stone, comes in after his wife dies to have his will rewritten. It turns out that he is a neighbor of Evelyn, who takes a liking to Sam and begins to help him out by stopping by his house once or twice a week with groceries. After two years, during which Evelyn and Sam continue to be friends, Sam asks Timothy to rewrite his will for the purpose of leaving Evelyn half of his estate. Is it ethical for Tim to draft Sam's will with this provision? Is it ethical for Evelyn to assist in the preparation of the will? If the will is challenged, what will the court consider in deciding whether to void the gift? Would it make any difference to your answer if Sam had no other relatives? Would it make any difference if Sam and Evelyn had a sexual relationship?

5. Frank Fink, an intellectual property paralegal, works in a boutique law firm, Edmund & Sun, which specializes in technology. The firm puts together its regular clientele of venture capitalist clients with clients who have ideas for high-technology companies. The firm is often approached by start-up companies that need funding. Is it ethical for Edmund & Sun to represent both the venture capitalists and clients that need funding? How might the interests of these two clients conflict? Are consents needed? Assume that VC, a venture capitalist entity, and SU, a start-up company, are put together by Edmund & Sun and VC agrees to fund SU to the tune of $5 million. May Edmund & Sun draft the incorporation agreements, stock arrangements, and contracts involved? May Edmund & Sun take as its fee a 2-percent interest in the new company? If a dispute arises between VC and SU, may the firm mediate? May the firm represent one of the parties in the litigation that ensues? Both of the parties? May Frank invest his own money in the client's new company?

6. Jerry Jones works for Biotech Corp. as an executive assistant to the president. She leaves the company and works as a freelance secretary for executives. She is contacted by lawyer Bonnie Butler, who hires her to organize documents obtained in discovery from Biotech, which Butler is suing on behalf of another former employee. Has Butler done anything wrong? Is the information that Jones learned as an executive assistant confidential? What if she had signed a confidentiality agreement? What if Butler knew that Jones had confidential information when she hired Jones? What will happen if Biotech brings a motion to disqualify Butler?

DISCUSSION QUESTIONS AND PROJECTS

1. If you worked in a law firm and were getting a divorce, would you find it acceptable to have two different lawyers in your firm represent you and your spouse? What if you were getting married and needed a prenuptial agreement?

2. Do you think firms should be bound by ethics rules against representing matters that create issue conflicts? Explain your reasoning.

3. What would you do if you worked for an attorney who had such a heavy court calendar that she or he was constantly rescheduling court dates and delaying motions and trials?

4. What would you do if you knew that your firm had a conflict of interest problem that it was not addressing internally? Would it make any difference in your actions if the firm was knowingly ignoring the problem?

5. Draft a letter to a client explaining a recently discovered potential conflict based on your previous employment.

6. What are your state's ethics rules on conflicts of interest?

7. Does your state or local bar have any special guidelines or ethics opinions on the application to paralegals of conflict rules? Are there any cases in your state involving firm disqualification because of a paralegal conflict of interest?

8. Do you think paralegals should be subject to the same rules on conflicts as those governing lawyers? Why, or why not?

9. What would you do as a paralegal if a client of an attorney with whom you work asked you to invest in his or her business? To buy property from him or her? Do you think that entering into these transactions would create a conflict of interest?

10. Do you think that a paralegal's co-writing a screenplay with a former client about the client's life creates a conflict of interest? What about a current client?

11. Would you lend a client money for living expenses? Would your answer be different if lending the money would keep your client from accepting a low settlement offer because of the client's dire financial condition?

12. What would you do if an elderly client wanted to leave you a substantial gift in his or her will? Would it make any difference if the client had no other living relatives? If the client wanted to do this because of an estranged relationship with his or her children?

13. What would you do if a client gave you a valuable piece of jewelry? Would it make a difference if the gift was intended as thanks for your work on a case? What if the client promised to give you a personal "bonus" if your firm prevailed in the case?

14. What would you do if you worked for a firm that had all new clients sign an agreement limiting the firm's malpractice liability to $10,000?

15. Do you think the rules prohibiting conflicts involving relatives should be extended to nonrelatives? What about roommates? Long-term live-in relationships? In-laws? Is it any "safer" for closely related lawyers and paralegals to work in the same firm? What kinds of problems might this situation create?

16. Interview paralegals at five local law firms and ask them about their policies and procedures for establishing screens and conducting conflicts checks. Also find out how effective they think screens are.

17. Do you think it is possible to screen an employee in a small law firm — for example, a firm with one lawyer, one paralegal, and one secretary? What if the firm had two lawyers, two paralegals, and two secretaries?

18. What should you do if a firm that has offered you a job does not request information to do a conflicts check?

SELECTED CASES

In re American Home Products, 985 S.W.2d 68 (Tex. 1998) (conflicts rules apply to freelance paralegals).

In re Complex Asbestos Litigation, 232 Cal. App. 3d 670, 283 Cal. Rptr. 732 (1991) (firm disqualified for paralegal conflict; screens endorsed).

Hayes v. Central States Orthopedic Specialists, Inc., 202 Okla. 30, 51 P.3d 562 (2002) (screening for paralegals allowed).

Leibowitz v. District Court, 78 P.3d 515 (Nev. 2003) (overturned strict rule of disqualification in cases of paralegal conflicts).

Phoenix Founders, Inc. v. Marshall, 887 S.W.2d 831 (Tex. 1994) (screen endorsed for paralegal conflict).

Smart Industries Corp. v. Superior Court, 876 P.2d 1176 (Ariz. App. Div.1 1994) (screen endorsed for paralegal conflict).

Zimmerman v. Mahaska Bottling Company, 19 P.3d 784 (Kan. 2001) (disallows screening for paralegals where screening would not be allowed for lawyers).

SELECTED REFERENCES

ABA Model Code Disciplinary Rules 5-101 through 5-107 ABA Model Rules 1.7 through 1.11

ABA Formal Opinion 88-356 (1988)

NFPA Ethics Opinion 93-3 [re conflicts of interest]

NFPA Model Code EC-1.6(a) through (g) [conflicts]

5

Advertising and Solicitation

This chapter explains the rules governing lawyer advertising and solicitation, how they evolved, and how they apply to paralegals working with lawyers. Chapter 5 covers:

- key cases affecting the ways that lawyer advertising is regulated
- the current status of legal advertising and marketing
- ethics rules governing advertising
- advertising rules as they apply to paralegals
- ethics rules prohibiting direct solicitation of clients
- advertising and solicitation on the Internet

A.   Advertising

1.   The Advent and Evolution of Lawyer Advertising

In 1977, the landmark case of *Bates v. State Bar of Arizona*, 433 U.S. 350, upset decades of ethics rules prohibiting lawyer advertising. These rules date back to the first state codes and first ABA Canons issued in 1908. The early rules prohibited virtually every form of advertising except business cards. Later, inclusion of biographical information on approved lists of lawyers was permitted.

The **political and social environment** surrounding the *Bates* decision was one of growing consumer awareness. The public was also coming to realize that most citizens did not have access to legal services; at the same time, the cost of legal services was rising dramatically. During the late 1960s and throughout the 1970s, new nontraditional methods of increasing access to legal services were being developed. Legal aid and public interest law firms began opening their doors. The first prepaid legal insurance plans were established. Storefront legal clinics that handled common legal problems at lower cost than traditional firms began to crop up. The organized bar and the public shared the realization that not only were most middle- and lower-middle-income citizens unable to afford an attorney, but most did not even know how to go about finding one.

The ABA Model Code, adopted in 1969, contained the **traditional restrictions** on lawyer advertising. Only business cards, announcements of attorney personnel changes within a firm or of a new address, and Christmas cards to existing clients were permitted. The ABA had made some slight modifications in these rules in the mid-1970s to accommodate the special needs of legal aid organizations and prepaid legal insurance plans. It was not until *Bates* that sweeping changes were made in the ethics codes of every jurisdiction.

In the *Bates* case, two Arizona lawyers advertised low-cost legal services in a local newspaper and were disciplined by the state bar. Their challenge to restrictions on lawyer advertising was ultimately heard by the U.S. Supreme Court, which struck down the restrictions as violative of the First Amendment. The Court held that lawyer advertising — like other forms of commercial speech — was protected, and states could prohibit advertisements only in limited ways. States could only prohibit **false, misleading, or deceptive ads** and could provide for **reasonable time, place, and manner restrictions**.

Several Supreme Court decisions that followed *Bates* struck down attempts by states to restrict lawyer advertising. In *In re R.M.J.*, 455 U.S. 1991 (1982), the Court held that a practitioner could advertise the **areas of law** in which he practiced in language other than that specified in the state ethics code because the language the lawyer used was not misleading and the code was unnecessarily restrictive. The court also allowed the lawyer to advertise the jurisdictions in which he was licensed to practice. In *Zauderer v. Office of Disciplinary Counsel of Supreme Court of Ohio*, 471 U.S. 626 (1985), the Supreme Court reversed a state supreme court ruling that disciplined a personal injury attorney for placing a newspaper ad that pictured the intrauterine device that was the subject of litigation. The Court held that the attorney had the right to publish ads **directed at readers with specific legal problems** so long as the ads were accurate and not misleading.

In 1988, the Supreme Court in *Shapero v. Kentucky Bar Association*, 486 U.S. 466, held that state ethics codes could not prohibit truthful and nondeceptive **direct mail advertising**. The language the Court found unconstitutional in the Kentucky code was identical to ABA Model Rule 7.3, which was then revised. Prior to *Shapero*, ethics rules had classified direct mail advertising with telephone and in-person solicitation and had prohibited it completely. In *Peel v. Attorney Registration and Disciplinary Commission of Illinois*, 496 U.S. 91 (1990), the Court struck down state prohibitions on statements on a lawyer's letterhead indicating the lawyer's **certification as a specialist**. Although the certifying agency in the case — the National Board of Trial Advocacy (NBTA) — was not recognized by the state, the NBTA was shown to have objective and verifiable criteria for the certification of a civil trial specialist. This ruling resulted in changes in several state codes that had restrictions similar to those of Illinois.

Peel was followed by another case endorsing the use of a designation by an organization not approved by a state agency. In *Ibanez v. Florida Dept. of Business and Professional Regulation*, 512 U.S. 136 (1994), the Court held that an attorney/certified public accountant who advertised her certified public accountant (CPA) and certified financial planner (CFP) designations could not be reprimanded by the Florida Board of Accountancy for false, deceptive, and misleading advertising because the ad was truthful and the CFP designation was publicly recognized by potential clients.

The pattern of the court striking down state prohibitions on lawyer advertising was finally broken in 1995 in the case of *Florida Bar v. Went For It, Inc.*, 515 U.S. 618 (1995). In this landmark case, the Supreme Court upheld **restrictions on targeted direct mail advertising** sent to accident and disaster victims. Florida, like many other jurisdictions, had adopted a rule prohibiting such ads from being sent within 30 days of the accident or disaster. In upholding the prohibition, the Court cited heavily to bar studies that showed how negatively such letters were viewed by the public, which saw the lawyers' conduct as an invasion of privacy and as an unscrupulous practice designed to take advantage of vulnerable people in tragic circumstances. No major cases on lawyer advertising and solicitation have been decided by the U.S. Supreme Court since this case.

2. The Current Ethics Rules

The ABA Model Code was amended after *Bates* to comply with that decision (DR 2-101 through 2-105). The code prohibits false, fraudulent, misleading, deceptive, self-laudatory, or unfair statements or claims in public communications and delineates the specific information that may be used in print or broadcast media advertisements. The code requires ads to be "dignified," a requirement that would probably not be upheld by the Court. Special rules dictate that copies of broadcast and other ads be retained for stated time periods and that lawyers who advertise fees abide by the advertised fee for specified periods. Another provision prohibits a lawyer from compensating anyone in the media for giving him or her publicity. Some states adopted an alternative version of the ethics rules on advertising that permits any advertising except that which is false, fraudulent, misleading, or deceptive.

False/misleading communications Contain material misrepresentations of fact or law or omit necessary material facts

The ABA Model Rules (7.1 through 7.5), which have been adopted in most states, follow the less restrictive and less specific approach to advertising, by prohibiting only *false or misleading communications.* The Rules define false and misleading communications as containing material misrepresentations of fact or law or omitting necessary material facts. The previous version of the rule, followed in many states, also prohibits communications that create an **unjustified expectation** about results or imply that results can be achieved by **violating the law** or ethics rules or statements that **compare** the lawyer's services to other lawyers' unless factually substantiated.

A few states specifically prohibit **testimonials**, contending that they are inherently misleading, create unjustified expectations, or are self-laudatory. A growing number of jurisdictions allow testimonials, usually with the requirement that they include information about payment to the endorser and/or the status of the endorser as a client, or have disclaimers to avoid unjustified expectations. The U.S. Supreme Court has refused the opportunity to review this issue twice. A **list of clients' names**, with their approval, may be used in advertising in all jurisdictions. **Dramatizations** in radio and television ads are also disfavored by many in the organized bar, but are becoming increasingly common and are tolerated in most states. Several states permit them, usually with disclaimers that advise the viewers that the ad is a dramatization and does not guarantee similar results.

Many states' rules are more restrictive than the ABA Model Rules. Some prohibit all lawyer **comparison advertising**. Other states prohibit statements regarding past performance on the grounds that they are inherently misleading and create false expectations. Several states specifically prohibit predictions of success; these claims would probably be found to be misleading even without a specific prohibition in the code. Claims about quality are generally prohibited because they are incapable of objective measurement. **Fee information** and comparisons are generally permissible, although some states have adopted specific language to describe fees.

Lawyers may advertise through virtually any medium, including telephone and online directories, legal directories, newspapers, periodicals, outdoor signs, radio, television, direct mail, and the Internet. **Direct mail, e-mail, and recorded communications** must include the words **"Advertising Material"** at the beginning and end, and if the communication is direct mail, the words must appear on the outside of the envelope. Most states require lawyers to keep copies of ads and records on when and where they were used, whatever the method of advertising, for a stated period, usually between two and six years. Some also require that ads be submitted to a specified agency. Some states require specifically worded **disclaimers** in ads. The rules also prohibit **payment** to a person for recommending legal services except for the cost of ads, charges for legal service organizations or lawyer referral services, or payment when a lawyer buys another lawyer's practice.

Certification may not be stated unless the lawyer is certified by a state- or ABA-accredited program and the name of the certifying entity is clear. Most states' rules prohibit the statement that a lawyer is "specialized" or a "specialist" in a practice area unless he or she is certified as such. Some states' rules and the proposed revisions to the ABA Model Rules allow the terms **"limited to"** or **"concentrated in"** to describe a lawyer's particular area of practice.

Trade names are permitted under ethics rules so long as they do not imply a connection to a government agency or legal services organization; however, some states have strict limits on the use of trade names. Firms with multijurisdictional practices may use the same firm name in all states but must show the states where lawyers are licensed to practice. Lawyers in public office cannot be listed in a firm's name or on its letterhead unless the lawyer is actively and regularly practicing with the firm. Finally, lawyers cannot state or imply that they practice with a partnership or organization unless they do in fact. For example, lawyers who share office space but are not partners cannot hold themselves out as partners by means of their firm name or letterhead.

As indicated in Chapter 2, paralegals' **names and titles** may be listed on letterheads and business cards in most jurisdictions. Earlier restrictions on nonlawyers being listed on letterheads and having business cards have been revised in most jurisdictions because of changes in the rules on lawyer advertising brought about by *Bates* and the cases that followed it. Paralegals' names may also be included in lawyer advertising of all kinds. The NFPA Model Code's DR 1.7 also endorses the use of paralegals' names and titles in lawyer communications. Three ethics opinions specifically endorse the use of "CLA" and "CLAS" on letterheads and business cards.

Paralegal titles must clearly reflect the role of the paralegal and cannot mislead the public to believe that the paralegal is a lawyer.

Some ethics opinions on the subject have been issued, including a fairly restrictive one issued in 1992 by the New York State Bar Association Committee on Professional Ethics. Opinion 640, the first opinion issued by a bar on the **titles** that may be used by paralegals, endorsed the use of "paralegal" and "senior paralegal," which unambiguously convey the nonlawyer status of the paralegal. It recommended against the use of several other titles: "legal associate," "paralegal coordinator," "public benefits specialist," "legal advocate," "family law advocate," "housing law advocate," "disability advocate," and "public benefits advocate." The committee objected to these titles on the ground that they are likely to be confusing to the public, which would be misled about the non-lawyer status of someone with one of these titles.

A final concern about **letterhead and business cards** relates to their use by persons outside the firm, which should be carefully monitored. For example, several ethics opinions advise against allowing clients to use lawyers' letterhead to send correspondence without attorney review. Business cards, of course, must not be used for unethical solicitation.

3. Current Issues and Trends in Lawyer Advertising

The legal profession's initial resistance to lawyer advertising was tremendous, based mainly on the notion that it would deprofessionalize and commercialize law practice. Strong support for these beliefs still exists in many segments of the legal community; however, studies show that the vast majority of the lawyers in this country engage in some form of advertising. More firms than ever are using advertising as part of a marketing plan to attract clients.

Although many lawyers attribute the declining image of the legal profession to advertising, the public does not. The public considers advertising as a source of information and only begins to perceive it as objectionable when it becomes "invasive." It is also clear that an increasing number of people find lawyers through advertising.

Legal **marketing** has become a small support industry to the legal profession. Consultants, Web site designers, and legal public relations and marketing firms abound. Many larger firms have their own in-house legal marketing personnel. Legal marketing specialists have their own organization, the National Association of Law Firm Marketing Administrators. Many firms have become sophisticated marketers, using tactics to attract clients in ways never dreamed of when *Bates* was decided.

Legal advertising takes many forms and is designed to target many different kinds of potential clients. Larger traditional law firms have strategic marketing plans that identify potential clients and develop ways to attract their business. Virtually all law firms have Web sites that provide information on the firm's lawyers and the nature of their practice. Most have **firm brochures** that describe the backgrounds of the firm's attorneys and the nature of their practice. Many also have regularly published **newsletters** for clients to update the clients on the latest firm triumphs and to inform them of changes in the law that may encourage the clients to have legal work done. Many hold social events and educational seminars for clients and send press releases to the media to announce significant events in the firm — for example, when the firm wins an important case or a prestigious new partner joins the firm.

Combined with the increased competition for corporate clients, the phenomenon of advertising has created a new atmosphere in larger law firms. Great value is placed on **rainmakers** who can bring in business. A lawyer's ability to work well with clients and keep them satisfied is essential to success in a firm. Law firms try to establish a high public profile by donating funds to worthy causes, participating in community and civic activities, taking pro bono cases that will generate favorable publicity, and encouraging their lawyers and paralegals to participate in a wide variety of civic and professional activities outside the firm. Many firms sponsor in-house seminars or send lawyers to continuing education programs that train lawyers how to better market their services and how to enhance client relations. Many firms give seminars at trade shows in industries from which they draw clients — an example of "niche marketing."

Some large firms use **client surveys** to assess the attitudes, needs, and levels of satisfaction of their clients. Surveys, conducted either orally through structured interviews or in writing, aim to identify the importance of various factors in meeting clients' needs and to find out how the firm's responsiveness, communication, services, and fee structure are perceived. Theoretically, client relations are improved simply by virtue of conducting the survey, and the information gained may be used to enhance services and to remedy weaknesses. Sophisticated research surveys are also being used by a few major firms, sometimes in conjunction with a client, to gain information about a particular industry or trend. The firms then use the results to sponsor firm events for clients and prospective clients and to craft press releases and articles for publication in bar, industry, or specialinterest periodicals. Many firms have sought to **"brand"** themselves, making changes to the firm name to make it easier to recall (and eliminating the punctuation); developing taglines used in publications; promoting the values they hold or their specific expertise. Some firms have advertorials in major newspapers or on the Web.

Smaller firms also engage in **advertising**. The more traditional small firms use the same kinds of marketing activities as large firms. But many small firms are specialized; they handle one or two kinds of legal matters and seek a clientele that might not otherwise have a ready referral to an attorney. Personal injury firms have led the way in lawyer advertising, most noticeably with television and radio spots, but also with billboards, flyers placed on cars or doorknobs, posters on telephone poles, and even ads on the backs of grocery store receipts. Firms that handle immigration, family law, workers' compensation, Social Security benefits, and bankruptcy frequently use these techniques as well. Direct mail advertising of targeted persons who may need a specific kind of legal service is employed by some firms. Some lawyers have 900 telephone numbers to dispense legal advice, and others have catchy 800 numbers that are included in print, radio, or television ads.

Lawyers use various kinds of Internet communications to reach prospective clients. Most law firms now have **Web sites** that, like firm brochures, provide background information on the lawyers in the firm and the areas in which the firm practices. Web sites also include articles about legal issues of interest to clients. Some have catchy names to draw in clients who are searching the Internet for a lawyer. Some lawyers participate in *chat groups* and have used direct e-mail to attract clients. Many lawyers post advertisements and articles on Internet bulletin boards, participate in trade group seminars online, and have their own blogs where they provide information and opinions about legal issues of the day.

Chat group
Discussion carried on electronically over the Internet, which can be live or synchronous

Web sites that provide legal information have also sprung up. These sites have lawyers who answer questions from inquirers who have a legal problem. Lawyers sometimes answer these queries for free; other times they are paid by the Web site. Many lawyers who participate hope that they will gain clients this way. Another use of the Internet to increase access to legal services has been created by Web sites that **match up prospective clients with lawyers**. In these sites, the client usually spells out his or her legal problem, and participating lawyers "bid" for the case. Lawyers have to be careful about the sites they associate with or link to, as some have been less than scrupulous in the way that they advertise to clients. Some lawyers have been disciplined for running afoul of the rules; others have been badly and publicly embarrassed.

The use of the Internet to attract clients has raised **new ethical issues** that fall into many areas of the ethics rules. Are the lawyers who answer questions on Web sites for people with legal problems giving advice or providing legal "information"? If clients pay a fee to the Web site to have their questions answered, is the lawyer engaging in fee splitting with the Web site owner? Is direct e-mail of prospective clients advertising or solicitation, and which rules apply? Is a Web site more like a television ad or a firm brochure? If an attorney states a legal opinion in a chat group or a legal Web site, is the attorney forming an attorney-client relationship with the person posing the question? Is the attorney violating unauthorized practice rules in states in which he or she is not licensed to practice but where the opinion is read? Is it inherently misleading to advertise on the Internet when the attorney is not licensed in all the states where the ad may be read? Are firms that match up lawyers and clients acting as referral services that must be approved by the state bar or court?

Some states have issued ethics opinions or new rules that explain how the ethics rules on advertising and solicitation apply to electronic communications. A few generalizations can be made about the ethics of electronic advertising and solicitation:

- It is not unethical for a lawyer or law firm to have a **Web site or blog** providing information about the firm and legal issues so long as other ethics rules on advertising are followed. The applicable rules prohibit false and misleading statements, require lawyers to retain copies of the material for review, specify language about certifications, and mandate inclusion of the lawyer's name in the "advertisement."
- A lawyer's Web site must state the **jurisdictions** in which the lawyers in the firm are licensed to practice law and should contain disclaimers to warn prospective clients that they can practice only in those states. This information and the disclaimers are needed to prevent the public from being misled about where a lawyer can practice and to protect against UPL.
- Advertising on the Internet, including direct e-mail, constitutes "**advertising**," not solicitation, so lawyers can use the Internet to advertise as long as the existing ethics rules on advertising are followed.

Most lawyers have **disclaimers** on their Web sites indicating that information provided therein is not legal advice and that no attorney-client relationship is established by virtue of the prospective client sending a lawyer an e-mail. Disclaimers also warn that such communications are not privileged and state the jurisdictional limits of the lawyer's practice.

The 2001 revisions to the ABA Model Rules classify "**real-time electronic contact**" with prospective clients, such as in live chats, as solicitation, not advertising, making these forms of communication subject to more rigorous restrictions than those that apply to advertising. Another related issue concerns when an attorney-client relationship is formed in electronic communication. Some experts believe that an attorney-client relationship may arise in **threaded discussions** and chat rooms if a lawyer gives advice that is specific to the client's problem. If a lawyer-client relationship does arise without the lawyer checking for conflicts, the lawyer could be placed in a conflict situation. If the client follows the advice and is harmed by the results, the lawyer may be sued for malpractice.

At least one state, Tennessee, has disciplined a lawyer for soliciting on the Internet by sending a direct e-mail *spam* to more than 10,000 Internet users, including users in jurisdictions in which the lawyer was not licensed to practice. Some states have determined that lawyers are not permitted to be listed in lawyers' directories on the Internet, and several states classify fee-charging directories as profit-making referral services that lawyers are prohibited from using. Many firms use direct e-mail with current clients, sending newsletters and the like.

Spam
Direct unsolicited e-mail to a large number of Internet users

Many commentators would like to see **uniform national ethics rules** concerning Internet communications. The great variation among states in their handling of advertising and solicitation exacerbates this already difficult new area of ethics; a lawyer may be in compliance with the local jurisdictional rules but in violation of the rules in another state where the communication is read. Further, the lawyers in states with more restrictive advertising rules are at a competitive disadvantage because they are more limited in what they can say, how they can say it, and where they can say it. Differences in rules on advertising in directories, how one's areas of expertise can be described, and whether extensive disclaimers are required make advertising on the Internet especially challenging for lawyers in restrictive jurisdictions.

B. Solicitation

The changes in ethics rules that loosened restrictions on lawyer advertising have not changed the basic rules restricting the conduct of lawyers in soliciting clients directly, either **in person or by telephone**. The foundation for these restrictions is strong and remains virtually unquestioned by the profession. The rules reflect concerns about the intimidation, undue influence, and unfair bargaining position that a lawyer may have when he or she confronts a prospective client face-to-face or on the phone. The ethics rules have a long-standing prohibition against "ambulance chasers" or *"runners and cappers,"* agents of lawyers who prey on accident victims by soliciting them directly at the scene of an accident or while they are in a hospital as the result of an accident. This kind of overreaching conduct, especially when it is directed toward clients who are vulnerable and not in a position to make a rational or well-thought-out choice about selecting counsel, clearly offends most lawyers and the public.

Runners and cappers
Agents of lawyers who prey on accident victims by soliciting them directly, usually at the accident scene or hospital

Several cases have addressed this issue. The leading case upholding restrictions on direct solicitation is *Ohralik v. Ohio State Bar Association*, 436 U.S. 447 (1978), which was decided at about the same time as the *Bates* case. This case involved an attorney who solicited an accident victim both by telephone and in person, including making a visit to the victim in the hospital. Aggravating the solicitation violation was the attorney's refusal to stop the solicitation after the potential "client" refused representation.

The U.S. Supreme Court case of *Edenfield v. Fane*, 507 U.S. 761 (1993), caused speculation that the Court might strike down some of the restrictions against direct solicitation by lawyers. In that case, a Florida CPA sought relief from regulations that prohibited direct solicitation of clients. The Court held that such restrictions are a violation of free speech in a business context where prospective clients are sophisticated and experienced business executives. This decision has not, however, caused any jurisdiction to do away with prohibitions on lawyer solicitation of clients and no other related cases have come before the Court.

An **exception** to rules against direct solicitation of clients is made in cases involving organizations that seek to represent plaintiffs in cases that further a specific **political principle**, such as freedom of speech or association, or civil rights. Examples of such organizations are the National Association for the Advancement of Colored People and American Civil Liberties Union. The leading cases in this area are *NAACP v. Button*, 371 U.S. 415 (1963), and *In re Primus*, 436 U.S. 412 (1978). Some states have adopted an alternative provision that takes a different approach to the exception for politically motivated solicitations. This version of the rule allows personal contact with the prospective client if "under the auspices of a public or charitable legal services organization; or . . . a bona fide political, social, civic, fraternal, employee or trade organization" whose purposes include providing or recommending legal services.

The ABA Model Code prohibits lawyers from soliciting employment **in person** or by **telephone.** Model Rule 7.3 solicitation includes **live telephone** and **real-time electronic contact**. To meet the definition of solicitation, the lawyer's financial gain has to be a significant motive. Exceptions are carved out for other **lawyers, family members, close personal friends**, and **clients.** Speaking or writing about legal matters is not considered soliciting employment so long as the lawyer is not emphasizing his or her own experience or reputation or giving individual advice. The Model Rules also prohibit lawyers from soliciting when the prospective client has asked not to be solicited or when the solicitation involves "coercion, duress or harassment." Generally, courts have also carved out an exception for attorneys seeking to contact members of a class in a **class action suit**.

Some states have adopted additional provisions that prohibit any direct or written solicitation of persons who are in a **vulnerable physical, emotional, or mental state**. California's rules state that communications transmitted at the scene of an accident or en route to a health care facility are presumed to violate rules against solicitation.

Finally, there is a split in the jurisdictions over the use of **prerecorded telephone messages**. Some states classify these messages as direct telephone solicitation and prohibit them, but others find this method to be more like direct mail advertising and do not prohibit them per se. The ABA rules classify them as "communications," i.e., advertising, not solicitation, as these messages are much like direct mail.

A lawyer who attempts to use **agents** or intermediaries to circumvent rules against solicitation will be held responsible in a disciplinary action for the conduct of his or her agents, under general principles of agency law and ethics rules. Despite these very clear rules, instances of unethical solicitation are not that uncommon, especially by lawyers using agents. For example, agents of lawyers, including accident investigators, have been found soliciting business at the scene of airline crashes and other major accidents. Some states are attempting to overcome the difficulties inherent in stopping unlawful solicitation by creating disaster response teams of volunteer and staff lawyers who go to the scenes of major accidents and disasters to warn victims about unlawful solicitation and to deter lawyers from engaging in such conduct.

A few state bars have found arrangements where **independent nonlawyers** providing legal services have referred clients to lawyers to constitute unlawful solicitation, usually coupled with fee splitting. Some personal injury lawyers offer a referral fee to anyone who brings a new case to the firm, often accomplished through the agent's unethical in-person or telephone solicitation. These violations are not often the subject of discipline because only the parties involved are aware of them, and no one is willing to report them and thus lose a source of income.

The NALA and NFPA ethics codes do not address advertising and solicitation directly, but do prohibit a paralegal from engaging in any act that is unethical (see NALA Canon 3(c) and NFPA DR 1.3). Likewise, the ABA Model Guidelines for the Utilization of Paralegal Services require the lawyer to ensure that the paralegal's conduct is compatible with ethical rules (see Guideline 1 and ABA Model Rule 5.3).

REVIEW QUESTIONS

1. When were prohibitions on lawyer advertising lifted? Under what leading U.S. Supreme Court case?
2. How did the recognition in the 1960s and 1970s that many Americans do not have access to legal services affect the movement toward acceptance of lawyer advertising?
3. What kinds of lawyer advertising were permitted under the 1969 ABA Model Code?
4. What kinds of restrictions may states place on lawyer advertising after the *Bates* case?
5. Why do many lawyers dislike lawyer advertising?
6. What kinds of advertising do lawyers most commonly use?
7. What do the key court decisions since *Bates* say about lawyer advertising?
8. What kinds of restrictions do some states place on lawyer advertising?
9. Do lawyer ads have to be "dignified" under ethics rules?
10. In what media can lawyers advertise under the ethics rules?
11. What are the rules governing lawyer advertising of specialization and certification?
12. What are acceptable restrictions on direct mail ads to accident victims?

13. Are law firms allowed to use trade names? Under what circumstances?
14. May paralegals be listed on lawyers' letterhead? Their business cards?
15. Are lawyers prohibited from soliciting clients in person? On the telephone? Why?
16. What are the exceptions to the direct solicitation rule?
17. May lawyers use paralegals to solicit clients directly?
18. How common are violations of the ban on direct solicitation?
19. What job titles for paralegals are and are not acceptable?
20. What kinds of advertising and solicitation are being done on the Internet? What do ethics rules say about it? Are online chats considered to be communications/advertising or solicitation? What about threaded discussion? Blogs?

HYPOTHETICALS

1. A group of lawyers and nonlawyers form a profit-making company that is called "Foreclosure Fighters." The company represents people whose houses are being foreclosed. Foreclosure Fighters has a strong public interest mission to help people who are being treated unfairly, but it does charge a fee to the client. The goal of the representation is to forestall or stop the foreclosures. Are there any ethical issues involved in this scenario? May the company advertise its services using its name? May it solicit clients directly under the public interest exception to the solicitation rules? Would it make any difference if it were a nonprofit company?

2. Pam Pearson is a paralegal who works for a small personal injury law firm called Jones & Johnson. Her cousin, Marge Marshall, is injured in a car accident and is in the hospital. Pam asks Jan Jones, one of the name partners in the firm, for permission to leave an hour early to go see Marge in the hospital. Jan says yes, and adds, "Be sure to tell Marge that we can represent her." Should Pam do this? Is it unethical? Does it make any difference that Marge is in the hospital? Does it make any difference that Marge is a relative of Pam's?

3. Nathan Norris, a business paralegal, goes to work for Ollie Owen, who handles small business matters, including some that are litigated. Ollie wants to run an ad in the local business newspaper and asks Nathan to research the ethics rules and opinions to be sure that the ad is okay. The proposed ad would say: "Ollie Owen, experienced business and trial lawyer. Never lost a case. Handles some matters on contingency — no recovery, no fee." Examine each aspect of this ad and determine if there are any ethical violations. Would it matter if Ollie had only been in practice a year? Would it matter if Ollie settled all his cases and had never done a trial? Note that in most contingency

cases, the client has to pay the costs even if he or she loses. What advice should Nathan give Ollie? How should the ad read?

4. Ruth Reardon works for a criminal lawyer, Sammy Swanson. As a paralegal, Ruth sometimes goes to the county jail to talk with clients who are awaiting release. One day when Ruth is going to the court-house, Sammy hands her a stack of flyers about his services and asks her to hand them out in front of and inside the courthouse and jail. The flyer is on letter-size paper and looks like a business card. It has Sammy's name, address, telephone number, and e-mail address and the words, "Specializing in criminal defense work. Call collect any time night or day. Free initial consultation. $150/hour." May Ruth hand out these flyers? May she post them on bulletin boards and walls in the courthouse or jail? If the state has a certification program and Sammy is not certified as a criminal defense specialist, may he use the word "specializing"? If not, what alternative language may he use? Is it okay for the hourly fee to be stated? What if Sammy decides to raise his fees the next week? What if Sammy asks Ruth to hand out regular business cards?

5. Thomas Tucker is a paralegal working for Victoria Vernon, who handles workers' compensation cases. Victoria wants to produce a television ad about her services and asks Thomas to play the part of an injured client who gets a good recovery because of Victoria's ser-vices. In the ad, Thomas would be asked to say, "I was desperate and didn't know where to go. Then I found out about Victoria. She is incredible. She got me a great settlement. I can start my life all over. She is the best workers' comp lawyer in the state." During one part of this statement, Thomas is seen in a factory with a large machine falling on him. During the other part, he is seen standing in front of the local U.S. Court House. Should Thomas participate in this ad? What might be objectionable about it under current ethics rules discussed in this chapter? What do some states require on such ads?

DISCUSSION QUESTIONS AND PROJECTS

1. Locate the rules governing advertising and solicitation in your juris-diction. Compare them to the ABA Model Code and ABA Model Rules.

2. Using the *Bates* case, make a list of the reasons that support banning lawyer advertising and a list of those that support minimal restrictions on lawyer advertising. Which side of the argument do you find more persuasive?

3. Collect examples of as many different kinds of lawyer ads as you can find in your area. Check the Yellow Pages, billboards, television, radio, Internet, and so on. Rate these ads according to their

(1) usefulness and information value, (2) effectiveness in recruiting clients to a firm, and (3) degree of dignity or offensiveness.

4. Call five local law firms and find out what they are doing to bring in clients, including what methods of advertising they use. Collect their firm brochures, newsletters, and other advertising materials and rate them the same way you did the ads in Question 3.

5. Do you think advertising has hurt or helped the public image of lawyers? Has it made legal services more accessible?

6. Do you think that dramatizations in television and radio ads should be restricted? Why or why not? How?

7. Do you think testimonials should be prohibited? Why or why not?

8. May an ad say that an attorney is an "expert"? "Highly qualified"? "Competent"? Why or why not?

9. May an ad say that a firm specializes in "quickie divorces"? "Guaranteed visas"? Why or why not?

10. May an ad say the fee is $150 an hour without any additional information? Why or why not?

11. May a firm in a jurisdiction that allows trade names have the name "Public Law Firm"? "Legal Defenders"?

12. May a law firm print its name and phone number on pens that are given out to clients? On shirts donated to the local Little League team? On city maps sent to new residents?

13. Go on the Internet and find sites that offer legal advice or information and that match lawyers with prospective clients. What ethics rules are implicated in these sites? Did you find any sites that you believe are operating unethically? What potential ethics violations do you see?

14. Check your state's ethics rules and advisory opinions and find out what they say about Web sites, advertising on the Internet, chats, blogs, etc.

15. Write an ethics rule that covers advertising and solicitation on the Internet and is constitutional under *Bates* and its progeny.

16. Do you think restrictions on in-person and telephone solicitation are appropriate? Can you think of a way to allow direct solicitation while addressing concerns about overreaching and intimidation? Read the *Edenfield v. Fane* case for guidance.

17. Should political and public interest organizations be excused from restrictions on in-person solicitation? Why or why not?

SELECTED CASES

Bates v. State Bar of Arizona, 433 U.S. 350 (1977) (struck down state rules prohibiting advertising of legal services).

In re Cartmel, 676 N.E.2d 1047 (Ind. 1997) (paralegal placed ad that violated rules and lawyer was suspended).

Edenfield v. Fane, 507 U.S. 761 (1993) (struck down restrictions on CPAs that prohibited solicitation of business clients).

Falanga v. State Bar of Georgia, 150 F.3d 1333 (1998) (distinguishes vulnerable accident victims from the business clients in *Edenfield*).

Florida Bar v. Went For It, Inc., 515 U.S. 618 (1995) (upheld restrictions on direct mail advertising to accident victims).

Ohralik v. Ohio State Bar Association, 436 U.S. 447 (1978) (upheld restrictions on lawyer solicitation).

Peel v. Attorney Registration and Disciplinary Commission of Illinois, 496 U.S. 91 (1990) (struck down restrictions on advertising of certification and state licenses).

In re R.M. J., 455 U.S. 1991 (1982) (struck down restrictions that prohibited advertising of a lawyer's practice areas).

Shapero v. Kentucky Bar Association, 486 U.S. 466 (1988) (struck down restrictions on direct mail advertising).

Zauderer v. Office of Disciplinary Counsel of Supreme Court of Ohio, 471 U.S. 626 (1985) (struck down restrictions that prohibited advertising a picture of an IUD).

SELECTED REFERENCES

ABA Model Rules 5.3, 7.1-7.5

ABA Model Code DR 2-101 through 2-105, 9-101 ABA Model Guideline 1

NALA Canon 3(c)

NALA Guideline 1.3

NFPA DR 1.3

6

Fees and Client Funds

This chapter examines the role that financial matters play in the attorney-client relationship and covers the ethics rules and cases that guide conduct relating to fees and client funds. Paralegals are involved in client-related financial matters in many ways, from handling client trust funds to billing clients for their time. Chapter 6 covers:

- fee arrangements made with clients, including fixed fees, contingency fees, and hourly fees
- alternative fee arrangements
- factors in determining if a fee is unethically excessive
- unethical billing practices
- communication of fee agreements with clients
- terms included in fee agreements
- award of attorney's fees under fee-shifting statutes
- inclusion of paralegal fees in fee awards
- fee-splitting and referral fees
- partnerships between lawyers and nonlawyers
- client funds and client trust accounts

A. Fee Arrangements with Clients

Several different methods are used to charge clients for legal services. The method selected depends mostly on the nature of the services being rendered. The most common methods of billing are fixed fees, contingency fees, and hourly fees.

1. Fixed Fees

Fixed fees
Fee for legal services based on a set amount

Fixed fees (also known as *flat fees*) usually are used for **routine legal services**, ones for which the attorney knows the approximate amount of time needed to complete the work. In this instance, the client is paying for the lawyer's expertise as much as for the time expended. Typical services for which a fixed or flat fee is charged are filing a default divorce, forming a corporation, or handling a simple wage-earner bankruptcy.

A variation on the fixed fee is a fee that is based on the **percentage of the worth** of the matter being handled, either by statute or by practice. In probate matters, for example, the fee usually is based on a percentage of the value of the estate, according to statute. It is common practice in some states for a lawyer to charge a percentage of the value of a real estate transaction for handling related negotiations, document drafting, and the closing of the transaction. Although calculated as a percentage, these kinds of fees are not to be confused with contingency fees in litigated matters, in which lawyers take the risk of not collecting a fee if they lose the case.

2. Contingency Fees

Contingency fees
Fee depends on the successful outcome of a case and is based on a percentage of the recovery

Contingency fees are usually based on a **percentage of the recovery** in a case, usually a dispute that is litigated or may lead to litigation if not settled first. Sometimes a fixed fee is made contingent on the outcome in a case, giving it the most important attribute of a contingency fee — risk. Contingency fee arrangements typically are used by plaintiffs' attorneys in civil litigation, such as personal injury or medical malpractice. The risk to lawyers in handling cases on contingency is that they get no compensation if they lose.

Although the contingency fee is now well accepted in the United States (it is not used in England or Canada), it was resisted by the American bar until the early twentieth century. Contingency fees were thought to stir up litigation and to encourage attorneys to engage in unethical conduct to win cases. Gradually, the bar came to recognize the value of the contingency fee as a means to provide access to legal services for those who have a legal claim but who cannot otherwise afford a lawyer.

Despite the widespread use of contingency fees in **personal injury and medical malpractice** cases, ethics rules still place some limitations on their use. Contingency fee arrangements are not permitted in any state in **criminal defense** cases because they are thought to encourage corruption and discourage plea bargaining (ABA Model Rule 1.5(d)(2)). Most jurisdictions also have rules prohibiting contingency fees in **family law** matters where the fee is contingent on securing the dissolution of the marriage or on the amount of support, because such fee arrangements are thought to discourage reconciliation and settlement. In addition, a contingency arrangement in divorce matters is considered unnecessary because the court may award attorney's fees to the spouse without the means to pay them (ABA Model Rule 1.5(d)(1)).

Other limitations on contingency fee arrangements have been codified into state ethics rules or statutes that restrict the **percentage** of the fee. For example, the Federal Torts Claims Act, 28 U.S.C. § 2678, places the maximum fee at 25 percent. Some state statutes, including California's Business and Professions Code § 6146, limit the percentage that can be charged in medical malpractice cases.

Many jurisdictions require that contingency fee agreements be in **writing** even though other kinds of fee agreements are not required to be in writing. State ethics rules often require ads that mention contingency fees to disclose that clients are liable for costs even if they lose their case. Finally, contingency fees are subject to special judicial scrutiny for reasonableness and are disallowed if the percentage is considered exorbitant or the fee is well out of proportion to the work done or the risk taken by the lawyer.

Contingency fees have been a perpetual subject of debate within the legal profession. "Tort reformers" regularly call for prohibitions and limits on fees. Despite the controversy, the use of contingency fees has expanded as clients and their lawyers consider alternatives to the hourly fee. Increasingly, corporate clients request contingency arrangements in business litigation, even on the defense side, and some states use contingency fees for lawyers that collect overdue child support.

While a typical contingency fee in a personal injury matter is one-third of the recovery, most personal injury lawyers charge on a **sliding scale** that reflects both the amount of risk to the attorney and the time and effort expended as the case moves forward. For example, the lawyer might charge 25 percent if the case settles before trial, one-third if it goes to trial, and 40 percent if it is appealed.

Sliding scale
Method for determining contingency fee based on both the amount of risk to the attorney and the time and effort expended

3. Hourly Fees

Hourly fees are the most common method of billing in matters other than plaintiff civil litigation. Charging for time was not always standard practice. Charging by way of hourly fees started about 40 years ago and quickly became a deeply ingrained practice. Most large firms bill

Hourly fees
Fee based on hourly rates and the amount of time actually expended

107

mainly by means of **hourly rates**, with every lawyer and paralegal keeping close track of the time spent on client matters, usually in increments of either six or ten minutes.

Hourly rates are based on the **expertise** and other **qualifications** of the person billing, the nature and complexity of the services performed and, of course, the **market**. For example, a senior partner in a major law firm who handles complex securities transactions may have a billing rate of $750 to $1,000 an hour. The time of a midlevel associate with five years' experience, however, may be charged at $300 to $500 an hour, and a five-year paralegal's time may be charged at $100 to $150 an hour.

In the last decade, some law firms have experimented with other forms of billing and have considered how to move away from hourly billing as the norm. Part of the impetus for this move is attributed to the increased efficiency of law firms through specialization and the use of technology. Firms that have developed highly valuable expertise and means of producing documents quickly and efficiently want to avoid being penalized for their efficiency and receive fair compensation, not just for their time, but also for the value of their services. Clients are also calling for changes in the way legal services are priced, as they seek ways to lower legal fees and structure fee agreements that allow them to plan and budget more accurately and to assess the value and productivity of the services. Many large corporations and government issue requests for proposals to law firms, asking them to bid for the legal work on projects. Decisions about who gets the legal work depend largely on which firm has the best expertise for the work and provides the most attractive projections and arrangements for legal fees.

Many firms, including most large firms, use **alternative methods** of structuring fee arrangements, such as charging a percentage of the value of a transaction, charging a premium for achieving results that are especially beneficial to the client, and charging a fixed fee that reflects the value of the services to the client without regard to the time expended. Fees that are capped at a predetermined amount, discounted hourly rates for major clients, blended hourly rates arrived at by averaging rates for all firm lawyers and paralegals, contingency fees in defense matters, and hybrids of several different billing methods are now all commonly used. Some firms also use task-based billing, in which clients are charged a predetermined flat fee for a specific function, such as taking a deposition or representing a client at a particular kind of hearing.

More changes in billing practices are on the horizon as law practice responds to market conditions and factors such as the use of technology. To meet standards of ethics and performance paralegals must be proficient in technology and demonstrably efficient and productive in the work they do on client matters. Paralegal managers and lawyers who supervise paralegals must promote skill development for paralegals, assign work that matches the paralegal's expertise, and delegate appropriately to avoid duplicative time and inefficiency. Paralegals should be trained on the job about methods of time keeping, guidelines on what constitutes billable work, and expectations about billable hours.

Paralegal time is typically charged directly to clients just as attorney time is in firms that use the hourly billing model. When utilized properly, paralegals are engaged in legal work that, were it not for the paralegal, would have to be done by an attorney. And because paralegal time is billed to clients at lower rates than attorney time is, the cost to the client is lower. Guideline 8 of the ABA Model Guidelines for the Utilization of Paralegal Services (ABA Model Guidelines) provides that lawyers may charge for paralegal services. State guidelines specifically endorse this customary practice, which was validated by the U.S. Supreme Court in *Missouri v. Jenkins,* 491 U.S. 274 (1989) (with regard to statutory fee awards). The comment to NALA Model Guideline V also discusses the practice of billing clients for paralegal time and fee awards that include compensation for paralegal work. (Section C below discusses this topic further.)

B.   Ethics Rules About Fees

Most states' ethics rules prohibit lawyers from agreeing to, charging, or collecting an **unreasonable** fee. Some states use the term "**excessive fees**" instead of unreasonable fees; at least one state, California, prohibits *unconscionable* fees. **Illegal** fees are also prohibited. Illegal fees include those that exceed statutory limits, such as those set by the Federal Torts Claims Act, and fees that have an illegal purpose. The ABA Model Code, which speaks in terms of "clearly excessive," and the ABA Model Rules, which prohibit "unreasonable" fees, both list several factors used to determine whether a fee is unethically high:

Unconscionable
So unreasonable as to render a contract unenforceable, usually because the terms are so favorable to one party

1. the time and labor required, the novelty and difficulty of the questions involved, and the skill requisite to perform the legal service properly
2. the likelihood, if apparent to the client, that the acceptance of the particular employment will preclude other employment by the lawyer
3. the fee customarily charged in the locality for similar legal services
4. the amount involved and the results obtained
5. the time limitations imposed by the client or by the circumstances
6. the nature and length of the professional relationship with the client
7. the experience, reputation, and ability of the lawyer or lawyers performing the services, and
8. whether the fee is fixed or contingent

Model Code DR–2–106 and Model Rule 1.5.

The reasonableness of fees has been litigated extensively, mainly in cases involving statutory fee awards and fees awarded under the provisions of a contract (discussed below in Section C). Guidelines can be drawn from litigation over fees and from disciplinary cases. Although all the factors on the ABA list are generally considered by courts and disciplinary bodies in determining if a fee is unethical, the **amount of time spent** still tends to be the most important. In fee dispute cases and disciplinary matters, the client's understanding of the fee agreement is also a critical factor.

Probably the most widespread ethical problem relating to fees is one that is not addressed directly by either ethics codes or case law. It is also one that paralegals may face during the course of their careers. It is the practice of **inflating the figures** for time spent on client matters.

Lawyers and paralegals in firms that depend on hourly billing have seen a steady increase over the last 20 years in firm expectations for billable hours. And the value of fee-generating lawyers and paralegals is measured largely by how much revenue those people produce for the firm. In the early 1980s, 1,200 billable hours a year was a common standard of performance; whereas the expectation for lawyers has nearly doubled to 2,000 hours or more.

Although most of the pressure to bill falls on highly compensated associates trying to make partner, paralegals feel it, too. Firms have also learned that they have to delegate and monitor paralegal work carefully to ensure that their use of paralegals is profitable. Many firms, especially those that utilize paralegals extensively and bill by the hour, have also adopted strict **guidelines on paralegal billable hours**. The pressure to bill has created an incentive to engage in improper billing practices, such as double billing, billing full rates for recycled work product, overbilling, overstaffing, billing for overhead costs, padding hours, doing unnecessary work for clients, and spending excessive amounts of time on matters that do not warrant it, sometimes called "churning."

Cases of prominent attorneys **overbilling** and billing personal expenses to clients have given this issue a high profile. Some cases have involved padding hourly bills in corporate, insurance defense, and criminal defense cases; others have involved charging personal expenses, including clothes, travel, meals, and gifts, to clients. Examples abound in the press, with new scandals coming to light with some frequency. Disciplinary cases on excessive fees have involved overcharging for legal research and driving time to an unnecessarily distant library, doubling the costs of process servers and independent contractors, billing clients for more than 24 hours a day, charging fees and costs that were agreed in advance not to be charged, and multiplying the time spent by billers (e.g., by $1\frac{1}{2}$) to ensure a profit. In one high-profile case during the last three years, a former client suing for malpractice claimed that the lawyers charged for their time when they were actually surfing the Internet, a matter that could be proven with technology records. In another, a highly compensated partner in a firm charged $30,000 in personal telephone calls to a client and claimed that he did so to hide the amount of time he was spending on personal matters from his partners. **Corporate clients** have taken proactive steps to prevent themselves from becoming the victims of unscrupulous billing practices and excessive legal bills.

Corporate clients sometimes request firms to make proposals for services, establish strict budgets for a legal matter beyond which a firm may not bill, and utilize task-based billing. Clients want detailed information on the cost of services so they can evaluate services and negotiate future billing arrangements. Many corporations restrict the costs they will pay. For example, corporations may reimburse for coach airfare only and refuse to pay surcharges on computerized legal research or for secretarial overtime or computer use. Some corporate clients conduct **audits** of bills to turn up errors and improper practices.

The ABA and several other bar associations have issued ethics opinions addressing billing practices. Among the practices found objectionable are *double billing,* such as billing more than one client for the same hours (e.g., travel time to and from court appearances for more than one client on the same day); **surcharges** on services contracted with outside vendors, such as expert witnesses and freelance paralegals; and **charges beyond reasonable costs** for in-house services like photocopying and computer searches. Some opinions call for full disclosure of the basis for charges when the fee agreement is made and subsequently when the client is billed. Some emphasize that the charges must also be reasonable, which covers charges for unnecessary work and for hours not actually worked.

Double billing
Billing more than one client for the same hours

Paralegals have been implicated in some cases. For example, paralegals in one case billed time for deposition summaries at a rate that was about a fourth of the average speed. In another case, a paralegal billed 43 hours in one day. In some cases, paralegal billing rates were double the market rate or the client was billed at paralegal rates for routine clerical work such as copying and filing. A few well-publicized cases in the insurance industry have forced insurance defense lawyers to rethink what work they assign to paralegals because insurance companies refuse to pay paralegal rates for work they consider to be clerical.

Billing abuses are not only inherently dishonest and unethical, but also detrimental to the one who engages in them and to the firm. Good firms do not send bills to clients without first examining them for fairness and accuracy. If a bill is excessive, the partner who is responsible for billing the client can and should adjust it and "write off" excessive time. The written-off time is usually allocated back to the person who billed it and deducted from his or her total billable hours.

The firm that does not **review bills** or adjust them in this fashion is running the risk of having a dissatisfied client or of losing a client. Egregious billing abuses may result in discipline and malpractice lawsuits. Some commentators believe that excessive legal fees caused by dishonest billing practices have been a leading factor in the revolt by clients against

111

the high cost of legal services and in the lowered esteem in which lawyers are held by the public.

Paralegals should not themselves engage in unethical billing practices and have an obligation to report this kind of conduct to a supervising paralegal or lawyer. A paralegal should not continue to work in a firm that permits unethical billing. The NFPA Model Code calls attention to the proper paralegal role in billing under DR 1.2. EC-1.2(c) and (d), which tell paralegals to prepare thorough, accurate, and honest timekeeping and billing records and specifically notes billing abuses such as those mentioned in this chapter.

C. Terms and Communication of Fee Arrangements with Clients

As soon as possible after a lawyer and client agree to representation, the lawyer should fully explain the terms of the fee agreement to the client. Many states (including New York and California) require the scope of representation and information on fees and costs to be communicated to the client in writing. However, the ABA Model Rules do not require all fee agreements to be in writing, so paralegals should check the controlling ethics rules on fee agreements carefully.

The ABA Model Code does not have a disciplinary rule requiring **written fee agreements** but advises lawyers to reach a "clear agreement" about fees, reduce the agreement to writing, especially in the case of contingency fees, and fully explain the reasons for the fee arrangement. ABA Model Rule 1.5(b) states that the scope of representation and the fee agreement should be communicated within a reasonable amount of time, "preferably in writing." Contingency fee agreements must be in a written form and signed by the client and must include the method and percentage(s) by which the fee is to be calculated and provision for payment of costs (that is, whether they are deducted before or after calculation of the fee and whether the client is liable for them if the case is lost). A written statement showing the calculations is required at the conclusion of the matter (ABA Model Rule 1.5(c)).

Written fee agreements are favored because they promote clear **communication** between the lawyer and client and prevent disputes over fees. In addition, they protect both parties in the event of a dispute. Courts typically construe unclear fee arrangements against lawyers; therefore, it is in the lawyer's interests to have a completely clear agreement. Most state bars have standard forms that attorneys are encouraged to use.

As indicated in Chapter 2 on unauthorized practice of law, paralegals should be alert to the **traps** in discussing fees directly with new clients. Only an attorney can agree to represent a client and in doing so to set and communicate the fee arrangement and meet the ethical obligation to explain the arrangement fully to the client. The paralegal may act as a liaison to the client, answering questions about fees and costs, but should not enter into the contractual agreement with the client on the lawyer's behalf.

The ABA Model Guidelines state that **establishing a fee** is one of the few specified functions that a lawyer cannot delegate to a paralegal. Guideline 3(b) advises that a lawyer may not delegate "responsibility for establishing the amount of a fee to be charged for a legal service." The NALA Code of Ethics and Professional Responsibility provides in Canon 3(b) that "a paralegal must not . . . establish an attorney-client relationship [or] set fees."

The fee agreement or letter of engagement should cover fully:

- the **scope** of the firm's services
- **responsibilities** of the client and the firm
- the method of determining the **fee** (that is, hourly, fixed, contingency, or some other method)
- **hourly rates** for different professionals if services are billed hourly
- **costs** the client is obligated to pay and when they are to be paid (that is, out of the client's recovery after the attorney's fee is calculated, in the case of contingency arrangements, or at specified regular billings)
- **termination** rights for both parties
- disposition of **client files** at the end of the matter
- the method and **time of fee payment**
- **the procedure** for and frequency of billings, if applicable.

Fee agreements must be clear about the use of paralegals and paralegal billing rates. Fee agreements that are ambiguous on this point may be interpreted against the lawyer and result in lost fees for paralegal time. Further, lawyers cannot bill the time spent by paralegals as their own.

Fee agreements should contain a provision indicating that the agreement is **privileged**. It is wise to include language indicating that the firm is not guaranteeing a particular result. If the client does not speak or read English proficiently, the agreement should be in a **language** that the client does understand. The signature clause should include an acknowledgment that the client has read and understood the terms of the agreement, and the client should be given sufficient time to read and reflect on the agreement before signing it. If the lawyer is providing limited services, this matter should be carefully addressed to ensure that the lawyer does not become responsible for work that is not contemplated to be part of the representation. Finally, fee agreements may contain provisions indicating how fee **disputes** and malpractice claims will be handled — for example, by mediation or arbitration.

In some instances, attorneys may require a *retainer* or *advance,* which is paid at the commencement of the agreed-upon work. Although frequently called "retainers," **advanced fees** are usually refundable, in that the attorney earns the fee as the work progresses and will refund to the client any portion that is unearned when, for whatever reason, the services stop. *Retainer fees* are nonrefundable, in essence acting as a minimum fee regardless of the amount of work done and as a guarantee that the attorney will be available to handle the representation. A non-refundable retainer is ethically acceptable so long as the client fully understands the arrangement and the fee is not excessive, considering the factors previously discussed. Advances must be deposited into a **client trust account** until earned, whereas nonrefundable retainers may be deposited directly into a firm operating account. (Client trust accounts are discussed below in Section G.)

> **Retainer**
> Fee paid at the commencement of agreed-upon work to assure the availability of the lawyer to handle specified matters

Matters for which an hourly fee is charged represent a higher potential for disputes with clients because, without an **estimate** of the number of hours a project will take, the client will have no idea what the ultimate bill for services might be. It is good practice for the attorney to provide the client, if at all possible, with an estimate or several estimates depending on how the matter might play out and to update the estimate if the situation changes as the matter proceeds.

Payment of **costs** requires special clarity in fee agreements, as clients may not be aware of the kind of costs that can arise and may resent paying many small charges when they are already paying high fees. The kinds of costs that are billed directly to clients vary somewhat from firm to firm but, as a rule, all lawyers expect clients to pay direct expenses that the firm pays to an entity outside the firm, such as filing fees paid to courts and government bodies, transcripts of depositions and trials, experts' reports and testimony, out-of-the-area travel expenses, outside printing, and messengers. Most firms also charge for copying done within the firm and for long-distance telephone calls. Some firms, by agreement with clients, also charge for costs that might ordinarily be thought of as part of overhead, such as secretarial overtime, computer use, and even air-conditioning in the event the firm must work extra evening and weekend hours for a client. Costs should be itemized on the bill to the client.

Although not in widespread use, the majority of jurisdictions permit lawyers to accept payment of legal fees by **credit card**. Some state rules have limitations, including one that the attorney not increase fees to cover expenses of participating in such a plan. Some states also specifically permit lawyers to help clients work out financing for the payment of fees with a bank. Lawyers may accept property or an **interest in a client's business** in payment of fees; however, when doing so, they must honor conflict of interest rules (see Chapter 4) and consider whether the fee is reasonable under the circumstances.

D.   Statutory and Other Court-Awarded Fees

As a general rule, litigants in the United States must pay their own legal fees. This practice is different from that in England, Canada, and most other European countries, all of which have some form of *fee shifting*. In England and Canada, for example, attorney's fees in litigation are awarded to the prevailing party.

> **Fee shifting**
> Award of the attorney's fees to the prevailing party

Exceptions to this general rule have come about in the last 30 years in court decisions and legislation, and through the wider use of contractual fee provisions. Courts have awarded attorney's fees in cases in which a **common fund** that benefits persons other than the parties has been created as a result of the litigation; in which the litigation resulted in a common benefit to the public or some portion of the public, even though no fund was created; similarly, in which the plaintiff acted as a "private attorney general" vindicating a legal right that also benefits others and for which the plaintiff's actual damages are relatively small; and, finally, in actions for malicious prosecution, for abuse of civil process, or for those taken in bad faith. This last category of fee shifting is also supported by legislation in some states. **Contractual provisions** for attorney's fees that are charged when a dispute arises under the contract are now common and are generally enforced by the courts.

Fee-shifting statutes have proliferated — hundreds of state and federal statutes provide for the award of attorney's fees in specified kinds of litigation. Fee-shifting statutes generally apply to the kinds of litigation that the legislature wants to encourage as a matter of public policy (for example, protecting civil rights) and award fees only to prevailing plaintiffs, not to defendants. Like contingency fees, statutory fees enable plaintiffs who might not otherwise be able to afford a lawyer to bring a legal action to vindicate their rights. And as with contingency fees, the lawyers in these cases run the risk of not being compensated if they do not prevail.

Conflict of interest problems may arise in cases involving statutory fees when the interests of the client clash with the interest of the lawyer in maximizing the fee award. For example, an offer to settle may satisfy the client but not include sufficient fees for the attorney or may satisfy the attorney because the fee is sufficient but not the client because the recovery to the client is too low. Lawyers must always be aware of the potential for this kind of conflict and keep the client's best interests in mind when advising whether to accept an offer.

Most important to paralegals in the area of statutory fees is the land-mark decision of *Missouri v. Jenkins,* 491 U.S. 274 (1989), in which an award of attorney's fees that included **compensation for paralegal work** under the federal civil rights statute was upheld. The lower court had awarded fees that included compensation for paralegal time at hourly market rates. The state of Missouri contended, first, that the statute provided only for lawyer time, not paralegal time, and second, that if paralegal time was compensable, it should be compensated at cost, not at a market rate that includes a profit to the law firm. In upholding the award of fees that included compensation for paralegal time, the Court construed the attorney's fee statute broadly, finding that it did include compensation for paralegal time and that the recognized measure of market value, not cost, was the appropriate one for setting the fee.

This was a critical decision for paralegals: A court decision that had gone the other way would have acted as a disincentive to the utilization of paralegal services by firms that work on statutory fee cases and cases where fees are may be awarded under the provisions of a contract. Thousands of cases awarding paralegal fees as part of attorney's fee awards have been decided in state and federal trial courts since *Missouri v. Jenkins.* This case was also the first U.S. Supreme Court decision in which the role of paralegals was discussed at any length. The Court endorsed the use of paralegals as a praiseworthy innovation and an effective means of containing the costs of legal services. Finally, *Missouri v. Jenkins* resolved an issue that had been in dispute throughout the country: Several state and some federal appeals courts had interpreted attorney's fees statutes not to include paralegal fees at all or had used the cost of paralegals (i.e., their compensation), not market rate, to calculate the awards.

After *Missouri v. Jenkins*, several states **amended statutes and/or court rules** to clarify that attorney's fee awards include paralegal fees at market rates. A few states continued to resist interpreting their statutes the way that the Supreme Court did in *Missouri v. Jenkins.* For example, Michigan and Idaho courts held that general attorney's fee statutes should not be read to allow an award that includes compensation for paralegal time and called on the legislature to amend statutes to allow market rate compensation for paralegal time. As a result, Michigan adopted a court rule allowing court-awarded attorney's fees to cover paralegal work, and Idaho finally amended its Rules of Civil Procedure in 1999 to allow paralegal fees to be included in attorney fee awards. Most recently, the U.S. Supreme Court struck down a decision in which the Court of Appeals for the Federal Circuit disallowed compensation for paralegal time at market rates in fee awards under the Equal Access to Justice Act. (See *Richlin Security Service Co. v. Chertoff,* 128 S.Ct. 2007 (2008).)

An important issue in fee-award matters involves the kind of information that must be supplied in fee petitions to the court to justify the **award of paralegal fees**. Some trial courts have denied paralegal fees on the grounds that the work done by paralegals was clerical in nature, and therefore not the kind of work intended to be covered by an award of attorney's fees, or because there was inadequate information as to the qualifications of the paralegals, the nature of their work, the customary practice of billing separately for their services, and the market rates charged for their services. Other courts have reduced the amounts requested for paralegal work because the work was not sufficiently documented and justified or the petition contained what appeared to the court to be too high a profit margin.

Documentation supplied to the court when seeking fees should include:

- **credentials and experience** of the paralegals
- detailed **descriptions** of the work performed, including the number of hours spent on each discrete task
- information on paralegal **compensation**, overhead allocated to paralegals, and hourly rates
- **market data** on practices and rates in the legal community

Additionally, it is preferable for a firm to have a **range of rates** for paralegals, depending on their experience and the level of work they are performing. Not all paralegal work requires the same level of sophistication and expertise, and some judges are keen on matching the rate to the task.

Some court rules specify what is required for the award of paralegal fees. For example, California Bankruptcy Court Rules for the Northern District allow fees only if (1) the services they rendered would have to have been done by a lawyer if the paralegal had not performed the services, (2) the paralegal has special training and is not primarily a secretary or clerical worker, and (3) the fee application has a resume or summary of the paralegal's qualifications.

A few courts have reduced fee awards for an attorney's time when the work billed at the attorney's rate could have been done by a paralegal. These cases demonstrate the growing appreciation within the judiciary of the contribution paralegals make to improving the cost-effectiveness of and access to legal services.

Finally, in a case of first impression, a California federal trial court in 2005 deducted the requested compensation for paralegal work that had been done by personnel who were not qualified as paralegals under the California statute governing paralegals. (See *Sanford v. GMRI,* CIV-S-04-1535 DFL CMK (E.D. Cal. 2005).)

In 1993, the ABA House of Delegates adopted a resolution "support[ing] the award of paralegal/paralegal fees to law firms or attorneys who represent prevailing parties in a lawsuit where statutes or current case law allow for the recovery of attorney fees." This resolution parallels Guideline 8 of the ABA Model Guidelines for the Utilization of Paralegal Services, which endorses both recovery for paralegal time in statutory attorney fee matters and the billing of clients for paralegal time.

E. Fee Splitting and Referral Fees

Ethics rules in every state carefully control the way in which lawyers and nonlawyers are compensated. These rules are designed with a number of important policies in mind: to prevent the **unauthorized practice of law,** to guard against interference with the lawyer's **independent professional judgment,** and to discourage unethical direct **solicitation** of clients by agents of the lawyer.

Ethics codes have long limited the splitting of fees **between or among lawyers** who are not members of the same firm; however, these rules are gradually giving way to some fee-sharing arrangements among lawyers. The ABA Model Code and Model Rules (DR 2-107 and Model Rule 1.5(e)) allow fee splitting between lawyers, but only under certain conditions, including client consent, proportionate division of fees to services, and a reasonable total fee.

The older rules, followed in some states, mean that an attorney may not pay a referral fee or a portion of a client's fee to another attorney simply for referring a case. Referral fees in either of these forms have long been thought to be unprofessional and to increase the cost to the client. However, a growing number of states have in recent years revised rules to permit *forwarding fees* and to omit the requirement that the fee division be proportionate to services, thereby effectively allowing referral fees. Proponents of referral fees say that they serve the client's interests by encouraging a thoughtful referral to a competent attorney, and point out that clients are protected because the rules require the fee to be reasonable.

Forwarding fees
Fee paid by one lawyer to another for referring a case

Fee splitting with nonlawyers, including paralegals, is absolutely prohibited because of concerns of unauthorized practice, interference with the lawyer's independent professional judgment, and direct solicitation. The ABA Model Code and Model Rules (DR 3-102 and Model Rule 5.4) prohibit fee splitting with nonlawyers except when a lawyer dies and fees are paid to his or her estate, and to compensate nonlawyer employees through bonuses and profit-sharing arrangements. The Model Rules also make an exception that allows a lawyer to pay for the purchase of the practice of a deceased, disabled, or disappeared lawyer. All states have some version of the prohibition on fee splitting and referral fees with nonlawyers. In addition, such agreements are unenforceable because of illegality.

The ABA Model Guidelines follow the standard prohibitions against fee splitting with nonlawyers in Guideline 9. Most state guidelines on paralegal utilization specifically prohibit fee splitting but emphasize that **retirement plans and bonuses** based in part on a firm's overall profitability are acceptable. Neither NALA nor NFPA has a specific prohibition against fee splitting or referral fees in its code of ethics.

An early ABA ethics opinion endorsed the inclusion of nonlawyers in **profit-based compensation** and retirement plans, and other state and local ethics opinions have followed suit. Bonus plans that compensate paralegals and associates whose billable hours exceed a set minimum and bonuses based on firm profitability have been approved. Other ethics opinions advise that lawyers may not compensate paralegals on a contingent basis and may not compensate them only when fees are collected from a client or only when there is a recovery in a case.

The ethics rules and the opinions interpreting them make it clear that it is not acceptable for an attorney to pay a paralegal for **referring a case**, either directly or by means of a bonus, increase in compensation, or payment of a portion of a fee received from the client. Lawyers may not pay a paralegal, under any circumstances, a percentage of a fee from a specific client or case. Several cases in which lawyers were disciplined for unethical fee arrangements with nonlawyers have found that a "bonus" tied to a particular client or case is not acceptable. However, it is appropriate to pay bonuses and other compensation based on overall firm profitability. This kind of arrangement breaks the direct link between a paralegal's action and a specific client, thereby eliminating concerns about unauthorized practice and incentives to solicit clients by unethical or overly aggressive methods. Such bonus plans are commonly used by firms who want to reward paralegals for their contribution to making the firm profitable. It should be noted that a few states, however, still have ethics opinions that appear to prohibit compensation to nonlawyer employees based on overall firm profitability.

A few other exceptions to the prohibition against fee splitting with nonlawyers do exist. As mentioned above, fees may be paid to the **estate of a deceased lawyer**. A lawyer may pay a fee to an approved **lawyer referral service**. Lawyer referral services are regulated by ethics rules and usually must be approved by the state bar or some other entity. Many are run by local bar associations. Lawyer referral services charge either a flat fee or a percentage of fees. Another exception is the prepaid legal plan, under which a member pays a fee for entitlement to a range of services, and the fee is divided between the lawyer and the plan sponsor. All jurisdictions permit such fee splitting when the plan is nonprofit; some jurisdictions specifically prohibit lawyer participation in profit-making prepaid legal services plans. Lawyers may also split a court-awarded fee with a nonprofit organization that employed, retained, or recommended the lawyer in the matter (ABA Model Rule 5.4(a)).

F.   Partnerships Between Lawyers and Nonlawyers

The same theories underlying the prohibitions on fee splitting with non-lawyers form the basis for rules prohibiting lawyers from entering into partnership with nonlawyers for the purpose of practicing law. The ABA Model Code and Model Rules both prohibit a lawyer from forming a partnership with a nonlawyer if any of the activities of the partnership consist of the practice of law (DR 3-103 and Model Rule 5.4(b)).

This rule is sometimes implicated when lawyers are disciplined for aiding in the unauthorized practice of law, fee splitting, and unlawful solicitation if the arrangement with the nonlawyer looks like a partnership or business venture where the nonlawyer has a meaningful voice in the operation of the firm. Virtually all jurisdictions have a rule prohibiting such arrangements, and most states that have guidelines for the utilization of paralegals reiterate this rule as it applies to paralegals.

Multidisciplinary practice
A business model under which law firms and other professionals form partnerships to deliver legal and other related services to clients

Because of the changing nature of law practice and the desire of law firms, especially large law firms, to be full-service providers for their clients, some lawyers sought to modify this ethics rule to allow for **multidisciplinary practice.** However, the rules have not been changed either by the ABA or by states and at present only the District of Columbia allows other professionals, such as economists and lobbyists, to be partners in law firms.

G. Client Funds and Property

1. Client Trust Accounts

The **mishandling of client funds** is probably the leading cause of disciplinary sanctions of attorneys. A typical scenario is a sole practitioner with cash-flow problems who "borrows" funds from a client trust account to pay bills until a big settlement comes in. A shortfall in a client trust account can also result from sloppy bookkeeping and management practices. The attorney will sooner or later find that a client's money just isn't there, and the client will report this to the state or local bar and possibly to the local prosecutor's office.

Commingling
The mixing of client funds with lawyers' funds

Client trust account
Bank account set up by a lawyer in which funds are kept that belong to one or more clients

The most important ethics rule related to client funds is the requirement to keep the client's money separate from the attorney's — in other words, not to commingle client and law firm funds. The rule against **commingling** also applies to funds from third parties held by the lawyer. Lawyers must have a separate bank account — called a **client trust account** — to hold clients' funds. Some clients may warrant having their own individual client trust account if the lawyer handles large amounts of funds or transactions for them. Both the Model Code and Model Rules and every jurisdiction require client trust accounts (Model Code DR 9-102(A) and Model Rule 1.15(a)). Some ethics rules specify that the client trust account must be in the state where the lawyer is situated; others allow another location with client consent.

Lawyers hold client funds for many reasons. Typically, funds in client trust accounts are estate or trust distributions, funds to be distributed at a real estate closing or on settlement of a matter, advanced fees, and awards of which the attorney is owed a portion under a contingency fee agreement.

In the case of funds that are to be **divided between the client and the attorney**, the funds must remain in the client trust account until they are earned by the lawyer and she or he prepares an accounting for the client indicating how the funds are to be divided under the fee agreement. In the event that a dispute arises over the fee, the amount in dispute must be kept in the client trust account until the dispute is resolved. A minority of jurisdictions allow advanced fees to be deposited into a lawyer's operating account. Remember that advances are different from retainers, which are nonrefundable and paid directly to the lawyer.

In addition to commingling of funds, *conversion* of funds and embezzlement can be the basis for discipline and criminal charges against the lawyer. Commingling refers only to mixing client funds with those of the attorney and does not require any intent to harm the client or actual harm to the client. Conversion is the misappropriation of the client's funds for the attorney or firm use. Conversion may take place when the attorney draws funds from the client trust account for personal use, for payment of firm expenses, or — more rarely — to cover another client's shortfall.

> **Conversion**
> The tortious deprivation of another's property without justification or authorization

Disciplinary bodies are not sympathetic to most defenses that lawyers use to defend their actions in commingling cases, including their intent to return the funds or the actual restoration of the funds. Lawyers' personal or financial problems or financial mismanagement are also not excuses; in fact, they may be considered aggravating circumstances as they may lead to repeated incidents of mishandling of client funds. Blaming office personnel is also an ineffective defense.

Some states, like California, have advisory opinions indicating that it is acceptable for lawyers to permit nonlawyer personnel to sign checks on client trust accounts; however, some states specifically prohibit nonlawyer personnel from serving as a signatory and many experts promote the practice of having the lawyer sign to guard against nonlawyer negligence and embezzlement.

Interest on Lawyers' Trust Accounts and Client Security Funds

Most jurisdictions in the United States have a program under which the interest on certain client trust accounts is used to fund the bar disciplinary system, client security fund, or legal services for the poor, specified by the state's bar, legislature, or supreme court. Hundreds of millions of dollars are raised annually through these programs, known as

IOLTA
Interest on Lawyers'
Trust Accounts

IOLTA (Interest on Lawyers' Trust Accounts). These plans can be **mandatory, voluntary, or "opt-out."** A voluntary program is one in which a lawyer must affirmatively decide to participate; an opt-out program means that all lawyers participate unless they affirmatively declare *not* to. The plans ordinarily cover only client funds that are too small in amount or are to be held for too brief a period to earn interest for the individual client. The majority of jurisdictions have voluntary or opt-out plans, or some hybrid of the two, although a growing number of plans are being converted to mandatory status.

Client security fund
Fund set aside to reimburse clients who have lost money or property due to lawyer misconduct

IOLTA plans are different from *client security funds*, which reimburse clients who have lost money or property as a result of lawyer misconduct. Almost all states have some kind of client security fund in addition to IOLTA. Funding of client security funds may come from bonding insurance or IOLTA.

The **constitutionality of IOLTA** programs has been upheld in the face of challenges that claim that individual clients have property rights in the interest generated in these accounts and that these rights are violated when the interest, however small, is not paid to the clients.

2. Other Client Property and Files

The lawyer and paralegal have a duty to protect client property in addition to the duty to protect client funds. The ethical obligation to **safeguard** usually requires that property be placed in a safe deposit box. Property covered by these rules typically includes titles to real estate or valuable personal property, jewelry, and securities. If a safe deposit box is shared with other clients, the items must be identified and labeled.

Lawyers have a duty to keep **accurate and complete records** of client funds and property. The ethics rules in each state include a specific number of years, ranging from five to seven, that records must be kept. Some states have very specific requirements for record keeping. A few jurisdictions provide for random audits of client trust accounts and some for annual certification or verification of compliance with record-keeping rules. Many states conduct **audits** in conjunction with disciplinary actions.

The kinds of bookkeeping mechanisms that a firm uses to comply with ethics record-keeping rules vary from firm to firm. Several state bars have adopted model guidelines or standards, which usually require cash receipts journals for each account, disbursement journals for each account (with separate ledgers for each client showing monthly trial balances), monthly reconciliations of balances, bank statements, cancelled checks, and records of other client property received and distributed. Other duties regarding client property are to:

- **notify** the client on the receipt of funds or property
- **deliver** client funds or property promptly
- provide a full **accounting** to the client on request

Model Code 9-102 and Model Rule 1.15(d).

Lawyers may breach their duty if they have lax **office procedures.** Sometimes a third party has a claim against the client funds; in this situation the lawyer may have a duty not to turn over the funds to the client until the various parties' rights are clarified. The notion of what is "prompt" delivery can become an issue in disciplinary actions. The best practice certainly requires action within the month in which funds are received, if not more quickly. And, finally, although neither the ABA Model Code nor the Model Rules require them, regular periodic accountings to clients (monthly or quarterly) are advisable rather than accountings only on a client's request.

All jurisdictions also have some special rules that require attorneys to **turn over** papers, funds, money, and unearned advanced fees on termination of representation. These rules emphasize the lawyer's obligation to protect the client's interest, a duty that extends even after the representation ends.

One final matter in this area is the handling of **client files** after work on a matter is completed. Firms should have policies on retention of files, turning files over to clients, destroying files, and security for files maintained electronically and in off-site storage. Because the client file is the property of the client, the lawyer should not destroy old files without first informing the client and getting permission, and/or giving the client the chance to keep the file. Care should always be taken to retain important papers such as wills, deeds, securities, and tax returns. It is good practice to include a provision about the handling of client files in the engagement letter or other agreement for representation.

The rules governing the handling of client funds and property are especially important to paralegals because they often must implement attorneys' instructions relating to client funds and property and may be delegated substantial responsibility for handling these matters. Checks and property may come directly to the paralegal. Lawyers should have procedures for handling client funds and property. In small firms, a paralegal may perform some of the bookkeeping and record-keeping functions. The paralegal must know the rules well enough to identify mistakes and improprieties. It is not unusual for an attorney in trouble to blame the nonlawyer employee for poor office practices that have resulted in disciplinary action against the attorney. Although such excuses do not mitigate the attorney's misconduct, they can harm the paralegal's reputation.

NALA's Code does not address client property and funds directly. NFPA's ethics rules call on paralegals to be "scrupulously thorough and honest" in handling client assets (NFPA EC 1.2(e)).

REVIEW QUESTIONS

1. What are fixed fees? For what kinds of work are they typically used?
2. What are contingency fees? For what kinds of cases are they usually used?
3. What are the traditional objections to contingency fees? What are the most important modern limitations on contingency fees? What is a sliding-scale contingency fee?
4. What are hourly fees? In what kinds of legal matters are they typically used?
5. What is the authority for paralegal time to be billed separately to clients? What is the advantage to the client?
6. Why do some firms use alternatives to hourly billing? What kinds of new fee arrangements are being developed? How do these affect paralegals?
7. What factors may be taken into account in determining if a fee is excessive?
8. What is an example of an illegal fee?
9. What kinds of billing abuses sometimes take place in law firms, and why? What are some of the risks of these abuses?
10. What is double billing? Is it ethical?
11. What are a lawyer's duties relating to the fee arrangement when he or she undertakes representation?
12. Under what circumstances must a fee arrangement be in writing?
13. May a paralegal tell a client what the firm's fee schedule is? Do the rules permit a paralegal to negotiate a fee arrangement with a client?
14. What is the difference between a retainer and an advanced fee? How are they treated differently by the firm?
15. What provisions should a written fee agreement contain?
16. What kinds of costs are usually charged directly to the client?
17. What is the purpose of "fee shifting"?
18. Give some examples of fee-shifting statutes.
19. What was the holding in *Missouri v. Jenkins?* Why is this decision so important for paralegals? What has happened in state and federal courts as a result of this case?
20. What information should be included in a request to the court for paralegal fees as part of an award of attorney's fees?
21. Can a firm that uses paralegals who do not meet the statutory requirements for paralegals in California get compensation for those paralegals' time at market rates? Why or why not?

22. What are the rules about referral fees? What is the basis for these rules? Do the same rules apply to lawyers and paralegals?
23. What are the rules about fee splitting?
24. What kinds of retirement, bonus, and profit-sharing plans for paralegals are permitted under the ethics rules?
25. Why do the ethics rules prohibit lawyers from being partners with nonlawyers in a law practice?
26. What are the duties of lawyers and paralegals regarding client funds?
27. What is IOLTA? Do many states have such a program? Are such programs constitutional?
28. What is a client security fund? How are the funds from these programs used?
29. Describe the difference between the commingling and the conversion of funds. Which is more serious?
30. Is mishandling of client funds common? Why?
31. How might a paralegal violate ethics in the handling of client funds?
32. When a lawyer receives a check for a judgment or settlement and the case was taken on contingency, what should he or she do with the check?
33. Do the facts that an attorney is very busy, has high staff turnover, and has not had a bookkeeper in months mitigate against charges of commingling of funds?
34. What are the lawyer's duties with regard to client property held for the client?
35. What are the lawyer's duties pertaining to client funds, files, and property when representation ceases?

HYPOTHETICALS

1. Wendell Wilson is a paralegal with a small law firm, Xavier & Young, that handles family law matters and criminal defense work. The firm just took on a new case involving the divorce of a wealthy couple, the Applebys. The firm is representing the wife, Anna Appleby. Wendell is asked to prepare an agreement with the client concerning the representation with the following provisions:

    1. The firm agrees to represent the client only concerning the divorce matter.
    2. The client agrees to pay the firm an amount equal to 25 percent of the annual spousal support that the firm gets for the client.
    3. The client agrees to hold the firm harmless for any errors its paralegals make in the handling of the matter.

    Are these provisions ethical? Why or why not?

125

2. During the divorce proceedings, Ms. Appleby becomes increasingly distraught about her husband's conduct. One day in a rage she attacks him with a fireplace poker. He is not badly injured but the police are called and Ms. Appleby is charged with assault and battery. The firm agrees to represent her in this matter, too, but wants a separate agreement under which the firm will be paid hourly rates ranging from $85 an hour for paralegals to $500 for the trial lawyer involved, and a $10,000 bonus if the firm can get the charges dismissed. The client agrees to this fee arrangement during a conference with the lawyers and paralegals but the agreement is not put in writing. Are there any ethical problems with this agreement?

3. Wendell gets disgusted with the ethics at Xavier & Young and decides to go to work for a large law firm that has a civil litigation department handling major lawsuits. This firm, Allison & Beals, has billing guidelines that require paralegals to put in 1,800 billable hours a year. If it takes eight hours on the job to produce seven billable hours, how many hours a week will Wendell have to work to reach the firm goal? After the first month on the job, Wendell gets a report showing that he billed 150 hours but that 20 hours were written off as being duplicative of the work that an associate did. What should Wendell do? Wendell becomes concerned toward the end of the year that he will not meet the required quota. He does not have enough work to warrant working overtime to make up for the hours. What can he do? Another paralegal, Zina Zumbrun, tells Wendell that she sometimes adds a tenth of an hour to each hour's work to make up for the time written off. What should Wendell do about this? Is it ethical for him to do what Zina does?

4. Carl Carlsmith is a paralegal working on some major civil rights litigation. He and his firm have spent years on the case and have finally prevailed. The firm's senior partner, Danielle Dupree, asks Carl to draft a request for fees that includes his time. The petition he drafts contains the following language: "Compensation is also requested for paralegal time spent by Carl Carlsmith, paralegal, who spent 1,000 hours drafting pleadings and correspondence, summarizing depositions, filing and organizing documents, and locating and interviewing witnesses. $300,000." Will the court grant this fee award? Why or why not? Be sure to look for more than one reason. Redraft this petition, adding all the requisite information and correcting anything else that is in error.

5. Emily Emerson, a paralegal, works for a medical malpractice firm, Freed & Gant. A friend of hers knows someone whose surgery was botched. Emily suggests that the person call the firm to talk to the senior partner about taking the case. This prospective client, Horace Hanson, calls Emily first and asks, "What does your firm normally charge for this kind of case?" Has Emily done anything wrong at this point? Can Emily answer Horace's question? What is she

permitted to say? Later, Horace comes in and meets Fred Freed and the firm decides to take the case. The next day at work, Emily is greeted with a dozen roses and a check from the firm made out to her for the amount of $500. May Emily keep the flowers? The money? Why or why not? Another paralegal in the firm, Inga Inglewood, comes in to see the flowers and says casually to Emily, "Wait until you see what you get when the case is over!" What should Emily do now?

6. Emily leaves Freed & Gant after a few months for the firm of Kranston & Knight. Kranston offers Emily a signing bonus, a salary that is $500 a month higher than her pay at Freed & Gant, great benefits, and a bonus plan based on the following formula: 1 percent of the firm's net revenue annually, plus 5 percent of her monthly salary as of the end of the year, plus 5 percent of the net recovery in every litigated matter that Emily has worked on. Is Emily's compensation package acceptable? What about the bonus plan? Be sure to look at each element of the plan.

7. Larry Langsford is a paralegal working for a sole practitioner, Martha Monroe. Larry handles all the bookkeeping for the office in addition to all the paralegal work in a variety of practice areas. One day Martha comes in very distraught and asks Larry for all the firm checkbooks. She leaves and does not come back the rest of the day. The next day, Larry notices that a check from the client trust account is missing. What should he do? The following day, a big settlement check comes in. Martha instructs Larry to deposit the check in her operating account, to pay all the office bills, and to pay the client his share of the recovery. What should Larry do? Later, Larry is filing some documents in files in Martha's office and discovers several checks in the bottom of a file cabinet. These undeposited checks appear to be from clients and insurance companies. What should Larry do?

8. Nancy Nussbaum is a paralegal for Overton & Price, a firm that handles estate planning and real estate transactions. A wealthy client, Ronald Roland, comes in one day and asks Nancy to keep some jewelry for him for safekeeping while his house is being remodeled. Should she do this? If the firm agrees to do this, where should the jewelry be kept? Suppose that one day Nancy is looking for a file in Oliver Overton's office and comes across the jewelry in a file cabinet. What should she do?

DISCUSSION QUESTIONS AND PROJECTS

1. Contact five local law firms and find out:

   a. what kinds of fee arrangements they use for legal work (for example, contingency fee for personal injury, fixed fee to form a corporation, hourly fee to negotiate a deal)

     b. their hourly rates for lawyers and paralegals

     c. what costs they bill directly to clients

     d. whether they require that all fee agreements be in writing (ask if you may have a copy of a standard fee agreement if the firm has one)

2. Do you believe that the special restrictions on contingency fees (for example, in criminal and divorce cases) are warranted? Why or why not?

3. Do you believe the ethics rules should require all fee agreements to be in writing? Why or why not?

4. Should the percentage of attorney's fees in contingency cases be limited by statute or ethics codes? Why or why not? What do you think is the reason for limiting the amount of contingency fees in medical malpractice cases?

5. Do you think the trend to use alternative methods of fee structures — for instance, task-based, value, or premium billing — in lieu of traditional hourly rates is a good one? Why or why not?

6. What would you do if the supervising attorney in a matter continually wrote off your time as excessive, diminishing your billable hours?

7. What would you do if a client called and wanted to know the firm's hourly rates to handle certain kinds of legal work?

8. What would you do if a prospective personal injury client with a good case came into the office seeking representation and the attorney was out of town for two weeks?

9. What would you do if you knew that a lawyer was inflating the costs on clients' bills?

10. You are flying across country for client X and en route do some work for client Y. How do you bill your time?

11. Do you think the United States should have the kind of two-way fee shifting that England and Canada have? Why or why not?

12. Outline the arguments in the *Missouri v. Jenkins* majority opinion and dissent on the award of compensation for paralegal time in statutory fee awards. Which side do you find more convincing and why? Outline the arguments for charging paralegal fees at market rate as opposed to cost. Which do you find more convincing and why?

13. Are there cases on paralegal fees in your state? Are these supportive of paralegal fee awards?

14. Are there any statutes or court rules in your jurisdiction that provide for paralegal fees awards as part of attorney's fees awards?

15. Do you think that courts should examine the credentials of paralegals when they consider whether to compensate for paralegal time? Should the federal court refuse to award compensation for paralegals who do not meet statutory requirements, even if the statute does not

state that it is intended for this purpose? Why or why not? If a state has voluntary certification, like Ohio or Texas, should the courts require that paralegals have it in fee award cases? Should they adjust the paralegal's rate according to whether or not the paralegal is certified?

16. Do you think the rules prohibiting fee splitting are well founded? Why or why not? Do you think the rules should be different for lawyers and nonlawyers?

17. Do you think the rules prohibiting referral fees are well founded? Why or why not? Does your jurisdiction allow attorneys to pay or receive referral fees? Is it common practice?

18. May a personal injury firm pay a $500 bonus for every case a paralegal brings in? May a paralegal be paid one-third of the fee when the case is settled?

19. Call five local law firms and find out if they have pension or profit-sharing plans for their paralegals or pay bonuses to their paralegals. Ask them how the amount of the bonus is determined.

20. Do you think the rule prohibiting paralegals from becoming partners in law firms is well founded? Why or why not? Do you think this rule should be changed? Ask some lawyers and practicing paralegals what they think. Has your jurisdiction considered adopting a rule that would allow multidisciplinary practice?

21. Is it ethical or acceptable for an attorney to keep the deed of trust to a client's real estate in the attorney's desk? In the client file? Under the floor board in the attorney's attic? Why or why not? What if the property were a valuable diamond ring? Stock certificates?

22. What is wrong with an attorney putting client funds in the firm's account if he or she plans to replace them in two days? Would it make any difference if the period were two weeks? If the client owed fees to the attorney? If the attorney were doing this for the benefit of another client and did not benefit himself or herself in any way?

23. What kind of IOLTA does your state have — voluntary, opt-out, or mandatory? How do attorneys pay the fund? What are the funds used for? How much money is currently in the fund?

24. Does your state have a client security fund? How is it funded? How much money is in the fund? What kinds of payments have been made from the fund?

25. What would you do if your attorney-employer is very careful about handling client funds but keeps no records other than bank reports and withdrawal slips?

26. What would you do if you discovered that a settlement check come in and had been deposited six months ago and the client had never been notified?

27. Draft a provision on handling of client files after the matter is closed.

28. Does your state or local bar have rules on how long lawyers should retain client files?

SELECTED CASES

Absher Construction Co. v. Kent School District, 79 Wash. Ct. App. 841, 917 P.2d 1086 (1995) (appellate court case upholds fee award with paralegal fees and sets forth list of criteria for determining if fees should be awarded).

Doe v. Condon, 341 S.C. 22, 532 S.E.2d 879 (S.C. 2000) (State Supreme Court adopts ethics opinion that prohibits lawyer from allowing paralegal to give estate planning seminars for public and from paying the paralegal under a plan that is based on the number and value of cases the paralegal handles).

F.D.I.C. v. Singh, 148 F.R.D. 6 (D. Me. 1993) (no paralegal fees in Maine attorney's fee statute).

First NH Banks Granite State v. Scarborough, 615 A.2d 248 (Me. 1992) (paralegals are covered by attorney's fee statutes).

Hines v. Hines, 129 Idaho 847, 934 P.2d 20 (1997) (legislature must change attorney's fee statute to include paralegal time).

In re Bass, 227 B.R. 103 (Bankr. E.D. Mich. 1998) (petition for fees with clerical tasks, the role of the paralegal, and an improper compensation plan).

In re Hessinger & Associates, 171 B.R. 366 (Bankr. N.D. Cal. 1994) (bankruptcy court sanctions attorney for fee splitting, excessive fees, and partnership with nonlawyers).

Kansas v. Barrett, 207 Kan. 178, 483 P.2d 1106 (1971) (attorney disciplined for client trust account violations; blaming staff is no defense).

Joerger v. Gordon Food Service, Inc., 224 Mich. App. 167, 568 N.W.2d 365 (1997) (appellate court refuses to award compensation for paralegal time under attorney's fees statute and calls on legislature to amend statute).

Missouri v. Jenkins, 491 U.S. 274 (1989) (landmark U.S. Supreme Court case upholds award of attorney's fees that included compensation for paralegal time at market rates).

Richlin Security Service Co. v. Chertoff, 128 S.Ct. 2007 (2008) (U.S. Supreme Court overturns Court of Appeal decision disallowing paralegal compensation at market rates in fee award under Equal Access to Justice Act, reaffirming the *Missouri v. Jenkins* precedent).

Sundance v. Municipal Court, 192 Cal. App. 3d 268, 237 Cal. Rptr. 269 (1987) (Court upheld award of fees that included time paralegal had volunteered).

Taylor v. Chubb, 874 P.2d 806 (Okla. 1994) (Oklahoma Supreme Court case upholds award of attorney's fees with paralegal fees at market rates).

Vitac Corp. v. Workers' Compensation Appeal Board, 578 Pa. 574, 854 A.2d 481 (Pa. 2004) (attorney fee statute in workers' compensation matter includes reasonable fees for paralegals).

SELECTED REFERENCES

ABA Model Rule 1.2 [scope of representation]

ABA Model Rule 1.5 [fees] ABA Model Rule 1.15 [safekeeping property]

ABA Model Rule 5.4 [fee splitting and referral fees, and partnerships with nonlawyers]

ABA Model Code DR 2-110, 9-101 [scope of representation]

ABA Model Code DR 2-106, 2-107 [fees]

ABA Model Code DR 5-103, 9-102 [safekeeping property]

ABA Model Code DR 2-103, 3-102, 5-107 [fee splitting and referral fees]

ABA Model Code 3-103 [partnerships with nonlawyers]

ABA Formal Opinion 93-379 (1993) [cites certain billing practices as unethical]

ABA Informal Opinion 875 (1965) [lay employees may not make fee arrangements or agree to undertake representation on the lawyer's behalf]

ABA Informal Opinion 1440 (1979) [nonlawyers can be included in profit-sharing and retirement plans]

ABA Formal Ethics Opinion 338 (1974) [endorses the use of credit cards for legal fee payments]

Federal Bankruptcy Law (11 U.S.C. § 330) [act amended to allow paralegal compensation in attorney fee award]

NFPA Ethics Opinion 95-4 [the ethics of billing for nonprofessional clerical work]

Competence

This chapter addresses competence, one of the essential elements of lawyers' and paralegals' professional responsibilities. Failure to perform competently for clients is grounds for both legal and disciplinary remedies. Chapter 7 covers:

- definitions of lawyer and paralegal competence
- key components of competence for paralegals, including

  - knowledge
  - skills
  - thoroughness and preparation
  - diligence and promptness
  - communication with clients

- sanctions for incompetence, including disciplinary actions and malpractice suits
- trends in malpractice
- avoiding malpractice
- factors affecting paralegal competence

A. Introduction

Lawyers are bound to represent clients competently by both **ethics codes** and common law rules of tort liability for **professional negligence**. The duty to represent a client competently also makes the lawyer responsible for the work of paralegals and others in the law firm; the ultimate responsibility for the competent handling of a client matter rests with the lawyer.

Paralegals should consider their own competence one of their highest duties, both because they desire professional status and treatment and because they share with the lawyer the moral and ethical responsibility for providing quality legal services. As discussed in Chapter 1, paralegals should also be mindful of their own personal tort liability in the event a client brings a malpractice case.

A clear all-encompassing definition of competence is not easy to state; competence cannot be defined quantitatively and the range of acts that fall within its scope expands over time. Most definitions begin with the requisite legal knowledge and skill needed to perform competently, and add values and attitudes that are needed to apply knowledge and skills.

B. Legal Education

Legal knowledge for lawyer competence generally means, at a minimum, a **law school** education of three or four years followed by a bar examination, which primarily tests substantive legal knowledge and judgmental-analytical ability. Although slow to change, law schools have made changes in the last several years to make the education of aspiring lawyers more practical. Clinical programs along with courses on lawyering skills, mediation training, and trial techniques have been added to the traditional law school curriculum. Teaching ethics and embedding skill development across the curriculum have become part of the law school experience in many forward-thinking schools. The bar examination has been modified to include performance testing along with multiple-choice and essay questions.

In addition to formal legal education, the requisite legal knowledge and skills to practice competently encompass many things not covered in school. Newly admitted lawyers learn **on the job** from more experienced lawyers in the firms that hire them. Some of this training is informal: learning by example, by models available in the firm, and by trial and error. Some on-the-job training is more formal: some large firms and governmental agencies, such as offices of prosecutors and public defenders, have formal in-house training and mentoring programs.

A lawyer must continue to develop legal knowledge and skills throughout his or her career. Formal **continuing education** programs are offered by firms, bar associations, and private entities. Forty-three states have mandatory continuing legal education. Ideally, attorneys are committed to keeping abreast of changes in the law and to developing their talents to the fullest. Such is the aspiration of the professional — it is not predicated on mandates from the state, but is a matter of commitment and integrity: Lawyers are driven by a commitment to serving clients in the most effective way possible and, for many lawyers, to achieving justice. Most lawyers experience a strong sense of personal satisfaction from doing their work well.

C. Paralegal Education

Paralegals share a lawyer's commitment to education and skill development. Because in most jurisdictions paralegals do not have to comply with state-mandated educational standards the responsibility for achieving and maintaining competence through education and skill development rests firmly with paralegals and the lawyers who employ them.

As described in Chapter 1, **paralegal education** programs were first developed as the paralegal profession was just getting started about 40 years ago. The first half-dozen programs were established around 1970. There are now approximately 1,100 paralegal programs situated in a wide variety of institutions, including two- and four-year colleges (both public and private), multidisciplinary and freestanding proprietary institutions (some of which are vocationally oriented), and correspondence and online schools. Unlike the law school curriculum, the paralegal curriculum is not standardized, and offerings vary widely in length, content, format, level of sophistication, and degree of specialization. Good programs of all types teach an appropriate balance of substantive law and practical job skills.

About 260 of these paralegal programs are approved by the **ABA**, which means they have met guidelines on curriculum, admissions, faculty, administration, staff, facilities, finances, library, and support services, such as counseling and placement. ABA approval, first granted in 1975, is the only kind of specialized accreditation or approval of paralegal educational programs available. It is purely voluntary and is not formally recognized by the federal government. The ABA has never sought such recognition. The American Association for Paralegal Education also promotes quality in paralegal education through education, model curricula and courses, networking, and sharing of best practices.

Formal paralegal education is increasingly becoming a minimum requirement for entering a paralegal career, although firm hiring standards vary throughout the country. States considering regulation of paralegals usually set minimum paralegal education requirements. For example, one of two ways that one can qualify as a paralegal under the California state statute is to complete a program of at least 24 semester credits of paralegal courses. Not all legal employers require formal paralegal education, but most favor candidates who have formal training over those who do not. In some cities, a baccalaureate degree alone is the hiring standard in large law firms. Smaller firms often consider previous legal work experience more important than formal education.

Because a lawyer who utilizes a paralegal's services is responsible for determining that the paralegal is competent to perform the tasks assigned, lawyers should require high levels of education and training. Whether or not employers require it, paralegals should acquire the appropriate formal education to meet their professional obligation of competence. This education should include not only a basic paralegal program, but also regular and frequent **continuing education** that covers new practice areas, updates paralegals in their area of practice, and enhances paralegal skills. Continuing education is available to paralegals in many forms, especially because paralegals may take courses that are designed for lawyers and courses offered specifically to paralegals. Continuing education for lawyers is readily available through state and local bar associations and independent providers. Courses for paralegals are provided by paralegal programs; local, regional, and national paralegal associations; and independent organizations. State regulatory schemes are likely to mandate continuing education for paralegals, as does the California legislation. State voluntary certification programs in Texas, Ohio, Florida, and North Carolina (described in Chapter 1) are also designed for paralegals to demonstrate competence and require continuing education to maintain certified status.

Both NALA and NFPA promote competence and education to their members. NALA's Code of Ethics Canon 6 requires paralegals to maintain a high degree of competency in the legal profession. NALA offers its *Certified Legal Assistant/Paralegal* (CLA or CP) and CLA Specialist examinations, discussed in Chapter 1. Educational and experiential requirements must be met to sit for the examination, and CLAs must also meet continuing education requirements to maintain their certified status. NFPA Model Code DR 1.1 contains a strong statement concerning competence and education. This statement tells paralegals that it is their professional responsibility to maintain competence through education, training, and work experience. NFPA offers the PACE examination to candidates with a degree and two years of experience. *Registered Paralegals* who pass the PACE test must participate in continuing education. Both NALA and NFPA hold annual national educational seminars and encourage their local chapters to provide frequent continuing education courses. As noted in Chapter 1, the other associations serving paralegals also offer certification examinations.

Certified Legal Assistant or Paralegal Certification for paralegals offered by NALA for passing the Certified Paralegal examination

Registered Paralegals Certification offered by NFPA for passing the Paralegal Advanced Competency Examination

D.   A Definition of Competence

Competence cannot be defined solely in terms of formal education and professional skills, although these are essential preconditions to competence. Competence itself has full meaning only when it is applied to the tasks at hand — to the specific legal work to be done. At this point, factors other than knowledge and skill determine whether work will be carried out competently. Most state ethics codes follow the ABA Model Rule in defining competent representation as requiring:

- **legal knowledge, skill, thoroughness, and preparation;**
- reasonable **diligence and promptness**; and
- **communication with clients** to keep them informed about the status of their matters, to comply with reasonable requests for information, and to explain matters so that clients can make informed decisions.

Ethics rules and cases interpreting them can be synthesized into a list of qualities that comprise competence for lawyers and paralegals alike.

1.   Knowledge

Both lawyers and paralegals must have appropriate **formal education**, both legal and general, that enables them to communicate well in both oral and written form; that provides them with knowledge of substantive law and procedure; that has developed their analytical and judgmental abilities; and that has provided them with the information and skills needed to resolve legal issues.

The bodies of knowledge needed by the lawyer and the paralegal naturally differ because the lawyer exercises independent professional judgment in deciding how to proceed, whereas the paralegal participates in the steps preliminary to these decisions (for example, by interviewing clients and conducting legal and factual research) and in the actions that implement these decisions (for example, by drafting a document).

Increasingly, the legal knowledge needed to be competent is highly **specialized**. The law has become more complex, and most practitioners emphasize no more than a few areas of practice. This trend away from general practice is also reflected in the growing number of states that have specialized certification programs for lawyers, by the departmentalization of large firms, and by the proliferation of "boutique" firms that devote themselves to one or two very specialized areas of law. As a result of specialization, lawyers have a duty to refer complex, specialized cases to a lawyer with appropriate expertise if

137

they don't have that expertise themselves. Paralegals, especially in urban areas where highly specialized legal services are needed by clients, must also be specialists to act competently. Most paralegal education programs, unlike law school, include specialty courses, and most paralegal continuing education programs are devoted to specialized or advanced coursework. NALA offers advanced specialty examinations in a variety of practice areas, as does the State Bar of Texas in its certification program for paralegals.

Orientation and formal **on-the-job training** have become important elements of legal training. Many large law firms offer formal inhouse training programs for lawyers and paralegals, which not only orient them to the firm's "way of doing things," but also cover substantive knowledge and skills. Many firms have courses for lawyers on advocacy skills and trial techniques; courses have been developed for paralegals on topics such as doing legal research, managing databases, and handling document productions.

Keeping abreast of changes in law and practice is critical, as is regular updating of technology skills. Ample opportunities exist for errors to be made on documents by anyone who is not careful while working with technology. For example, key documents or entries might be lost; errors can be made by selecting the wrong form, using the wrong paragraphs, or changing some but not all names, numbers, or provisions. Confidential information can be revealed inadvertently by sending documents with metadata. Evolving standards of competence now require lawyers to conduct online legal research, which yields more up-to-date and accurate results than can be achieved by working with books and paper supplements.

2. Skills

Skills are acquired through formal education and through training and experience on the job. The term *skills* refers primarily to the **execution of tasks** and the implementation of decisions about how to proceed in a matter, as opposed to the mastery of a body of substantive principles and legal information. Lawyers and paralegals both must have the ability to apply their skills to the resolution of legal problems in carrying out their respective roles. Skills needed most by paralegals include drafting and analyzing documents, summarizing information, handling procedural matters, gathering and organizing information, and conducting legal research. Lawyers need different skills, such as trial advocacy and negotiating. Studies on the utilization of paralegals show that lawyers retain the complex and sophisticated tasks and delegate to paralegals legal functions and duties that require strong organizational and oral and written communication skills.

3. Thoroughness and Preparation

In applying knowledge and skills to any legal problem, both lawyers and paralegals must be careful and complete in their information gathering, analysis, application of judgment, and actions. Neglecting to learn all the facts, to fill out forms properly, or to be **meticulous about every detail** can have devastating consequences for the client. Because paralegals are especially valued for their knowledge of the facts in the cases they work on and for their attention to detail, thoroughness is one of the most critical aspects of paralegal competence. An example of failing to act competently in this area is omitting a necessary and important provision in a legal document, which may result in a failure to protect the client's interest and may give rise to a malpractice suit.

Related to thoroughness is **preparation**. Most successful lawyers credit much of their success to their careful and thorough preparation. Paralegals play an important part in preparation because they are often delegated considerable responsibility for preliminary tasks. For example, paralegals often organize documents and information before trial and draft and organize documents for real estate closings. The paralegal, attorney, and other law firm personnel must work together as a team in preparation. Lawyers rely on the preparation done by paralegals while they are readying for their distinct role (representing the client in court, for instance).

4. Diligence and Promptness

Legal knowledge and skills are not of any value unless applied to a client's case in a timely and attentive manner. Diligence in this context requires **persistent attention to the legal matter** to ensure that it is resolved with the best possible outcome for the client. A lack of diligence or promptness is evidenced by delays that may cause harm to a client's case or cause the client unnecessary anxiety. Examples of failure to act diligently and promptly include missing court dates or appointments, frequently needing continuances, missing a statute of limitations, not pursuing discovery, or in general taking an unnecessarily long time to act. Implied in the duty of diligence is the necessity for firm management that ensures against the missing of critical deadlines, scheduling of conflicting court dates, and so forth. Often, these important organizational tasks are delegated to a paralegal.

5. Communication with Clients

The importance of clear and complete communication with clients cannot be overstated. The good work of a competent lawyer and paralegal will not be recognized if the client is not fully informed about the status of a case at each step of the process. It may not matter how successfully the client's case is resolved if the firm does not return the client's phone calls or e-mails promptly. **Ongoing communication** with clients is an important and potentially large role for paralegals. Attorneys, especially trial attorneys, often are too busy to return clients' calls immediately or to make regular calls or written reports on how matters are proceeding. Paralegals are ideally situated to handle these communications and can be very effective in keeping clients informed and satisfied.

E. Sanctions for Incompetence

Malpractice
Improper conduct in the performance of duties by a professional, either intentionally or through negligence

Incompetence can be fatal to a client's rights and to a lawyer's or a paralegal's career. Failing to act competently in the handling of a case is the most common basis for *malpractice* actions against attorneys and for **disciplinary proceedings** — albeit when the incompetence is particularly egregious or persistent. Incompetence in the malpractice context is defined as the failure to exercise the level of care commonly observed in other professionals. The remedy is compensation for the loss of the client's legal rights — in other words, damages for losing a case in which the client would have prevailed if the lawyer had acted competently. Some cases also permit recovery to third persons who are damaged by an attorney's failure to act competently.

As discussed in Chapter 1, paralegals, including freelance paralegals, also may be named in legal malpractice actions. Most lawyers carry **malpractice insurance** that covers the actions of their employees, including paralegals; such insurance is mandatory in some states. Paralegals should be certain their employer has adequate malpractice coverage that also covers them.

Insurance carriers report that the most common bases for claims are:

1. substantive incompetence
2. management incompetence
3. poor communication skills and practices
4. fee misunderstandings
5. substance abuse and stress.

Incompetence as grounds for disciplinary action must normally be **severe or repeated** before sanctions are imposed. Frequently in disciplinary matters, lack of competence is coupled with other ethical violations, such as commingling or conversion of client trust account funds or failure to turn over client papers after representation is terminated.

Discipline for competence-related violations includes cases in which lawyers failed to supervise paralegals properly and aided in the unauthorized practice of law by allowing nonlawyers to give legal advice and to prepare legal documents without proper supervision or review. In recent years, some former clients have successfully used violations of ethics rules as a basis for malpractice suits. Because paralegals are not subject to discipline by the bar and not usually named in malpractice suits, the most likely consequence for paralegals who fail to act competently is to lose a position and to become unemployable.

Many malpractice and disciplinary cases involving competence relate to **procrastination** or to a lack of promptness, thoroughness, or communication. Typical scenarios include missing the statute of limitations, failing to proceed on a client's case after agreeing to representation, and not returning phone calls for an extended period, usually because the lawyer has not taken actions in the matter. These allegations are sometimes tied to financial improprieties as well, such as not returning advanced fees, not turning over settlement checks or clients' files promptly, or "borrowing" from client trust accounts. Some cases of this type are the result of mismanaged law offices — some, troubled attorneys.

Personal problems — such as financial, marital, or health problems — often interfere with the ability to function competently. The legal profession has a relatively high rate of substance abuse, as high as 20 percent by some estimates. A substantial proportion of lawyers with disciplinary records have alcohol or drug dependency problems and/or emotional and personal problems that prevent them from operating in an ethical and effective manner. Most state bars now have programs to help attorneys with these problems, either voluntarily before they begin to affect a lawyer's professional actions or as part of the sanctions imposed on a lawyer who has been disciplined.

F.   Trends in Legal Malpractice

Lawsuits against lawyers have steadily increased over the last decade. Some of this increase is from **third-party claims** by nonclients who were harmed by the actions of clients from whom they could no longer recover. Corporate **securities work** carries a high risk of third-party malpractice actions because of the additional duties to the purchasers of securities imposed by federal law. Under the securities laws, attorneys may be liable when material false or misleading statements are included in offerings. The result is the imposition on counsel of heightened duties of due diligence and fact checking. Private investors who lose money look to the lawyers who represented the promoters as possible defendants, especially when the promoters have no money.

Third-party claims against lawyers Claims by nonclients against lawyers whose acts in representing clients may have caused harm to the third person

141

The principles underlying third-party liability in securities cases have been applied in other business situations as well. They were broadly used during the **savings and loan** crisis of the 1980s and 1990s in lawsuits by the federal government against firms who represented failed thrift institutions. Most suits claimed that firms failed to advise their clients properly; in many cases, firms relied on information provided by clients. In some suits, the lawyers served on their clients' boards, exacerbating the malpractice issue because of the possible conflict of interest and exposure to details about questionable transactions. Similar cases have been brought in matters relating to environmental compliance.

Another area where third-party lawsuits against lawyers have become common is in **estate planning** work. When a gift to an intended beneficiary fails because of an attorney's negligence in drafting, the intended beneficiary may seek damages from the attorney, even though the attorney represented the testator, not the beneficiary. Similar cases have held attorneys who represented sellers in real estate transactions liable to buyers for making misleading statements that the buyer relied on in making the purchase. When plaintiffs look for a "deep pocket," attorneys with malpractice insurance coverage make attractive defendants. More extensions of third-party liability are likely in the future, especially in areas heavily regulated by the government, such as environmental law.

More and more cases are being filed against lawyers by former clients on the basis of conflicts of interest. Some cases have revolved around a firm's representation of two clients who have become adversaries. Some have concerned conflicts that arose when an attorney did business with clients or served on a corporate client's board of directors. Finally, several recent suits have been brought against lawyers for giving poor advice on settling claims, when the client later discovered that the claim was worth much more money. Among the related areas accounting for the rise in malpractice suits in the last decade are major lawsuits against large law firms that represented companies that failed.

Some states also allow lawyers to be sued under consumer fraud statutes. A split exists among the states that allow these suits, some allowing recovery when the lawyer acted unconscionably and others finding that lawyers are not subject to this kind of state regulation. At least five states (Louisiana, Texas, Connecticut, Washington, and Colorado) allow these suits and two (Illinois and New Jersey) do not.

To avoid malpractice, lawyers and their firms are advised to follow these good practices:

1. Lawyers should use carefully drafted **letters of engagement** and **letters terminating or declining representation**. These documents must spell out and limit the extent and nature of the representation and the expectations and responsibilities of the law firm and

the client, and should clearly indicate that the lawyer is not guaranteeing a particular outcome.

2. **Lawyers should screen clients carefully** and turn away prospective clients where warning signs are present. Difficult personalities and questionable cases should not be accepted.

3. Lawyers and clients should enter into complete and well-drafted **fee agreements** for each representation. The agreements should cover all the terms noted in Chapter 6. Fee agreements should be prepared and signed as soon as possible in the representation and should be followed meticulously.

4. Lawyers should charge clients **reasonable fees** that are in accord with the fee agreements. Bills should be detailed and should be reviewed before being sent. Excessive, duplicative, and inappropriate charges should be removed before sending bills. Billing should be done regularly and timely.

5. Clients' **phone calls and e-mails should be returned promptly**, preferably the same day. Lawyers and paralegals should take the time to educate the client about relevant law and procedures and show that they care about clients' concerns. Clients should be sent copies of documents and work product. Correspondence and other materials from clients should be promptly acknowledged.

6. Lawyers and paralegals should **listen to clients** carefully and try to understand their goals and expectations. Unrealistic expectations should be addressed immediately and thoughtfully.

7. Lawyers should exercise **independent judgment** on clients' behalf and should **respect clients' decisions**.

8. Lawyers and paralegals should be scrupulous in the handling of **clients' funds**, in keeping with the rules set forth in Chapter 6. Client trust accounts and related records must be perfectly maintained, with no commingling or other irregularities. Client files must be turned over promptly upon termination, and settlements must be paid promptly after receipt.

9. Lawyers and paralegals should know the **limits of their competence** and should seek guidance and consultation when in doubt about how to proceed on a matter.

10. If a client asks for advice or help in an **unsettled area of law**, lawyers should be sure that the client understands that the advice or actions are not based on clear, well-defined law.

11. Lawyers and paralegals must honor rules on **conflicts of interest**, by maintaining good records of the matters they have worked on, conducting meticulous conflicts checks, and carefully following related rules on accepting matters, protecting client confidentiality, and adhering strictly to ethical screens.

12. Lawyers should create a **firm culture** that is characterized by high ethical standards, including promoting quality work, knowing and following ethics rules and high levels of performance, identifying and

addressing problems that may lead to substandard work, and supporting continuing education of lawyers, paralegals, and staff.

13. Finally, law firms should have **good management systems** and well-trained personnel in place, especially concerning the following matters:

   - conflicts checking and establishing screens
   - protecting client confidentiality
   - calendaring deadlines, court dates, and the like
   - billing and time keeping
   - handling client property
   - managing client trust accounts
   - addressing ethical and performance problems

Paralegals play an important role in helping lawyers to **avoid disputes** with clients. Communication with clients is greatly improved when lawyers delegate to paralegals the responsibility for keeping clients informed, in writing and by phone. When clients call and the lawyer is unavailable, the paralegal can take or return the call. Paralegals can keep the lawyer informed of client concerns and keep clients informed of progress in the handling of the matter. Keeping accurate and detailed time records and alerting the lawyer to potential problems in time and billing matters are also valuable paralegal functions. Paralegals often have responsibility for monitoring deadlines and handling client funds, especially in small law firms.

G.   Factors Affecting Paralegal Competence

Paralegals need to be cognizant of the factors in their work environment that may either enhance their competence or detract from it. Because paralegals work under the direction and supervision of lawyers, they are not usually in a position to establish the quality standards for the firm or to set the professional tone that determines the attitude that employees at all levels take toward their work. Paralegals, especially those in small firms, do have influence over firm standards and culture, but in many employment settings, they are subject to the environment established by the lawyers. Given this situation, paralegals should seek out firms that have high standards of quality and encourage competence and professionalism. A paralegal may not be able to function in a competent fashion over time in a firm that does not value and support competence.

Paralegals are sometimes faced with competence-related ethical dilemmas. Perhaps the most common is being asked to perform a task that the paralegal does not have the **requisite knowledge or skill** to perform. This scenario presents an especially difficult dilemma for paralegals, who want to do challenging, interesting work and who know their value is in relieving lawyers from tasks that they would otherwise have to perform. Thus tension may arise between the paralegal's desire to take the assignment and his or her ability to handle the assignment competently. A new paralegal, just like a lawyer just out of law school, must learn on the job. With a strong education, good research and drafting skills, and self-confidence and motivation, a paralegals can usually learn how to perform assigned tasks by conducting research, finding a model in firm files, and consulting with other paralegals or junior lawyers. Paralegals may ask for more guidance from the lawyers who assigned the task or seek out assistance from another lawyer or a more experienced paralegal. Paralegal colleagues in other firms may be able to guide the paralegal to the necessary sources. In any event, the supervising lawyer should be made aware that the paralegal has not previously undertaken such a task, so that the lawyer will evaluate the work fairly and review it carefully.

A related concern is the proper **delegation, supervision, and review** of paralegal work by attorneys. The ethics and agency rules discussed above and in Chapter 1 make it clear that the lawyer is ultimately responsible for the work of the paralegal. This responsibility is described in ABA Model Guideline 1 and its comment and in ABA Model Rule 5.3. For a variety of reasons, attorneys do not always carry out their supervisory responsibilities as well as they should. Many lawyers are not skilled delegaters; they often do not give adequate information and instructions when assigning work to paralegals and others. Many lawyers are overloaded and simply don't take the time to delegate and review thoroughly. Proper delegation requires selecting the appropriately skilled person for the task and giving sufficient direction so that the finished product meets expectations. Information given to the one performing the task includes background on the matter and/or reference to appropriate files that contain relevant information; an exact description of the end product desired; references to sources that may be of assistance; deadline dates; and, if possible, an estimate of the time the task should take. If paralegals are assigned work without this information, they may spend too much time on the work, the end product may not be what was desired, or the project may be late, all of which reflect poorly on the paralegal's competence and dis-serve the client. The paralegal who works for a poor delegater must take the responsibility for getting the information and instructions necessary to complete the project correctly and on time by asking the appropriate questions, repeating back instructions to make sure that they have been understood, and reducing hastily given oral instructions to writing, usually in a short confirming e-mail sent back to the attorney.

Attorney review
Responsibility of supervising attorney to review work of paralegals

Paralegals also find that *attorney review* of their work is not always as thorough as it should be, especially when the paralegal is a long-term, trusted employee whose competence has been proven. Even if the paralegal is confident in the work product, the lawyer must review it. If a paralegal is aware that the lawyer is not reviewing adequately, the paralegal has an obligation to discuss the matter with the lawyer to encourage more careful review. The problem of inadequate review is exacerbated when a paralegal is working for an inexperienced attorney or for an attorney who does not have expertise in the area of law in which he or she is working. If the paralegal is very experienced, the lawyer may rely too heavily or even completely on the paralegal's expertise. Paralegals in this situation should take steps to ensure that their work is properly reviewed.

A **heavy workload** often interferes with the performance of lawyers, paralegals, and other law firm employees. Many factors contribute to an unreasonably heavy workload, including taking on too many cases, being poorly organized or managed, or not having adequate staff. Sometimes, especially in litigation, temporary crisis periods emerge before and during trial requiring everyone involved in a case to work long hours. Paralegals must be assertive in their dealings with lawyers so that they do not take on more work than they can competently handle. Too heavy a workload causes a decline in productivity and quality and increases the likelihood of shortcuts being taken and mistakes being made. A firm that continually operates in this crisis mode is not a good place to work — the work will not be done competently, the stress will be unhealthy, and the staff will not feel personally or professionally satisfied. Paralegals should avoid working for law firms characterized by constant pressure caused by excessive workloads. They also should be aware of the potential problems created by a temporary heavy workload. When a project or group of projects require long hours and create pressure over an extended period, the paralegal should talk to the appropriate person in the firm to see what measures can be taken to remedy the situation. Additional support staff and temporary paralegals to do the most routine paralegal and clerical work may relieve the situation, making it possible for everyone to function more effectively.

Paralegals should have a thorough understanding of their own **level of competence** and, while striving to learn and develop, should not get so far ahead of their knowledge and skills that they are no longer acting competently. Continuing education, inhouse training programs, and mentoring can address the need to build knowledge and skills. Paralegals who want long and satisfying careers are, in essence, always "in school." An honest **self-assessment** will help paralegals identify those personal characteristics that may affect their competence. Well-qualified paralegals know what particular talents and qualities they do and do not possess, and they maximize strong points and minimize deficiencies accordingly. They work to improve in areas of weakness, to strengthen and emphasize natural abilities, and to seek work that matches their attributes. A paralegal who is not a good writer should strive to improve those skills but should also avoid positions that require a lot of sophisticated writing. A paralegal who works well with people should seek a position that will make use of that ability, such as a job that involves supervision of others or frequent client contact.

Paralegals who are having **personal, health, or family problems** must consider how these problems affect their work. No one functions as effectively when he or she is troubled, worried, or distracted. Paralegals who are experiencing difficulties outside the office must be alert to the potential for a decline in productivity and accuracy and should take steps to ensure that quality is maintained. If the problems are serious or ongoing, paralegals in this situation may want to discuss these problems with a supervisor to get both the emotional and the practical support needed to carry on competently and to make sure that their behavior is not misinterpreted. Paralegals who have alcohol and drug dependency problems should seek professional help, and colleagues and friends in the workplace should encourage them to do so.

REVIEW QUESTIONS

1. What are the elements of competence?
2. Are lawyers responsible for the conduct of their paralegals?
3. If lawyers are responsible for the professional actions of their paralegals, why should paralegals be concerned about competence?
4. Describe and compare legal and paralegal education.
5. What education do lawyers and paralegals need in addition to their formal professional education?
6. What are some sources of continuing education programs for paralegals?
7. What do the NALA and NFPA ethics guidelines say about competence?
8. How do ethics rules define competence?
9. Do lawyers and paralegals need to have the same knowledge and skills to be competent? How do they differ? What skills might they need in common?
10. How does the trend toward increasing legal specialization affect competence?
11. What do law firms do to develop their paralegals' competence?
12. How does a paralegal demonstrate competence in preparing a case?
13. What does *diligence* mean? What is the paralegal's role in ensuring diligence?
14. What are some common problems associated with a lack of diligence or promptness?
15. Why is communication with clients included in the definition of competence? What role can a paralegal play in this area?

16. What are the possible consequences of a lawyer's incompetence? What are the possible consequences of a paralegal's incompetence?
17. Give some examples of common grounds for malpractice claims.
18. What is third-party liability? How does it affect lawyers who work in government-regulated areas of practice?
19. What kinds of cases might give rise to third-party malpractice claims?
20. Name some steps that a firm can take to prevent malpractice claims.
21. How should a paralegal respond if he or she is asked to perform a task for which he or she has no expertise?
22. What steps should a paralegal take if his or her supervising attorney gives incomplete instructions on a project?
23. What should a paralegal do if the supervising attorney does not carefully review his or her work?
24. What should a paralegal do if his or her workload is too heavy and cannot be handled in a timely, competent manner?
25. What steps might a paralegal take upon learning that another paralegal has a substance abuse problem that is affecting work?

HYPOTHETICALS

1. Anna Anderson just graduated from paralegal school, where she focused on probate and real estate work. Her best job offer is from a big firm, Billings & Conroy, which has asked her to work in the litigation department until there is an opening in probate or real estate. She is assigned to work for a first-year associate, Bob Brown, on a new antitrust case that has just come in. Bob asks Anna to draft a motion to dismiss the case. Anna has no idea how to begin and knows little about litigation, let alone the intricacies of federal court and antitrust law. What should she do? Anna figures out how to draft the motion and gives a very rough draft to Bob for guidance. He says it is fine and asks her to file it as is. Anna knows it is not very good and is concerned that Bob has not reviewed it carefully and may not know any more than she does about the law and procedure in the case. What should she do? Is Bob acting competently?

2. Carl Carlson is a freelance paralegal. He has been working in the probate area for 15 years and has a regular client base of lawyers with whom he works. Carl gets a call from a lawyer, Debby Dunton, who wants to meet him about handling some probate matters for her. At the meeting, Debby says, "I really don't know much about probate, but I need to take these few cases until I can build up my family law practice." What should Carl do? Can he put procedures in place to make sure that there are no problems working with Debby? Assume that Carl goes to work with Debby. She hands him a file of papers and

asks him to organize it and to do whatever needs to be done. What should he do?

3. Ellen Ellerby, a paralegal with Franklin & Gainsborough, works closely with another paralegal, Harry Henderson. In the last few months, Ellen has noticed that Harry is late to work a lot and is getting behind in his workload. He seems a little forgetful and disoriented. When they have time to talk during lunch one day, Harry confides that his marriage is rocky and he has been going out drinking every night with his buddies because he doesn't want to be at home. What should Ellen do? A few more weeks pass without change. One day, Ida Imerson, a lawyer in the firm, calls for Harry and he isn't in. Ida is looking for a complaint that Harry was supposed to draft. Ellen, who has Harry's password, searches through Harry's electronic files and sees that the complaint has been started but not finished and that the statute of limitations runs the next day. What should Ellen do now?

4. Jan Jones is a paralegal for a small firm, Kingfield & Knowlton. The firm has grown dramatically in the last year, and everyone is working 60 or 70 hours a week to keep up with the workload. Jan is at her limit of stress and believes that she cannot handle one more client matter. As Jan is leaving the office one day at 5 P.M. to pick up her child from child care, Kent Kingfield passes her in the hall and hands her a phone message from a new client and says, "Call this guy back and tell him that we will have the contracts ready tomorrow. Find the Smith file and draft the contracts, using the Smith contracts as a model. I need them by 9 in the morning." What should Jan do? What should the firm do to change the way it is working? Assume that Jan drops everything, calls the client, arranges for a friend to pick up her child, and drafts the contracts that night, working until midnight. In her exhaustion, she transposes some numbers and the consideration for the contract is stated incorrectly. She sees this after the contracts have been signed and sent to the other contracting party. What should she do?

DISCUSSION QUESTIONS AND PROJECTS

1. Check the local ethics code in your jurisdiction to see what provisions it contains on competence.
2. Get a listing and description of the disciplinary actions recently taken against attorneys in your state or county. (This information may be published in the local legal newspaper or on the state bar Web site or in its magazine.) What kinds of ethics violations appear? To what extent do these relate to competence? What proportion is related to competence?

3. Do you think states should set minimum levels of education for paralegals? Why or why not?

4. What would your model of paralegal education be if you were required to set minimum standards? Consider how much general college education and paralegal education should be included. How would your model look if it were an ideal model, rather than a minimum standard? Do you think that continuing education should be required? What kind and how much?

5. Do you think paralegals should have to take a licensing examination to demonstrate their competence? Why or why not?

6. Call five local law firms and find out:

   a. their hiring standards for paralegals
   b. whether they have inhouse orientation or training programs for paralegals
   c. whether they have a mentoring program for paralegals
   d. whether they pay the cost for their paralegals to take continuing education or other job-relevant courses.

7. Call your local paralegal association and get a listing of its continuing education programs for the upcoming year.

8. Check the Web sites for the four paralegal associations described in Chapter 1. Obtain the current informational materials on their certification programs. What are the requirements for taking these examinations? What is tested on these exams? What percentage of the paralegals in your area are certified by one of these organizations? Ask paralegals who are certified why they took the exam and how it has affected their careers.

9. To what extent is legal specialization important in your area? Does your jurisdiction have a certified specialist program for attorneys? If so, in what areas of law? How many lawyers are certified? Do most paralegals "specialize"?

10. Interview five paralegals who work in five different areas of the law. Ask them to list the functions they perform and the functions their attorney-supervisors perform. Compare the lists and look for common functions. Is there a difference in the competence needed by lawyers and paralegals? What generalities can you draw about the differences and commonalities?

11. Name and discuss some breaches of competence that can result from errors when using technology? How can these errors be prevented?

12. How can you tell whether a law firm encourages competence and quality?

13. Describe the extent to which an attorney should review the following work prepared by a paralegal:

    a. a form complaint
    b. articles of incorporation

    c. a trial notebook
    d. answers to interrogatories
    e. deposition summaries
    f. abstracts of documents in a computerized retrieval system
    g. a letter for the lawyer's signature
    h. a letter for the paralegal's signature
    i. a legal research memorandum
    j. notes of a client meeting

14. What would you do if you worked for a firm that was always in an overworked, crisis mode?
15. What would you do if you knew that attorneys in your firm frequently took short cuts, such as not gathering facts carefully or not researching legal issues thoroughly?
16. Name three of your personal strengths that may help you in your career as a paralegal. Name three weaknesses that might interfere with your competence or success. Considering these, what should you do to maximize your strengths and minimize your weaknesses? What kind of work is best suited to you? What kind of work environment?
17. Look for articles in the local legal newspaper and bar journals about malpractice cases and bring them to class to discuss.

SELECTED CASES

Biakanja v. Irving, 49 Cal. 2d 647, 320 P.2d 16 (1958) (nonlawyer who drafted will and had it improperly witnessed held liable to heir who did not receive his intended inheritance under the invalid will).

Busch v. Flangas, 837 P.2d 438 (Nev. 1992) (malpractice case against law clerk who handled matter without lawyer supervision).

De Vaux v. American Home Assurance Co., 387 Mass. 814, 444 N.E.2d 355 (1983) (misfiled letter results in missed statute of limitations).

In re Gillaspy, 640 N.E.2d 1054 (Ind. 1994) (failing to act competently by allowing a nonlawyer bankruptcy service to prepare petitions and other documents without lawyer review).

People v. Smith, 74 P.3d 566 (Colo. 2003) (lawyer suspended for failing to supervise a paralegal who mishandled a client's divorce).

Pincay v. Andrews, 389 F.3d 853 (9th Cir. 2004) (court held that delegating calendaring of deadlines to a paralegal was not per se negligent).

Tegman v. Accident & Medical Investigations, 30 P.3d 8 (Wash. 2001) (paralegal working without lawyer supervision for a company handling accident cases is held to the same standard of care as a lawyer and found liable).

Webb v. Pomeroy, 8 Kan. App. 2d 246, 655 P.2d 465 (1983) (malpractice case against nonlawyer who acted as a lawyer in a real estate transaction).

SELECTED REFERENCES

ABA Model Rules, Rule 1.1 [competence]
ABA Model Rules, Rule 1.3 [diligence]
ABA Model Rules, Rule 1.4 [communication]
ABA Model Code, DR 6-101(A) [competence]
ABA Model Code, DR 6-101(A)(3), DR 7-101(A) [diligence and communication]
ABA Model Code, DR 9-102(B)(1) [communication]

Special Issues in Advocacy

This chapter describes the most critical of the many dilemmas that confront paralegals who work in litigation and the ethics principles that govern advocacy. Chapter 8 covers:

- the duty to represent clients zealously
- unmeritorious claims, delay, and abuse of discovery
- disruptive courtroom tactics and sanctions for those actions
- sanctions for disobeying court orders
- the court's contempt power and its use
- candor and honesty
- relationships and communications with judges
- contact with jurors
- contact with represented parties
- contact with unrepresented persons
- contact with witnesses
- trial publicity
- special rules for prosecutors

A.   Introduction

The practice of law has changed dramatically over the past 50 years in response to the proliferation of laws, their increased complexity, and their pervasive impact on so many areas of modern life and business. One aspect of these many changes is that **most lawyers no longer go to court regularly**. The majority of lawyers in this country do not litigate matters, either civil or criminal, and many lawyers never go to court. The areas of law in which these lawyers practice include corporate, tax, business transactions, real estate, estate planning, probate, environmental law, and intellectual property.

At the same time, many commentators and politicians contend that **society is too litigious**, as people look to the courts to handle all kinds of disputes, some of which are not well suited for judicial resolution. A debate flares up periodically about whether there has been a "litigation explosion." Politicians blame the rising cost of medical services and insurance on trial lawyers and the growth in litigation against corporations, doctors and hospitals, and government. Punitive damage awards are vigorously attacked and legislatures act to limit them. Judges and lawyers have worked to streamline the litigation process and to encourage, or sometimes mandate, alternative dispute resolution. In this environment, paralegals must be diligent in their efforts to meet high standards of performance and ethics and to stay current with the changing ethics rules, court rules, and cases that govern conduct in litigation.

Unlike lawyers, the **majority of paralegals work in litigation**. And, contrary to commonly held perceptions, most of the work in litigation is done out of court, before trial, preparing for trial. The role of the paralegal in litigation is expansive, including fact gathering, interviewing clients and witnesses, drafting pleadings and motions, conducting legal research, drafting discovery requests and motions, responding to discovery, preparing for trial by summarizing and indexing documents and depositions, organizing and overseeing the maintenance of databases, locating and preparing expert witnesses, and preparing demonstrative evidence. Many litigation paralegals accompany their attorney-employers to court and assist in court by taking notes, making observations about jurors' reactions to the proceedings, handling logistics and emergencies, and doing last-minute research. As the discovery experts in cases, paralegals frequently have a mastery of the facts and evidence, which is of tremendous help to trial lawyers who must concentrate their attention on presenting the case, examining and cross-examining witnesses, and making objections.

Because paralegals play such a major role in litigation, they need a strong understanding of the ethics rules governing advocacy. Violations of these rules are often not committed by lawyers acting alone; lawyers may act through another, like a paralegal, or may involve a paralegal without the paralegal being fully aware of the ethical breach.

Lawyers have an ethical **duty to represent clients zealously** (Model Code Canon 7 and Model Rule 1.3). Zealous representation entails exercising one's best efforts on the client's behalf within the boundaries of law and ethics. The duty to represent clients zealously has special meaning in the context of the lawyer's role as an advocate. It sometimes clashes with other legal-ethical duties or moral imperatives, such as the **lawyer's duty of candor to the court** and the proper administration of justice, the rules of client confidentiality, and the search for the truth that forms the basis of the adversary system. The following sections cover some of the situations where ethical prerogatives clash and concentrate on the ethics rules on advocacy that affect paralegals most directly.

B.   Unmeritorious Claims, Delay, and Discovery Abuse

Ethics rules, statutes and court rules prohibit lawyers from bringing **unmeritorious** or **frivolous claims** or **defenses** (Model Code DR 7-102 and Model Rule 3.1). Two specific kinds of acts fall into this category: (1) actions that serve only to harass or injure another maliciously and (2) claims or defenses that are unwarranted under existing law without the lawyer's having a good faith argument to change the law.

Violations of this rule most commonly occur when an attorney brings an **unwarranted action** to gain some advantage over the opposition, to force a party to expend funds to defend the action, or simply to earn fees. Lawyers can inadvertently violate the rule by bringing an action based on inaccurate information supplied by the client if the lawyer fails to conduct any independent check of facts. Lawyers should make a sufficient reasonable inquiry before taking action. An emergency might require action before there is time to investigate, but generally lawyers are advised not to proceed on the basis of a client's story alone.

An example of an unmeritorious claim is a plaintiff who sues his competitor without proper grounds under the law merely for the purpose of driving him or her out of business.

The ethics rules on unmeritorious claims do provide an important exception to the general rule against making claims or defenses that are not warranted by the law, that is, if the client is seeking to extend, modify, or reverse the law.

Related to unmeritorious claims are **abuses of the discovery process**. Conducting excessive or unnecessary discovery can be employed as a strategy to delay litigation, to burden the opposing counsel, to raise the cost to the opposition and, generally, to wear down the opposing party and counsel. Manipulation of discovery rules to gain tactical advantage, although not uncommon, causes judicial ire and increases the public's disdain for lawyers. All states and the federal courts have addressed discovery abuse by adopting statutes and court rules to streamline discovery, to expedite the pretrial stage, and to discourage excessive and unnecessarily lengthy discovery. Common rules set limits on the number of interrogatories that can be served on a party, establish strict deadlines for completion of discovery, and mandate alternative dispute resolution and pretrial settlement procedures. Most states and the federal courts also have rules to prevent abuses of electronic discovery, which in many cases has increased the cost and extended the time of litigation. Judges can and do impose sanctions for discovery abuse.

Discovery abuse is also prohibited by ethics rules (Model Code DR 7-102(A) and Model Rule 3.4(d)). Most states' ethics rules specifically forbid making frivolous pretrial discovery requests and failing to comply with proper discovery requests. Violations of this rule occur, for example, in requesting discovery that is beyond the scope of the case; flooding the opposition with irrelevant interrogatories; giving incomplete answers to interrogatories; requesting discovery of confidential, sensitive, or embarrassing information; or making unfounded objections to discovery. Or an attorney may respond to discovery, such as a demand for document production, by providing much more than what was requested and perhaps "hiding" a key incriminating document in volumes of unrequested documents. Other examples include cases in which counsel failed to name more than 20 witnesses, removed discoverable documents from records that were produced, and refused to produce discoverable documents that were known to exist.

The ethics rules also prohibit a lawyer from **delay** of litigation (Model Code DR7-102(A)(1) and Model Rule 3.2). These rules cover delaying pretrial procedures or the actual trial and require lawyers to make reasonable efforts to expedite litigation consistent with clients' interests. Some examples of unethical delays are postponements for a lawyer's personal convenience, deliberate frustration of the opposition's legitimate goals, and slowdowns for the purpose of financial gain. Examples of unethical delays for which attorneys may be sanctioned by judges are an attorney's refusing to respond to communications of opposing counsel; repeated failure to appear at hearings, settlement conferences, and depositions; unnecessary delays in filing motions to disqualify counsel; and failing to complete discovery in accordance with court rules, court orders, or statutes.

Sometimes violations of the rules against delay are caused by **incompetence**; disorganized or impaired lawyers may miss deadlines or not be able to keep up with their cases. But sometimes lawyers create intentional delays to gain a tactical advantage over the opposition. *Discipline* by the bar for bringing unmeritorious claims or defenses, abusing discovery, or causing unnecessary delays is relatively rare. When discipline does occur, it is usually in a particularly egregious case, such as a multiplicity of frivolous lawsuits or abuse or delay that is coupled with incompetence or failure to obey a court order. Because judges see the effects of ethics violations like these in the moment, the usual remedy is a swift sanction by the court under the court's **contempt power**. (See more on contempt in Section C below.)

Contempt power includes the imposition of **monetary sanctions**. Under federal statutes and procedural rules and under court rules and statutes in every jurisdiction, courts are granted authority to impose sanctions against lawyers, clients, or both for actions that are unwarranted, or for delaying or harassing conduct. The most frequently used rule in federal court is **Federal Rule of Civil Procedure 11**, which provides for appropriate sanctions against lawyers, clients, or both for filing unwarranted or other objectionable pleadings and papers. Rule 11 is supplemented by several provisions of the Federal Rules of Civil Procedure, which provide for sanctions for failure to respond to discovery and for acting in bad faith in discovery. Rule 11 also provides that the lawyer's signature on the document verifies that the facts in the pleading have evidentiary support, that the complaint is not being made for an improper purpose, and that the claims or defense are warranted under existing law or by a nonfrivolous argument to change the law. Sanctions include fines paid to the court and attorney's fees to the opposing party or parties. A judge may also dismiss a complaint with prejudice under Rule 11.

Rule 11 and related federal rules are intended to help alleviate unnecessary delays and paperwork in federal court, and are widely used by federal judges. The **amount of sanction** awards is sometimes quite substantial. Recent examples of cases in which sanctions were awarded include: using abusive language in a motion, filing an action unwarranted by law for purely political reasons, asking for an inflated amount of damages, and filing a motion to disqualify counsel purely to delay the proceedings.

Every state has specific court rules and/or statutes authorizing sanctions for the conduct described in this section, and case law recognizes the inherent authority of a court over its proceedings as the basis for imposing sanctions.

One other important remedy available to the victims of such conduct is a civil suit against the client, the lawyer, or both for *malicious prosecution* or *abuse of process*. Grounds for malicious prosecution exist when a civil lawsuit or criminal prosecution has been brought, without probable cause and with malice, after the defendant prevails in the action. Limited immunity for lawyers exists in some states if it is shown that the lawyer acted in good faith. An abuse of process action may be brought when the legal process is misused to achieve a purpose other than a legitimate legal purpose, such as filing a criminal complaint to force the defendant to pay a debt.

Malicious prosecution/abuse of process
Improper use of a civil or criminal process

C. Disruption in the Courtroom and Disobeying Court Orders

Trial lawyers are bound by ethics rules to conduct themselves in a dignified and courteous manner in court (Model Code DR 7-106(C)(6)) and Model Rule 3.5(c)). Most interpretations of these two rules have found that the Model Rule requires an intent to disrupt, whereas the Model Code does not.

Frequently, conduct that judges may consider disruptive is the result of a lawyer's efforts to represent a client zealously. Sometimes a lawyer's zeal rises to a level of enthusiasm that oversteps the bounds of acceptable conduct. Lawyers may also employ tactics in court that are intended to influence the jury or to throw the opposing counsel off track.

Some examples of **disruptive conduct** or dirty tricks in the courtroom are raising an unfounded objection to break opposing counsel's train of thought; making faces or gestures to the judge or the jury; asking a question that alludes to evidence known to be inadmissible; insulting the judge or opposing counsel — for example, by calling them names or accusing them of collusion, racism, incompetence, or bias; referring to the proceedings in an insulting or rude manner; and making unsupportable, inflammatory, or prejudicial side remarks to the jury. In another recent case involving disruptive conduct, a firm had its fees reduced for its hardball tactics, which included refusing to shake hands with opposing counsel, rolling eyes when opposing counsel spoke, and engaging in an ongoing monologue of verbal abuse of opposing counsel.

Disobeying a court order is categorized as disruptive conduct because it interferes with the smooth administration of proceedings and demonstrates disrespect for the tribunal (Model Code DR 7-106(A) and Model Rule 3.4(c)).

Although acts reflecting a lack of respect for the court may subject a lawyer to disciplinary action, the acts are more likely to elicit an immediate response from the judge. Judges may hold an attorney in **contempt** for offensive courtroom conduct and for disobeying a court order. The judges' contempt power is reserved for situations in which the administration of justice and orderly proceedings are immediately and substantially threatened. Generally, judges warn lawyers, sometimes repeatedly, before holding them in contempt. Contempt is punishable by jail time and may give rise to disciplinary proceedings.

Judges have imposed the contempt sanction on attorneys for a wide variety of disruptive actions, including continued argument of a point on which the court has ruled; continued mention of inadmissible evidence or prohibited arguments; absence from or tardiness for scheduled court dates; presentation of false evidence; the use of abusive, vulgar, and obscene language; disrespectful, irrelevant, or unjustified criticism of

Contempt
An act that obstructs the administration of justice, impairs the dignity of the court, or shows disrespect for the authority of the court

the court; implying that the defense attorney is unethical and dishonest; and engaging in a shouting match with the judge. Insults, sarcasm, and the like are not punishable by contempt unless they also obstruct the proceedings.

Although paralegals are not often in a situation in which they could engage in this kind of conduct, they need to be aware of and honor this important rule. Many paralegals working in civil litigation and criminal law attend court proceedings and are therefore in a position to abide by or violate this rule. NFPA Model Code EC 1.3(a) calls on paralegals to refrain from "conduct that offends the dignity and decorum" of the courts.

D.   Candor and Honesty

All ethics rules call for lawyers to be **honest** in their representation of clients. However, an important distinction exists between being honest and disclosing everything that the lawyer knows. Lawyers are not obligated to disclose evidence that is prejudicial to their client unless such information is not privileged and is requested through proper discovery or the lawyer is obligated to do so by some special rule of law, such as the rules governing prosecutors.

The ethics rules specifically prohibit a lawyer from making a **false statement of law or fact**; offering **false evidence**; and not disclosing **adverse controlling authority** when opposing counsel fails to do so (Model Code 7-102, 7-106, and 7-109, and Model Rule 3.3(a) and 3.4(a) and (b)). A lawyer who discovers that false evidence has been submitted to the court must correct the fraud. The lawyer must call on the client to rectify the fraud or must reveal the fraud to the court unless the information is privileged. Lawyers are bound absolutely to reveal a nonclient's fraud on the court promptly. Some states' ethics rules allow or require disclosure of false statements made in court even if the information is protected by the privilege. Finally, lawyers may not obstruct access to evidence; alter, destroy, or conceal evidence; or falsify or allow others to falsify evidence.

Some **examples** may be instructive. In one disciplinary case, an attorney was censured for failing to disclose to arbitrators that a doctor had changed his diagnosis of the condition of the client. In another case, a court ordered a default judgment against a defendant whose attorney refused to produce a witness who had avoided service. In another, a federal court ordered a default in a race discrimination case against a corporate defendant for altering and destroying key documents, leaving critical information out of affidavits, blocking access in court to relevant information, and intimidating a witness. A corporate defendant was

159

sanctioned more than $1 million for withholding documents that were favorable to the plaintiff's case. The same company was sanctioned for discovery abuses in more than 15 cases in a three-year period, for violations that included altering a training tape, destroying photographs of a scene, and refusing to produce training manuals and security tapes. Other recent cases have involved a lawyer requesting that his client be released from custody to attend his mother's funeral after it had already been held; a lawyer providing false information on the value of a client's property; a lawyer conveying property with the intent to defraud a creditor; and the lawyers on both sides of a case being required to take an ethics course after they repeatedly made frivolous objections and misstated the law and the facts.

Perjury
Criminal offense of making false statements under oath

Client *perjury* is a difficult legal and ethical dilemma for lawyers. The courts are not uniform in their handling of client perjury, and ethics rules and their interpretations also vary from one jurisdiction to the next. As a general rule in a civil case, the lawyer who knows that his or her client intends to commit perjury should not call the client to testify. Most courts either recommend or mandate withdrawal from representation or disclosure to the court if the client testifies dishonestly.

Client perjury in criminal cases presents even more difficult problems because of the client's right to testify and to be represented by competent counsel. The U.S. Supreme Court has held that withdrawal is the appropriate action (*Nix v. Whiteside,* 475 U.S. 157 (1986)). However, withdrawal may not be permitted by the court at the time of trial, and authorities are split on whether the lawyer in this situation should disclose the client's intended perjury as the basis for withdrawal. Some courts endorse a process in which the lawyer allows the defendant to testify in narrative form without the attorney's help. After perjury has occurred, most courts require the lawyer to seek withdrawal. If withdrawal is not granted, some require disclosure of the perjury. The ABA Model Rules require the lawyer to take remedial measures, including disclosure to the court if necessary (Model Rules 3.3 (a)(3) and 3.3(b)).

Many lawyers believe that **client and witness perjury** is widespread. Cases in which judges have referred conduct to prosecutors for investigation of perjury have involved relatives testifying falsely as alibi witnesses; spouses hiding assets in marital dissolution cases; a defendant in a patent case falsifying notes about the invention at issue (which was uncovered by a paralegal); and police lying under oath about the circumstances of an arrest, a search and seizure, or an informant. Some commentators believe that this dishonesty is a natural consequence of the adversarial system. Judges and most lawyers lament this situation but believe that it is unlikely to stop because perjury is so hard to prove and so rarely prosecuted.

One aspect of candor that litigation paralegals often encounter in their work is the requirement that **adverse controlling authority** be disclosed to the court. A paralegal who finds adverse authority while conducting legal research must report the authority to the attorney and must include it in appropriate documents filed with the court. The lawyer and paralegal can decide how best to deal with the authority by using other lines of argument, or attempting to distinguish the case or cases legally or factually from the client's case. Judges who discover that controlling authority was not disclosed may sanction the lawyer and report him or her to the disciplinary authorities, whether the omission was intentional or the result of a lack of competence in research or drafting.

Remedies for destroying, altering, or suppressing evidence imposed by disciplinary bodies and the courts are supplemented by **obstruction of justice** statutes at both state and federal levels. In addition to criminal charges against the lawyer and client, these statutes often provide for sanctions in the pending case, such as default, fines, dismissal, legal fees and costs, and civil causes of action by the injured party. Destruction of evidence also gives rise in some jurisdictions to a civil cause of action for *spoliation*, in which the injured party can collect damages for substantial interference with the ability to prove a claim or defense because the evidence is no longer available. And in some states, courts allow an adverse inference to be drawn from a party's failure to produce the evidence.

Spoliation
Destruction of evidence that may result in a civil cause of action for damages for interference with the ability to prove a claim or defense

E.   Relationships and Communications with Judges

Making false statements about the qualifications or integrity of a judge or making such statements with reckless disregard for the truth is a violation of ethics. This rule covers false accusations against a judge (Model Code DR 8-102(A) and Model Rule 8.2(a)). In most jurisdictions, the courts have held that the First Amendment does not protect lawyers who criticize judges inappropriately because of the strong state interest in protecting public officials and in maintaining respect for the courts. However, in a few notable cases, discipline of lawyers who criticized judges has been struck down on appeal. In one such case, the lawyer called a judge an anti-Semite and a drunk. In the other, the lawyer called a local judge "a midget among giants" in a letter to a newspaper. However, lawyers have been disciplined for implying to a client that they can influence a judge.

Ethics rules prohibit lawyers from attempting to **influence** judges or from implying that they can influence a judge. A lawyer may not give or lend anything of value to a judge except a campaign contribution in jurisdictions where judges are elected, and may not seek to influence

Bribery
The crime of giving or receiving something of value as payment for an official act

a judge by any illegal means, an act that constitutes the crime of **bribery**. Knowingly assisting a judge in violating the law or the judicial canons is also an ethical violation in states that follow the ABA Model Rules (Model Rule 8.4(f)). Implying or stating that one can influence a judge (or other public official) is forbidden by ethics rules (Model Code DR 9-101(C) and Model Rule 8.4(e)). Judges are bound by their own ethical canons and rules of conduct in every jurisdiction, and provisions of these judicial canons parallel the rules governing lawyers' relationships with judges.

Ex parte
Action taken by or on behalf of a party without the presence of the opposing party

Paralegals working in litigation need to know about the prohibition on *ex parte* **communications** with judges. To ensure fairness in the adversary process, lawyers and paralegals are prohibited from having contact with the judge in a case without the presence of the opposing counsel. Such secret communications might give the communicating party an unfair advantage or give an appearance of influence or favoritism (Model Code DR 7-110(B) and Model Rule 3.5(b)). Exceptions to these rules are made for special **ex parte proceedings** that legally do not require opposing counsel's presence, such as petitions for a temporary restraining order. The NFPA Model Code calls attention to the rules regarding ex parte communications in EC 1.2(b).

F. Contact with Jurors

Ex parte communications with jurors and prospective jurors, before and during trial, are expressly prohibited by ethics rules to prevent influence and bribery (Model Code DR 7-108(A), (B) and Model Rule 3.5(a) and (b)). Lawyers are prohibited from such communications even if they are not involved in the case. A lawyer may not circumvent these rules by using an agent such as the client or a paralegal.

Mistrial
Trial terminated and declared void prior to the return of a verdict

In addition to disciplinary action for such conduct, a *mistrial* is likely to be declared if ex parte communications with jurors come to light. The lawyer's intent or lack of intent to influence a juror is not relevant. A lawyer's research on prospective jurors by using an investigator to contact them and ask them questions from a standard questionnaire has been held to be impermissible and led to the criminal conviction and disbarment of the lawyer in one case. Even simple socializing during a break in a trial has been held to be grounds to declare a mistrial and to disqualify counsel. **Jury tampering** is, of course, a crime in every jurisdiction and under federal laws.

Communicating with jurors after the conclusion of a trial is forbidden in some states. Other states do not prohibit **post-trial communications**, which attorneys may have to help them evaluate their presentations, to find out what influenced the jurors, and to ascertain whether the jury deliberated appropriately. Most states' ethics rules allow post-trial communications under the conditions that communications may not be made if prohibited by law or court order, if made merely to harass or embarrass the juror, or to influence his actions in future jury service (Model Code DR 7-108(D) and Model Rules 3.5(c) and 4.4(a)).

Finally, some states' ethics codes require a lawyer to reveal to the court improper conduct toward or among jurors (Model Code DR 7-108(G)).

G.   Contact with Parties and Represented Persons

Lawyers are prohibited from **communicating with parties who are represented by counsel** and may communicate directly with the represented person's counsel only (Model Code DR 7-104(A)(1) and Model Rule 4.2). This rule is based primarily on concerns about overreaching conduct designed to gain advantage over an opponent by disrupting the trust between the lawyer and client or influencing the client when he or she is vulnerable because counsel is not present. Unethical solicitation is also a related concern. The two generally accepted exceptions to the general prohibition against such communications are when the party's lawyer consents to the communication and when a court order or law authorizes the communication.

Additional exceptions to the general rule prohibiting communication with represented parties are also made for certain situations: (1) when the represented party is not truly adverse, (2) when the represented person is seeking a second opinion or new counsel, and (3) when the represented person is dissatisfied with his or her lawyer over the representation or fee and is considering taking action against the lawyer. It should be noted that this prohibition does not restrict the parties themselves, who are free to speak to each other, although most lawyers warn their clients not to do so because of the potential for such conversations interfering with the representation in the case. Finally, the restriction applies even if the party is the one who initiates the contact. Remedies during proceedings may include **suppression of evidence** and **disqualification** of counsel. Ethical sanctions would likely follow, especially if the conduct has involved blatant dishonesty.

A lawyer may not circumvent the rules prohibiting contact with represented parties by asking a paralegal to communicate with represented persons in violation of these rules, and paralegals should be aware not to have such communications, whether on their own initiative or at the instruction of a lawyer.

H.   Contact with Unrepresented Persons

Ethics rules restrict the communications a lawyer may have with a **party not represented by counsel**. Lawyers are prohibited from giving advice to such a person if there is a possibility that this third person's interests may conflict with the client's. However, lawyers may advise the person to secure counsel. The ABA and most states' rules also prohibit lawyers from **misrepresenting** their interest in the matter and require lawyers to clarify any misunderstanding about their role. (See Model Rule 4.3.) If a lawyer is opposing a person who is representing himself or herself, the lawyer may, of course, communicate with that person directly, but should take special care not to take advantage of the situation.

Applying rules about communications with unrepresented persons in a corporate environment requires special care. Paralegals sometimes need to interview **employees and former employees** about matters that are being litigated or may be litigated in the future. Most cases hold that a lawyer may speak to unrepresented former employees of a corporation on the opposing side of litigation unless the employees were privy to privileged information. Current employees may be classified as represented persons if the corporation provides counsel to them. Members of a class in a class action are also considered to be represented parties.

Lawyers may not circumvent these rules by **using an agent**, such as a paralegal. Paralegals should be very careful when speaking with unrepresented persons — for example, persons who are potential witnesses or parties. Paralegals must refrain from inadvertently or intentionally misleading persons not represented by counsel about their interest in a matter and from giving them advice. An ABA Formal Ethics Opinion has concluded that a lawyer is responsible for the improper ex parte contacts of an investigator under his or her supervision if the lawyer did not try to prevent the improper contacts, told the investigator to make them, or failed to tell the investigator not to make them once the contact came to light (ABA Formal Opinion 95-396 (1995)).

I.   Contact with Witnesses

A few special rules govern lawyers' contact with witnesses. The first category of witness-related rules concerns the communication between the attorney and the witness. A lawyer is forbidden from **advising or causing a witness to flee the jurisdiction** or to hide to avoid testifying (Model Code DR 7-109(B) and Model Rule 3.4(f)). In addition to violating ethics rules, such conduct constitutes **obstruction of justice** and violates statutes that make it a crime to tamper with a witness or to delay, hinder, or prevent a witness from testifying.

A lawyer may not advise a witness to testify falsely (Model Code DR 7-109(A) and Model Rule 3.4(b)). Giving **false testimony** under oath constitutes the crime of *perjury*, and counseling a witness to do so is also a crime, called *subornation of perjury*.

Lawyers and their employees can and do interview witnesses in depth to ascertain as exactly as possible the content and consistency of witnesses' testimony and their credibility. If a witness's story changes, opposing counsel may use the inconsistency to attack the accuracy of the information and to impeach the credibility of that witness.

Ethics rules do not prohibit lawyers from **preparing witnesses**, including clients, to testify effectively. A witness who is familiar with courtroom procedure and who knows what questions counsel and opposing counsel will ask is more likely to be consistent and clear and less likely to become confused when being examined by opposing counsel. However, paralegals who handle witness preparation must be careful not to encourage witnesses to give false testimony and not to overcoach witnesses, with the result that their testimony seems "prepared" and perhaps false.

Coaching witnesses too much can backfire. For example, in a large asbestos case, one of the plaintiffs' law firms prepared a detailed memorandum to clients telling them how to testify, including what to say about their injuries. When the defense counsel was inadvertently given a copy of this memorandum and exposed it to the court, the firm stopped sending it to the plaintiffs and blamed an overzealous paralegal for writing it. The judge reported the matter to disciplinary authorities, but no action was taken against the lawyers involved.

The line between preparing witnesses to give their testimony effectively and encouraging them to testify untruthfully must not be crossed. As noted above, **perjury** is rarely prosecuted and hard to prove, especially when the witness is also a client and their communications are privileged. But judges and juries may perceive the deception and will, at the very least, discount the witness's testimony.

Lawyers and paralegals are prohibited from **harassing witnesses**, both inside and outside the courtroom. Lawyers may not engage in any conduct with the sole purpose of embarrassing, harassing, degrading, or burdening a third person (Model Code DR 7-106(C)(2) and DR 7-102(A)(1); Model Rule 4.4(a)).

Related to these ethics prohibitions about communicating with nonclients are statutes that prohibit the **tape recording** of a person without his or her permission. For example, a federal statute provides criminal and civil remedies for interception and disclosure of wire, oral, or electronic communications (18 U.S.C. §2511 and 2520) and prohibits the use of such communications as evidence in any court (18 U.S.C. §2515). Not all jurisdictions prohibit secret tape recording

Subornation of perjury
Criminal offense of encouraging another to commit perjury

of conversations, and some states have endorsed the practice. However, an ABA advisory opinion recommends against it on ethical grounds (ABA Formal Opinion 331 (1974)). Lawyers and paralegals should be familiar with state statutes and ethics rules and opinions before taping.

Lawyers may **pay witnesses for expenses** related to testifying. The usual and permissible expenses are travel and lost wages. **Expert witnesses** may also be paid a reasonable fee for their professional services. No witness may be paid a fee or bonus that is contingent on the outcome of a case, as this would provide an incentive for false testimony (Model Code DR 7-109(C) and Comment [3] to Model Rule 3.4(b)).

As discussed in Section D above, with regard to client perjury, a lawyer has special duties to prevent the introduction of **false testimony** and to take corrective measures if a witness gives false testimony. The ethical dilemma presented by a witness's false testimony is not difficult to resolve when the witness is not a client. The lawyer does not have an ethical duty to a witness, even if the witness's testimony would favor the client, that outweighs the lawyer's duty of candor to the court. A lawyer who knows that a witness intends to testify falsely should advise the witness not to do so and should refuse to call the witness if he or she persists in intending to commit perjury. Once a witness gives false testimony, the lawyer must inform the court (Model Code DR 7-102(A)(4); Model Rule 3.3(a)(3)).

J. Trial Publicity

Balancing the **right of free expression** and the **right to a fair trial** is sometimes a significant challenge. The public interest in big cases and the pervasiveness of the media sometimes clash with the smooth administration of the court system and assurance of a fair trial, especially in criminal cases. This tension most visibly presents itself in sensational cases, especially those in which the press seeks a presence by having cameras in the courtroom or when a judge issues a *gag order*.

Gag order
Court-imposed order that restricts information or comment about a case

The ethics rules on trial publicity have been hotly debated and revised over the years. Early Model Code provisions were found **unconstitutional**; Model Rules were adopted in the 1980s and revised in the 1990s. All states have some version of the newer rules, which vary from state to state but, in general, provide that a lawyer must not make a public statement "if the lawyer knows or reasonably should know that it will have a **substantial likelihood of materially prejudicing** an adjudicative proceeding."

The ABA and most state ethics rules list the kinds of information that presumably would or would not be prejudicial in the comment to the rule. Many states have also adopted a provision that permits lawyers to make statements to protect their clients in response to publicity not generated by the lawyer or the client (Model Rule 3.6).

Although **disciplinary actions** against lawyers for violations of these provisions are relatively rare, they do occur, usually in sensational cases that are closely covered by the media. For example, the lawyer representing underworld figure John Gotti was held in contempt for statements made in his media campaign, particularly for statements perceived by the court as intended to frighten potential jurors. The defense lawyers in the O. J. Simpson case were investigated for statements made to the media about Los Angeles police officers framing their client and then covering up their effort to frame him, but no charges were brought. Some courts impose gag orders to prevent lawyers from making any statements, which are sometimes struck down as unconstitutional prior restraints on speech.

Lawyer conduct in high-profile cases involves not only ethics principles but impacts public opinion about lawyers. Some polls have shown that a majority of people view lawyers more negatively because of their high profile in the media. Most people believe that lawyers use the media to influence opinion about their cases, and many believe that this conduct is inappropriate and unethical. However, there is also ample evidence that jurors are not influenced by the "trial in the press." Jury selection procedures are designed to screen out jurors who may have prejudged cases because of reports in the media, and jury sequestration protects against influence from reports in the media.

Paralegals should not allow themselves to be used by lawyers to circumvent the rules on trial publicity. Some states' ethics codes have a provision that requires lawyers to exercise reasonable care to prevent employees and associates from making prohibited statements. Model Code 7-108(J) and Model Rule 3.8(f) set forth prosecutors' duties to prevent employees from making unethical extrajudicial statements. A lawyer is responsible for such conduct under the general rules governing a lawyer's responsibility for acts of employees (Model Rule 5.3).

K.   Special Rules for Prosecutors

As representatives of the government and the people, prosecutors have a **special duty of truth and fairness** in the administration of justice. Prosecutors must seek not only to convict, but also to seek justice and to ensure that all citizens are afforded their rights. Ethics rules in all jurisdictions establish these obligations, and local laws frequently impose additional requirements.

One critical duty of the prosecutor is to not institute unsupported criminal charges and to not continue to pursue an unsupported action: **probable cause** is required (Model Code DR 7-103(A); Model Rule 3.8(a)). The rules also prevent prosecutors from abusing their discretion in prosecuting cases by singling out someone for prosecution on a discriminatory basis. Finally, prosecutors are required to **disclose information** that tends to negate or mitigate guilt or to reduce punishment (Model Code DR 7-103(B); Model Rule 3.8(d)).

Most states have ethics rules that require prosecutors to make reasonable efforts to see that accused persons know of their **right to counsel** and have an opportunity to secure counsel; not to obtain a waiver of rights from an unrepresented accused; and to exercise reasonable care to prevent employees and others involved with the prosecution from making prohibited *extrajudicial* statements (Model Rule 3.8(b) and (c)). Rules also limit a prosecutor's right to subpoena a lawyer to testify about a client or former client. A prosecutor may subpoena a lawyer only if the information sought is not privileged, is essential to the case and not otherwise available, and there is no other feasible way to obtain the information sought (Model Rule 3.8(e)). For additional guidance on ethical issues in the criminal area, see the ABA Standards for Criminal Justice, which include separate sections on the prosecutorial and defense functions.

Extrajudicial
An act that takes place outside the presence of the judge or jury

In addition to disciplinary sanctions for violations of the special rules for prosecutors, courts may impose remedies in a pending case if the defendant's constitutional rights have been violated. A court may reverse a conviction, suppress evidence, dismiss charges, or order a new trial. For example, in more than one case a murder conviction has been reversed on appeal when the appellate court found prosecutorial misconduct, including misrepresenting the law and the facts and intimidating witnesses. In two other recent cases, courts found prosecutors to have engaged in unethical conduct when one mistated the defendant's testimony and said that the defendant had been counseled to lie and in another when the lawyer spoke in the "voice" of the victim during closing arguments.

REVIEW QUESTIONS

1. Why do paralegals have to know about the rules governing advocacy?
2. What are the remedies for unethical conduct in litigation setting? Who imposes these remedies?
3. What is zealous representation, and what other ethics rules does it sometimes conflict with?
4. Define unmeritorious or frivolous claims, and give examples.
5. When can a lawyer make a claim that is not warranted under existing law?
6. What is the duty to investigate a client's story before filing an action?
7. Give examples of abuses of the discovery process. What are the possible consequences for the lawyer?

8. Give an example of an unethical delay. What other ethics violations might be involved in an unnecessary delay?

9. Name the remedies or sanctions that might result from bringing unmeritorious claims, abusing discovery, or causing unnecessary delays.

10. Under what circumstances may an action for malicious prosecution be brought? Abuse of process?

11. What kinds of sanctions may a court impose for unwarranted, delaying, or harassing actions? On whom are they imposed?

12. Give examples of actions by lawyers that would be disruptive in the courtroom. What do the ethics rules prohibiting such disruptions say? For what reasons might a lawyer be disruptive?

13. What is the most immediate remedy for disruptive conduct in the courtroom or disobedience of a court order?

14. What kinds of actions are prohibited and required by a lawyer's duty of candor?

15. What must a lawyer do if he or she discovers that a nonclient witness has given false testimony? What if the false testimony is given by a client in a civil case? In a criminal case?

16. What should a paralegal do if he or she discovers adverse controlling authority in the course of research?

17. What might happen if a lawyer presents false evidence or permits false testimony in court?

18. What are the rules governing lawyers' relationships with judges?

19. May a lawyer give a judge a gift? What if they are good friends?

20. Why are lawyers and their employees prohibited from having ex parte communications with judges?

21. What kinds of contact with jurors are prohibited by the ethics rules and why? What crime might be involved when a lawyer or paralegal tries to influence a juror?

22. What are the general rules about lawyers and their agents having contact with persons who already have a lawyer? Why? What are the exceptions?

23. What is the general rule about contact with persons who are not represented by counsel? What if the person makes the contact?

24. What must paralegals do when they are communicating with witnesses?

25. What actions might constitute harassing a witness? What crime (or crimes) might be committed in addition to violations of ethics rules?

26. May a lawyer pay a witness to testify? What are the applicable restrictions?

27. May a lawyer pay an expert witness? May the lawyer pay the witness more if the client wins?

28. What two important constitutional interests are being balanced in the ethics rules on trial publicity?

29. What kinds of extrajudicial statements are generally permitted by ethics rules? What kinds are prohibited?
30. May a lawyer have a paralegal speak to the press and reveal information about a pending case that the lawyer could not reveal under the ethics rules? Why or why not?
31. Why are prosecutors bound by additional ethics rules? Name four ethical duties that prosecutors have that other lawyers do not have.
32. What sanctions and remedies may be imposed for prosecutorial misconduct?

HYPOTHETICALS

1. Donna Duggan is a paralegal working for a criminal defense firm, Crane & Cook. She often interviews clients to gather facts and to assist in preparing them for trial. During one such interview, client Tommy Thorton, who has been charged with a number of crimes relating to a bank robbery, says, "I wasn't even there! Put me on the stand and I will tell the judge and jury!" Donna does not believe this because she has seen a videotape of the robbery and one of the perpetrators looks exactly like Tommy. In addition, all the bank tellers identified him in a lineup. What should Donna say to Tommy? What should she tell Calvin Crane, the lawyer handling the case? Later in the interview, Tommy says, "My mom and my sister will testify that they were with me at home watching television." What should Donna do with this piece of information?

2. Evan Eldridge is a paralegal working for Matilda Moniker, who handles lots of small lawsuits that often go to trial. Matilda asks Evan to contact opposing counsel in six cases and to tell them that she is ill and cannot take depositions as scheduled. Then she asks Evan to draft requests for continuances in three other cases, also based on her illness. Evan knows that Matilda is not ill and suspects that she is delaying the discovery process and trials because the suits are weak and she is overworked. Matilda later confides over drinks that she thinks the cases will have a better chance of settling with the delays. Is Matilda doing anything unethical? What should Evan do?

3. Fanny Franks, a litigation paralegal, is working for a large law firm defending the Oxxon oil refinery in a big toxic tort case. Fanny is in charge of the document productions and responses to discovery. George Gunderson, one of the lawyers on the case, tells her not to answer about two-thirds of the interrogatories that have been propounded and to draft objections to the rest based on irrelevance and privilege. Fanny reviews the interrogatories and sees only two that might be objectionable. She believes that George wants to make

these objections to wear down the opposition. Opposing counsel is a small law firm that is handling only this one case at the moment because the case is so big. Its existence depends on winning, and it currently has no other revenue. What should Fanny do? A few weeks later, Fanny is preparing the documents that will go to opposing counsel on a document production. She notices that a key internal memorandum from an employee to management about the toxicity levels at the site in question is missing from the documents she has been working with. What should she do?

4. Hanna Hanson, the chief trial lawyer for Hanson & Harding, asks paralegal James Jameson to accompany her to trial. When she arrives, she sees that the opposing counsel has two other lawyers with him. She tells James not to say anything that might reveal that he is a paralegal, not a lawyer, because she doesn't want to appear to be "outgunned." Hanna seats James at the counsel table and introduces him as her "associate." Has Hanna done anything wrong? What should James do? Hanna has a reputation for being a very zealous advocate. During the first day at trial, while the opposing counsel is making opening statements, she starts giggling and shaking her head. Later, when a damaging witness is being examined, she asks him what his IQ is and where he gets his clothes, both of which are not relevant to his testimony. Has she done anything wrong? What do you think the judge should do? What should James do? What if Hanna makes faces and rolls her eyes at James and giggles when opposing counsel is talking?

5. Larry Lemon is a family law paralegal working for Matthew & Morrison. One especially difficult divorce case they are working on is the Tyson divorce. The husband and wife don't have that much money and they have four kids. They are using all their money to pay attorneys and at this rate will be deeply in debt by the time the divorce is final. The lead lawyer, Marilyn Matthew, asks Larry to call the opposing party, Tim Tyson, to try to set up a meeting between Tim and his wife, their client, Tina Tyson. Marilyn says, "I know these two could work this out without all this expense if they just sit down without all these other people around." Should Larry do this? Later that day, while Larry is trying to decide what to do, Tim himself calls and asks for Tina's new home phone number, saying, "I just want to call and talk to her. I want to settle this thing between us without all the lawyers." Should Larry give him the number? What should he do?

6. Monica Middlebrook is a paralegal for the U.S. Attorney's office. Lawyer Nat Nottingham asks Monica to call Erik Ellington, a target in a major organized crime investigation, to see if she can "sweet talk" him into meeting her for an interview. Erik has a reputation as a "ladies' man" and is always accompanied by his lawyer and

bodyguards. Should Monica make the call? Later, during the trial, Nat tells Monica to copy and mail some documents to a crime reporter for the local newspaper. Among the documents is a copy of an anonymous letter to Erik from a woman named Sunny. The letter refers to a romantic tryst between the two of them and makes allusions to their using illegal drugs. Should Monica follow Nat's instructions? If not, what should she do?

7. Shane Samuels is a litigation paralegal working for the ImTox Corporation. Shane is asked to interview some employees who may know something about improper disposal of toxic waste. During his interview with Rachel Robinson, a truck driver, Rachel breaks down and starts crying and says, "All the guys cheat on the rules when they get rid of that stuff. Lately they have been putting it in my truck and going off to have beers. I was late getting home to my sick kid last night, so I just drove to the pier and dumped it in the bay." Shane knows Rachel can be charged with a crime for this act and that the corporation has not indicated that it will represent her. He also knows that if the crime is pinned on her and other employees who acted without the corporation's knowledge, the corporation may escape liability. What should Shane do?

DISCUSSION QUESTIONS AND PROJECTS

1. Why are there proportionately more litigation paralegals than trial lawyers?
2. Are you surprised that lawyers have duties that temper their duty to represent clients zealously?
3. What would you do if you interviewed a client who told you a story that you did not fully believe, and, on telling your supervising attorney, he or she told you to draft a complaint on the client's behalf based solely on the client's story?
4. How would you respond if your supervising attorney asked you to prepare a bankruptcy petition that you knew was unwarranted and designed solely to stop a foreclosure proceeding against your client?
5. Why are court-imposed sanctions such a powerful remedy for abuses in pleading and discovery?
6. Does your jurisdiction have rules or statutes comparable to federal Rule 11 and the other federal rules cited in this chapter?
7. How would you respond if the supervising lawyer asked you to shred documents that you knew were discoverable?
8. How would you handle adverse authority found in researching a case if you believe that it is not controlling?
9. Do you believe that the adversary system encourages perjury? Contact the local, federal, or state prosecutors and interview several

lawyers for their opinions on the matter and ask them how many prosecutions for perjury have been brought in recent years.

10. What would you do if your attorney-employer asked you to invite a judge who was serving in one of your cases to a social event you were planning? What would you do if your attorney-employer asked you to try to find out what a judge who was a friend of yours was thinking about a pending case?

11. Do you think lawyers and their employees should be prohibited from giving campaign contributions to judges?

12. What would you do if your supervisor asked you to give a sealed note to a juror during a recess?

13. Does your state have an ethics rule that governs communication with jurors after trial? Do you think lawyers should be able to interview jurors after a trial is over? Why or why not?

14. Why are lawyers not involved in a case prohibited from talking to jurors about the case?

15. What would you do if a co-plaintiff who was not represented by your firm contacted you to discuss changing lawyers? What if the party wanted to discuss the merits of the case? The performance of his or her lawyer?

16. What would you do if you were interviewing a potential witness who did not have an attorney, and you suddenly realized that he seemed to believe that you and your firm were representing him?

17. Suppose that one of your duties as a litigation paralegal is to prepare witnesses for trial. What would you do if you were preparing a witness and his or her story kept changing? What if the witness seemed to be changing his or her version of the facts to be more favorable to you? Suppose the witness, although generally favorable to your client, has some information that is adverse to your client. What do you tell the witness about how to handle this information while he or she is on the stand?

18. What would you do if you discovered that a client was sending anonymous threatening letters to a witness who planned to testify against her? Would it make any difference if you knew the witness's testimony would be false?

19. Does your jurisdiction have a statute that prohibits or limits the tape recording of conversations? What does it say about permission from the party or parties? About the admissibility of illegally tape-recorded conversations?

20. What would you do if your firm paid a witness, who was not an expert, a witness fee that was three times his normal salary?

21. Review the rules governing a lawyer's handling of client perjury. Do you think a lawyer should be bound to tell the court if her client commits perjury? Would you answer differently in criminal and civil cases? What does your jurisdiction's ethics rule say? Are there any cases on the issue in your jurisdiction?

22. What does your jurisdiction's ethics code say about extrajudicial statements or trial publicity? Do you think the rule strikes the right balance between free speech and fair trial? Have any lawyers in your jurisdiction been disciplined under the rule?

23. What would you do if your attorney-employer asked you to leak information to the press that you know is prohibited by ethics rules? Would it make any difference if you were certain that without press coverage of this information your client would be unfairly convicted of a serious crime?

24. Suppose you work for the local prosecuting attorney. What would you do if you uncovered information that proved a criminal defendant in a case was innocent? What if you went to the supervising attorney and he refused to drop the charges or to turn over the exculpatory evidence to the defendant's counsel?

25. What would you do if your supervisor, the prosecuting attorney, asked you to obtain a statement from a recently arrested person, and in doing so you discovered that the person had not been advised of her right to counsel? What if the accused had been advised of her right to counsel but had not yet been able to reach an attorney?

26. Obtain a copy of your state judicial canons and compare the relevant provisions to those for lawyers covered in this chapter.

SELECTED CASES

Chira v. Lockheed, 634 F.2d 664 (2d Cir. 1980) (case dismissed when lawyer and client refuse to move forward with discovery).

Crane v. State Bar of California, 30 Cal. 3d 117, 635 P.2d 163, 177 Cal. Rptr. 670 (1981) (sanctions for altering document and sending unethical threatening letter to represented party).

Eaton v. Fink, 697 N.E.2d 490 (Ind. Ct. App. 1998) (paralegal reveals lawyer-supervisor's presentation of false evidence and lawyer's defamation against her is dismissed).

Gentile v. Nevada State Bar, 501 U.S. 1030 (1990) (questions constitutionality of certain provisions of ethics rules on trial publicity).

In re Ositis, 40 P.3d 500 (Or. 2002) (lawyer disciplined for directing an investigator to pose as a journalist to interview a witness and possible adverse party).

In re White, 121 Cal. App. 4th 1453 (2004) (monetary sanctions and disgorgement of fees for filing frivolous habeas corpus writs produced by a mill where law students were unsupervised and other ethical violations were rampant).

Jorgenson v. County of Volusia, 846 F.2d 1350 (11th Cir. 1988) (sanctions for intentional failure to cite controlling authority).

Massey v. Prince George's County, 907 F. Supp. 138 (D. Md. 1995) (sanctions for failure of both sides to cite controlling authority).

Mississippi Bar v. Attorney ST, 621 So. 2d 229 (Miss. 1993) (endorses secret tape recording).

Omaha Bank v. Siouxland Cattle Cooperative, 305 N.W.2d 458 (Iowa 1981) (retrial after lawyers and jurors had drinks together during trial).

SELECTED REFERENCES

ABA Model Rules 3.1 through 3.9 [advocacy]

ABA Model Code Disciplinary Rules 2-109, 5-102, 7-102 [meritorious claims and defenses]

ABA Model Code Disciplinary Rules 1-102, 7-102, 7-106, 7-109 [candor]

ABA Model Code Disciplinary Rules 1-102, 7-106, 7-109 [fairness]

ABA Model Code Disciplinary Rules 7-107, 7-108, 7-109, 7-110, 8-101 [impartiality and decorum]

ABA Model Code Disciplinary Rule 7-107 [trial publicity]

ABA Model Code Disciplinary Rule 7-103 [prosecutors]

ABA Model Code Disciplinary Rule 7-104 [communication with represented and unrepresented persons]

NFPA Model Code of Ethics and Professional Responsibility, EC 1.2(a) [ex parte communications]

NFPA Model Code of Ethics and Professional Responsibility, EC 1.2(b) [communications with represented persons]

NFPA Model Code of Ethics and Professional Responsibility, DR 1.3 and EC 1.3(a) [decorum]

Professionalism and Special Issues for Paralegals

This chapter gives an overview of issues and challenges in professionalism that face paralegals today. Chapter 9 covers:

- the role of paralegals in the legal profession
- definition of professionalism
- special issues for paralegals, including

  - regulation of the occupation
  - paralegal education
  - utilization
  - overtime compensation
  - gender and related issues

- paralegal participation in pro bono activities

A.   The State of Professionalism in the Legal Field

A poor public image has plagued the legal profession for the last three decades. The involvement of lawyers in major corporate and political **scandals** has made the legal profession the target of criticism in the media and among the public.

Many people believe that society has become more **litigious.** Lawyers — and what many people consider an oversupply of them — have been blamed for the increase in litigation and in the size of judgments in civil cases. The public looks to the law to solve many of its problems, sometimes social and personal ones that in days past would have been dealt with in other ways. Public opinion polls show that lawyers rate well below most other occupations in the areas of honesty and integrity. Many clients polled believe that lawyers are **greedy,** unethical, hard to communicate with, and lacking in compassion and respect for others. The high salaries paid to lawyers — both new lawyers right out of law school and top corporate lawyers — have shocked and dismayed many Americans, who believe that such pay is unwarranted and out of proportion to the value of the work that lawyers do. High fee awards and ever-increasing hourly rates, now more than $1,000 for some lawyers, add to the perception of lawyers as overpaid and greedy.

Related is the public perception that lawyers manipulate the legal process, finding clever ways to circumvent the law to prevail. This goal of winning at all costs has made many lawyers seem like contentious and **overzealous** abusers of the system. Lawyers' involvement in highly publicized criminal cases, in the development of government policies on matters like torture, and in many business scandals have validated public opinion that lawyers' knowledge and skills are for sale to the highest bidder and that lawyers will not hesitate to use their talents to line their client's or their own pockets, whatever the cost to the public. Despite the poor regard in which lawyers are held, many clients seek out and expect "attack dog" behavior when they need legal representation. A related client complaint is that lawyers are too chummy with one another; some clients complain when their lawyers extend professional courtesies such as continuances to opposing counsel.

Lawyers recognize their poor image and acknowledge problems that trouble lawyers and the practice of law. Some studies estimate that at least half the lawyers disciplined for misconduct are **"impaired,"** usually because of some type of substance abuse. Law firms have become very "bottom-line-oriented," building in size and salary at astronomical rates and sometimes placing horrendous pressure on lawyers to bill an unrealistically high number of hours. This pressure leads many lawyers to inflate or pad bills, especially bills of wealthy clients. Higher **legal bills** drive clients away, creating a cycle of competitiveness and ever-higher billable hours. These conditions undermine firm **loyalty,** which once held most lawyers to one firm for their entire career. Lawyers commonly move several times and even prominent senior partners leave their firms for better opportunities. The overwhelming sense of law practice as a business first, a profession second, has caused great turnover and instability in law firms, which themselves dissolve and merge frequently.

Finally, the competitiveness and zeal of lawyers has led to **abuses** of the system, such as those described in Chapter 8. Many lawyers treat the litigation process as a game where tactics and strategy are more important than merit and substance. Bringing frivolous cases and motions, flooding an opponent with irrelevant and unwarranted discovery, and behaving discourteously and disrespectfully to other lawyers and even to judges have become the daily method of operation for some lawyers. Lawyers have hidden evidence of the harmful effects of smoking, backdated stock options, and misused consumer protection laws to shake down small business.

The bar and the press report stories monthly of lawyers charged with criminal conduct, often in relationship to their clients. Embezzlement, insider trading, and fraud by lawyers are not unheard of. Some prosecuting attorneys have created divisions to centralize prosecutions of judges, lawyers, and others working in the justice system. But lawyers are not the only ones in the legal profession to engage in improper conduct. Paralegals have been charged with embezzlement and insider trading in a couple of well-publicized cases. In one case, a paralegal and a lawyer were charged with attempting to defraud mortgage companies of millions of dollars.

Historically, there have been relatively few instances where lawyers openly reported misconduct within their law firms despite the **"snitch" rules** that are contained in most states' ethics rules. (See ABA Model Rule 8.3(a), which requires lawyers to report violations of ethics rules that raise a substantial question about a lawyer's honesty, trustworthiness, or fitness to practice.) Firms usually handle these matters internally and privately; however, they cannot always keep the lid on violations. Most courts that have addressed the matter hold that attorneys who report violations as required by the codes cannot be fired for these actions. A few states also have **whistleblower statutes** that protect employees from being discharged in retaliation for reporting violations. It should be noted that the NFPA Model Code requires paralegals to report ethical and legal violations under DR 1.3.

Snitch rules
Rules requiring lawyers to report unethical conduct

Whistleblower statutes
Protect employees and others from retaliation for reporting violations

The organized bar has attempted to address these problems in the legal community and to prove that the legal profession can regulate itself effectively in a variety of ways. Disciplinary systems that have been found lacking have been revamped. Bar-sponsored programs for impaired lawyers are found in every state. Court rules and statutes limit discovery and provide for severe sanctions against lawyers for abuse. Bar associations have launched public relations and professionalism campaigns to improve their image.

The organized bar encourages lawyers to engage in pro bono work and to support local charities and community activities. State and local bar associations and some courts have adopted codes of professional courtesy and civility or litigation guidelines, which advise lawyers how to conduct themselves.

Professionalism **guidelines** typically cover:

- client relations (including communicating frequently, advising mediation, resolving matters expeditiously, and not overcharging)
- relations with other lawyers and parties (including acting courteously, not engaging in delay or unmeritorious tactics, cooperating in scheduling and resolving disputes, not disparaging other lawyers, and not harassing the opposition)
- relations with courts (including advocating vigorously but with civility, being punctual, and being honest with the court)
- duty to the public and the profession (including keeping current in practice areas, supporting the profession, and upholding the profession's image)

Litigation guidelines usually contain rules covering continuances, extensions, service of process, communication with adversaries, discovery, and motions. They specify conduct that is courteous and honest and not designed to harass or unduly burden opponents.

Among the other recommendations to address these professional concerns coming from the organized bar are improvements in undergraduate education in **ethics,** teaching ethics and professionalism across the curriculum in law school, more aggressive judicial intervention in litigation, and more pro bono and public interest work. Some local bars offer client relations programs that attempt to improve lawyers' attitudes toward and treatment of clients. Increasingly, the conversation about these issues turns to the matter of morality and ethics in law practice. Ethicists have advocated that lawyers should examine the ethical and moral content of their actions and avoid separating their values and beliefs as persons from their conduct as lawyers.

Many lawyers have left the profession because of the problems that characterize law practice today. Some surveys show that as many as half the lawyers in practice would not become lawyers if they had it to do all over again. Some firms have started to deal with **quality of life issues** by creating counseling programs for troubled lawyers, providing part-time and flexible scheduling options, encouraging sabbaticals, increasing pro bono work, and establishing law firm cultures that place more value on collegiality and give lawyers and staff more time for their private lives. Legal newspapers publish surveys rating the satisfaction of associates working in the major firms, which provides incentive for firms to be good work places. Some firms have an inhouse ethics specialist or committee to help lawyers with ethical dilemmas and have established one-on-one or small group mentoring for new lawyers and paralegals to mitigate the negative effects of working in isolation and to build collegiality and trust.

Many studies have shown that lawyers are much more likely than people in other occupations to be alcoholics or substance abusers. Also, as noted in Chapter 7, there is also a strong correlation between disciplinary actions and substance abuse or emotional problems. In the last decade, many bar associations have been proactive in developing "legal assistance" programs to identify and help lawyers who are impaired before the impairment leads to unethical and destructive conduct.

Burnout and stress are major factors in conduct that lead to discipline. The pressures of billable hours, the competitive environment of the legal world, the lack of loyalty among clients and law firms, the constant burden of meeting other peoples' needs, the feeling of not having any control: All these factors contribute to burnout, detachment from relationships with others, loss of job satisfaction, and even chronic anger and anxiety.

This troubled milieu is the one in which paralegals find themselves working. These concerns, voiced both by the public and within the profession, affect the way in which paralegals are viewed and view themselves. A paralegal can be part of the problem — working for a firm that utilizes paralegals' talents principally to abuse the legal process and to accumulate wealth — or part of the solution — working for a firm that utilizes paralegals' talents to improve efficiency, to perform work competently and ethically, and to lower the cost of legal services to its clients. In the coming years, as the problems plaguing the profession and the proposals to solve them begin to shape a new image for law practice, paralegals can help determine what their image will be in that picture.

B.   Professionalization of the Paralegal Occupation

Paralegals are in a sometimes difficult and **ambiguous position** in the legal profession. Because they are not lawyers, they may not legally engage in certain activities carved out exclusively for lawyers. But they do engage in substantive legal work that otherwise would have to be done by lawyers and that is paid for by the client. The line between permissible and impermissible conduct is not always clear. Paralegals are part of the professional staff engaging in legal work, not part of the support staff, but they can never be full and equal partners in the law firm.

The parameters of paralegal job responsibilities are not clearly defined; evolve to meet client needs, new technology, and changes in the law and procedure; and vary from firm to firm.

The paralegal's role is not universally well understood, either by those in the legal profession or by the general public. Paralegals frequently must explain to lay persons what they do, even while they recognize that their role in legal services is evolving. Complicating this situation has been the increased use of the title "legal assistant" for legal secretaries and administrative assistants who do not do paralegal work. This phenomenon has driven most associations and many individual paralegals to favor the title "paralegal."

The dilemma posed by occupational ambiguity has many ramifications for the daily work lives of paralegals. The overriding question is how paralegals can forge a role for themselves — a professional role that holds them to high standards of ethics and performance while affording them the opportunity for long, satisfying, and challenging careers. Defining "professionalism" is an essential first step in this process.

Dictionaries define "profession" as an occupation that involves a special education and requires mental rather than manual labor. Sociologists define the term as an occupation whose members have the exclusive right to engage in certain activities that are intellectual in nature and require special education. Professions are bound by codes of ethics and are generally self-regulating. Philosophers tend to define *profession* as a calling that requires a special commitment to public service.

Legal paraprofessionals
Persons who perform legal work under the supervision of a lawyer

Paralegals usually are classified as ***paraprofessionals*** — that is, they perform legal work under the supervision of a lawyer but do not have the special education nor share in the societal prestige of the lawyer. Analogous to the paralegal are the many paraprofessionals in the allied health fields — for example, physical therapists, physician's assistants, and dental assistants.

The paralegal field has some characteristics that inhibit its **professionalization.** For example, many law firms do not require formal paralegal training, adopting nonuniform and sometimes substandard hiring qualifications. On the other hand, paralegals who have a formal education, frequently a baccalaureate degree and/or postgraduate certificate, find themselves overtrained for many of the tasks that they perform and unable to utilize fully their knowledge and skills. Prestige for paralegals is found mainly in the reflected prestige of the lawyers for whom they work. Paralegals' status is enhanced when law firms treat them well, affording them a meaningful career path and appropriate perquisites; alternatively, paralegals' status may be undermined by poor treatment.

Paralegals sometimes do not share a **common bond** with their paralegal colleagues, in part because they lack a shared educational experience such as that of lawyers and doctors. Aggravating this lack of bond is the fact that many paralegals view themselves as competitors within their firms, vying for the most interesting work and highest pay. Paralegals sometimes express their primary loyalty to the firm or to their supervising attorney, not to their chosen occupation. Many paralegals work in small or midsized firms where they may be the only paralegal, lending to their feelings of **isolation** from others. On the other hand, paralegal associations have been quite successful in building a strong sense of camaraderie and shared interests and responsibilities among their members.

Considerable progress has been made in the professionalization of the paralegal occupation. Levels of education, both general and specialized paralegal education, are rising. The duties paralegals are performing have greatly broadened and include more client contact and more sophisticated work. When surveyed, most firms report an expansion of paralegal duties and increasing dependence on paralegals. Billing rates and salaries are up. All four of the national associations that serve paralegals have certification programs to promote high levels of competence and recognition of paralegals. Voluntary state bar and state court certification programs have slowly started to take hold.

Many states have examined **regulation** of the paralegal occupation but few have made any meaningful progress toward a true regulatory scheme. Regulation now exists under state law in California, and other states have court rules or statutes that define and limit the use of "paralegal" and comparable titles. Many see regulation as a necessary step in the evolution of the profession, to distinguish it from other law-related positions and to give it enhanced and deserved prestige. (See Chapter 1 for a discussion of regulation.)

Persons entering the legal profession as paralegals should think carefully about and commit to certain kinds of values and attitudes that will serve them well and will guide them in their conduct as professionals. Building on ideas about the meaning of a profession that are commonly accepted in society, the following nine points comprise a list of qualities to which professional paralegals should dedicate themselves.

1. Commitment to Public Service

Paralegals should always remember that their highest goal is to assist in the delivery of legal services to the public — legal services that are delivered ethically, competently, and efficiently. In addition to being part of their daily work lives, this commitment also requires paralegals to engage in activities, such as pro bono programs, that improve the system of delivery of legal services overall. See Section D below for more on pro bono work.

2. Commitment to Education

Fulfilling this commitment includes participating in formal education, continuing education, and on-the-job learning that enhances knowledge and skills and continually develops the paralegal's potential. Education heightens the paralegal's ability to deliver quality legal services and enriches long-term career satisfaction.

3. Commitment to the Highest Standards of Ethical Conduct

Paralegals must know the rules of ethics that bind lawyers and paralegals and understand how these rules apply to them. Paralegals also must develop their own personal standards of ethics and morality that reach beyond the minimums imposed by law. Paralegals must be scrupulously honest in their relations with clients, courts, lawyers, and co-workers.

4. Commitment to Excellence

Paralegals must set high standards of performance for themselves and seek to meet those standards in all the work they undertake. They should approach each task with an attitude of seriousness and apply all their knowledge, skill, and talent to accomplish their work.

5. Commitment to the Paralegal Profession

Paralegals must view themselves as part of a common occupation, with interests and goals that are shared by other paralegals. They must support paralegal activities organized through professional associations, bar associations, and alumni associations. Paralegals must also engender collegiality with their colleagues, mentoring new paralegals and acting as role models and providing information and encouragement for those who aspire to the paralegal profession.

6. Commitment to a Strong Work Ethic

Paralegals must strive to do their best on every task and serve the clients of their firms diligently. They should be meticulous and thorough, organized in their work process, prompt in meeting deadlines, and always do more than the minimum. They should take pride in their work and always do work that merits that pride.

7. Commitment to Acting with Integrity and Honor

Paralegals must be courteous, respectful, and fair in their dealings with lawyers, other paralegals, support staff, clients, and others both within and outside their place of employment. They must demonstrate maturity, patience, and thoughtfulness in their actions, avoiding gossip, undue criticism of others, prejudice, and favoritism. This commitment also requires paralegals to show sensitivity to the needs and talents of others, appreciation for the differences in people's backgrounds, tolerance, helpfulness, and recognition and acknowledgment of the achievements of others.

8. Commitment to the Development of the Whole Person

Paralegals must not become so consumed by their work that they neglect the other aspects of their life, like family, friends, health, and personal interests and activities. They should seek to be well-rounded persons, with a variety of interests. Commitment to a profession need not prevent a person from leading a full life; in fact, a person who narrows his or her interests to work alone will not be as effective in relations with others and will not possess the sense of proportion and balance needed to fulfill his or her commitments as a professional.

9. Commitment to Exercising Good Judgment, Common Sense, and Communication Skills

Paralegals must use their understanding of human nature as a guide in their relations with others. They must listen to others carefully and communicate, both orally and in writing, clearly and persuasively.

C. Current Issues in Professionalism

1. Regulation

Regulation is central to the debate about the evolution of the paralegal field. Discussed in Chapter 1, regulation presents a complex set of issues that cannot be easily resolved. Within the profession, consensus does not exist about the need for and value of regulation, let alone about what such a plan should look like. The idea of regulating raises these difficult questions:

* Is there a need for regulation?
* Who should be regulated?
* Who should do the regulating?
* Should regulation be mandatory or voluntary?
* What level of regulation is appropriate?
* What educational requirements should be established?
* What kind of examination, if any, should be required?
* What, if any, tasks should paralegals be authorized to perform only if they are regulated?

2. Education

Education is another critical issue for paralegals. The lack of consistency in hiring standards and in uniformity of the curriculum offered by different schools prevents paralegals from having a shared body of knowledge and a shared educational experience, two important characteristics that distinguish occupations from professions. The lack of common educational experience also inhibits the development of collegiality among paralegals.

However, the diversity of offerings within paralegal education and the variety of pathways into the field have allowed the paralegal profession to flourish and to serve many needs in the legal world. Paralegals have a continuously expanding bank of job responsibilities, unhindered by a standardized, limiting education that trains everyone to perform the same tasks. The vastly varied work and life experiences that are brought to the profession by the wide variety of people who become paralegals have enriched both the career possibilities and legal profession itself.

As indicated earlier, educational achievement among paralegals is rising. Whereas the ABA and the American Association for Paralegal Education endorse two years of college as a minimum for entry into the paralegal field, IPMA, representing corporate counsel offices and large law firms, favors a four-year degree. Paralegal educators and paralegal associations continue to discuss appropriate minimal and aspirational levels of education for paralegals and the competencies that should be required of them.

3. Utilization and Treatment

The ambiguity that accompanies the development of a new profession has resulted in both underutilization of paralegals and disparities in the way that paralegal services are utilized. Even now, nearly 40 years after the advent of the modern American paralegal system, many lawyers still resist using paralegal services, especially those lawyers in small firms who believe that they cannot afford paralegals. Although all large law firms, corporate law departments, and most midsized firms employ paralegals, an estimated two-thirds of sole practitioners and small firms do not use the services of paralegals. Some lawyers do not understand how to utilize paralegals' talents and skills or are reluctant to delegate anything more than routine or repetitive work. Paralegals report that the lack of challenging work is a primary reason for job dissatisfaction, job changes, and paralegals leaving the profession.

Some lawyers and law firms treat their paralegals poorly — by not compensating them fairly, by not providing appropriate working conditions and clerical support, or by not giving them recognition when deserved — but still expect professional work and attitudes. Poor treatment results in high turnover within those firms and relatively high turnover in the occupation as a whole, as paralegals leave the profession dissatisfied with working conditions, compensation, and the nature of the work. However, surveys also show that the role of the paralegal has expanded, with more sophisticated work being assigned to senior paralegals, increased responsibility and compensation, and job titles and benefits that reflect a greater appreciation of paralegals.

4. Exempt Status

The issue of whether paralegals should be classified as *exempt or nonexempt* employees was resolved in 2004 when the Department of Labor adopted new Wage and Hour Rules, which established that paralegals are not generally exempt and therefore are entitled to overtime compensation under the Fair Labor Standards Act (29 C.F.R. 541). The new rules are in keeping with earlier U.S. Department of Labor Letter Rulings, which held that paralegals as a group may not be classified as exempt because they are not required to have advanced professional knowledge acquired through prolonged specialized instruction and study (usually at least four years of college) and are not generally involved in the performance of duties that require the exercise of discretion and independent judgment. Section 541.301(e)(7) indicates that the exemption is available for paralegals who hold advanced specialized degrees in other professional fields that they apply to their work as paralegals, such as engineering. Prior to the new Rules being adopted, paralegals and their associations were divided on the issue. Many believe that their classification as nonexempt is degrading and does not accurately reflect their professional work and status; others believe that they would not be fairly compensated for their long hours of work without overtime pay and that overtime pay does not lower their status or prestige. Most paralegals in

187

surveys report that they are paid overtime. However, not all firms have changed their policies since the new rules were adopted or pay all their paralegals in the same way. Some law firms that have career paths for paralegals classify the lower rungs of the ladder as nonexempt and the top level or levels as exempt, based on the nature and complexity of the specific responsibilities, including supervising other paralegals and the degree of independence exercised by the paralegal at each level. Often, senior and specialist paralegals and paralegal managers who supervise paralegals are classified as exempt.

5. Gender, Race, and Related Issues

The paralegal career continues to be a **female-dominated occupation** that serves a still male-dominated profession. Even though the proportion of women in law school has been about 50 percent for the last 20 years, only about one-third of the lawyers in this country are women. Other traditionally female-dominated professions like nursing and teaching have struggled very hard — not always successfully — to achieve status and recognition, fair treatment, good working conditions, and compensation that is based on the value, nature, and difficulty of their work.

Gender-related issues have come to the forefront in recent years in discussions about law practice. Ethics rules now bar attorneys from having **sexual relations with clients.** Some jurisdictions have experienced a rise in lawsuits against attorneys who have had sexual relations with their clients, and in some cases substantial judgments have been awarded.

High-profile **sexual harassment and sex discrimination** cases have been brought and won against several prominent lawyers and law firms. Some suits have been brought by women lawyers and some by support staff. Surveys show that half of the women lawyers in the United States believe they have been harassed. Most women do not report such incidents out of fear of retaliation and marginalization. Many firms have instituted sexual harassment policies that define prohibited conduct, establish procedures and sanctions, and include sensitivity training.

Bias in the legal profession on the basis of race, sex, or sexual orientation has been well documented. In general, women and minority lawyers make less money, are less likely to make partner, and are excluded from key committees and prestigious practice areas in their law firms. Most jurisdictions have adopted anti-bias provisions in their ethics rules that make it an ethical violation to discriminate in the operation of a practice and/or to disparage or humiliate someone on the basis of race, national origin, sex, sexual orientation, religion, age, or disability. The Americans with Disabilities Act has added new protection for disabled employees and other persons in their interactions with law firms.

The organized bar and law firms have recognized that the profession has been slow to bring underrepresented groups, like racial-ethnic minorities, gays and lesbians, and lawyers with disabilities, into the legal profession. The law lags behind nearly all other professions in the proportion of people of color. To address this challenge, many bar associations have started initiatives to promote diversity by having firms sign pledges, by encouraging firms to change recruiting and mentoring programs and to develop a firm climate that is conducive to success for people of different backgrounds. Some bar associations have diversity pipeline projects to address the places along the path to becoming a lawyer where many people from underrepresented groups are blocked out or left behind. Strong incentive exists for achieving greater diversity in the changing demographics of the general population and the clients that law firms serve.

D.   Pro Bono Work

The fact that the legal needs of the vast majority of Americans are going unmet is undisputed. Study after study has proven that most Americans — including poor and middle-income persons — do not have access to a lawyer when they need one. Most Americans cannot afford a lawyer and would not know how to find a lawyer if they needed one. Recent studies show that one-half to three-quarters of low-income households experience a civil legal need within a year's time and that only 10 to 20 percent of these seek a lawyer's help. Most of the people who try to handle legal problems on their own are ill-equipped to navigate the system. Many are afraid, face language barriers, and are unaware of resources like legal aid or pro bono help.

To cope with this problem, the organized bar has encouraged individual lawyers to engage in **pro bono** work and has sponsored a wide variety of pro bono programs to which lawyers can contribute their time and expertise. Several states have adopted **voluntary aspirational guidelines** for lawyers to do pro bono work. Only a few have mandatory rules, which can be fulfilled by making a donation in lieu of doing the work. Some law schools have a requirement for public service or pro bono work, and many law firms have policies that encourage their attorneys and paralegals to engage in such activities.

Pro bono
For free

During the past 15 years, there has been an increase in voluntary pro bono work being done by lawyers and law firms. The need for legal services is still unmet, however, and paralegals have an opportunity to help fill this need. Participating in pro bono activities as part of one's professional commitment not only produces psychic rewards, but also increases career satisfaction and self-esteem.

Guideline 10 of the ABA Model Guidelines for the Utilization of Paralegal Services encourages lawyers to facilitate paralegal participation in pro bono activities. Many state guidelines on paralegals follow suit. Lawyers have a duty to provide pro bono services under ABA Model Rule 6.1 and Canon 2 of the ABA Model Code, and the ABA has called on lawyers to fulfill this duty by aspiring to do 50 hours of pro bono legal services work annually. NFPA asks paralegals to aspire to do 24 pro bono hours annually (NFPA EC 1.4(d)).

Many law firms that do pro bono work include paralegals in these activities. Paralegals who do not have an opportunity to become involved in pro bono work through their jobs should seek activities on their own. Local bar associations and paralegal associations usually have several kinds of pro bono projects on which paralegals can work. Legal aid organizations and law clinics are always in need of volunteers.

Pro bono programs have been established in many specialized areas of law, thus affording paralegals a chance either to exercise their expertise or to learn a new area. **Examples** of some of the programs are court-appointed special advocates in juvenile and family law, consumer disputes, landlord-tenant matters, major public interest litigation (for example, housing or employment discrimination or children's rights), immigration, indigent taxpayers, elder law, bankruptcy, family law, mental health advocacy, domestic violence restraining orders and counseling, AIDS, and homelessness projects.

Paralegals who do pro bono work often find themselves working more **independently** than they do in their jobs; they are engaged in challenging tasks that they would not be delegated at work. Paralegals in legal aid settings very often have extensive client contact, as they handle intake interviews and help clients directly with matters not requiring a lawyer. Paralegals are called on in these settings to advocate for clients before administrative agencies, to conduct in-depth research, and to draft documents and memoranda.

In addition to skill development and growth, paralegals who do pro bono work derive the ultimate **satisfaction** of helping someone who needs help and who might not otherwise have gotten that help. Usually, the assistance needed and provided is of the most critical kind—for instance, keeping someone from losing a home or losing government benefits—and is a matter of survival to the clients.

REVIEW QUESTIONS

1. Give five reasons why the public image of lawyers is so poor.
2. What are lawyers doing to improve their public image?
3. What is a code of professional courtesy? What kinds of conduct does it require?

4. How can a paralegal make a difference in improving the professionalism and public image of the legal field?

5. Why are paralegals in an ambiguous position in the legal environment? Give at least three reasons.

6. How is *profession* defined?

7. What is a paraprofessional?

8. What is collegiality? Why is it difficult for paralegals to have collegiality?

9. To what extent are paralegals overtrained?

10. Describe the nine professional commitments that paralegals should make.

11. Name and discuss some of the issues facing today's paralegals.

12. What is the basis for classifying a paralegal as an exempt or nonexempt employee? What is the law currently?

13. Does the fact that paralegals are predominately female affect the career? How?

14. What is the current state of legal services for poor and middle-income Americans?

15. Have pro bono activities increased or decreased in the last decade?

16. What kinds of pro bono activities do lawyers and paralegals engage in?

17. What are the benefits to a paralegal of doing pro bono work?

18. How can a paralegal get involved in pro bono work?

19. What are some of the gender-related issues that paralegals face?

20. Is the legal profession racially and ethnically diverse? What is being done to address issues of diversity in the legal field?

HYPOTHETICALS

1. Ann Arista works for the law firm of Smith & Tory. Ann is a first-year paralegal. She is paid a monthly salary and a bonus at the end of the year. She works on document preparation for large lawsuits with a team of other paralegals and case clerks. She does not supervise anyone and has little discretion in her duties. She is hopeful that she will be promoted next year and begin doing more substantive paralegal work. Ann is not paid overtime. She often works more than eight hours a day, and for three straight months worked in excess of 50 hours a week. Is Ann being treated appropriately under the laws for exempt and nonexempt employees? Is she being treated fairly? What should she do? Suppose the firm offers her compensatory time off. Should she accept it?

2. Fred Fester is a senior paralegal with a large law firm. He works with one of the more flamboyant and successful trial attorneys, Sam Shore. Sam is known for being very flirtatious, especially with the young women in the firm. Fred walks into Sam's office one day and sees

him apparently kissing a young associate, Betty Block. Fred walks out embarrassed and Betty leaves a few minutes later in tears. What should Fred do? Suppose that a few weeks later Fred finds out that Sam has recommended against Betty's being retained by the firm.

3. Martin Morrison and Pamela Polk work for a large law firm that has a career path for paralegals. They call their paralegals by different titles as they move up the ladder: "case clerk," "junior legal assistant," "senior paralegal," "supervising paralegal," and "senior paralegal specialist." The firm's secretaries are unhappy with their status and pay. Some of them lobby for changes in their treatment. As a result, the most senior legal secretaries are given the title "legal assistant." Other legal secretaries are permitted to move into senior paralegal positions without meeting the usual educational requirements for those positions, and in some cases are given higher rates of pay. Some of these persons are capable of doing the paralegal work, and some are not. Martin and Pamela are really distressed and believe these changes undermine the credibility of the paralegals at the firm. What should they do?

DISCUSSION QUESTIONS

1. Do you think the legal profession deserves its poor public image? Why or why not?
2. Should the legal profession regulate itself?
3. Read a general interest newspaper every day for a month and clip out or print all the articles that mention lawyers. How many are favorable? What image do they present?
4. How can the legal profession overcome its poor image?
5. Do you think lawyers' salaries and billing rates are disproportionately high? Why or why not?
6. Do you think lawyers' increased mobility is a good or bad thing? Why?
7. Does your local bar association or court have a code of professional courtesy? Do you think a nonbinding code such as this is appropriate for a court or bar association to have? Why or why not? Should such a code be binding? Why or why not? Do such codes derogate the lawyer's duty of zealousness? Do they contribute to lawyers' "clubbiness"? Do they work?
8. Contact your local paralegal association and get salary surveys that ask about job satisfaction, career paths, pro bono work, and exempt or nonexempt status.
9. Contact paralegals at local law firms and ask them:

   a. if they regard their paralegal career as a profession
   b. if they are treated as professionals by their employers
   c. if they plan to continue as a paralegal indefinitely, and, if not,

- what they plan to do
- why they are leaving the career

d. if they are members of the local paralegal association
e. if their firm does pro bono work
f. if they do pro bono work
g. if their education and training are well utilized
h. if they are paid overtime
i. if they have experienced gender-related discrimination

10. Do you think paralegals are professionals or paraprofessionals? Is this distinction important to you? Why?
11. Do you think standardization in paralegal education would be good or bad for the career? Why?
12. How can paralegals build collegiality? Why is it important?
13. Do you think voluntary certification is good for paralegals? Why or why not? What about mandatory regulation? Why or why not?
14. Do you agree with the nine professional commitments for paralegals set forth in this chapter? Why or why not? How would you prioritize their relative importance? What would you add or delete?
15. Do you think regulation of paralegals would enhance their professional status? Why or why not?
16. Get the position papers on regulation of the major paralegal associations and compare the points of view and the rationale for the various positions. Stage a debate in your class with students or local paralegal association members arguing the points.
17. How can paralegals help overcome lawyers' reluctance to use paralegals' services? How can paralegals encourage lawyers to use their services more effectively and fully?
18. Check the Web site of your state and local bar associations to see if they are doing anything to address diversity in your legal community. Find statistics on the gender, racial-ethnic background and other groups within the bar in your state. Is your legal community as diverse as the general poplation? What are the barriers that inhibit a more diverse legal field? What is being done to change things? Do you perceive that the paralegal community is more or less diverse than lawyers are as a group?
19. Contact the local bar and paralegal associations and find out what kinds of pro bono opportunities are available to paralegals in your area.

SELECTED REFERENCES

ABA Model Rules of Professional Conduct, Rule 6.1 [pro bono service]
ABA Model Rules of Professional Conduct, Rule 8.3 [reporting misconduct]

ABA Guidelines for the Utilization of paralegal Services, Guideline 10 [continuing education, pro bono]

NALA Code of Ethics and Professional Responsibility, Canon 6 [education]

NFPA Model Code of Ethics and Professional Responsibility, Canon 3, EC 3.2 [reporting misconduct]

NFPA Model Code of Ethics and Professional Responsibility, Canon 1, EC 1.2 [continuing education]

NFPA Model Code of Ethics and Professional Responsibility, Canon 4 [public interest, pro bono]

Q. Johnstone & M. Wenglinsky, Paralegals: Progress and Prospects of a Satellite Occupation, pp. 183 et seq. (1985)

Green, Snell, Corgiat, & Paramanith, *The Professionalization of the Paralegal: Identity, Maturation States and Goal Attainment*, 7 J. Para. Ed. & Prac. 35 (1990)

Appendix A

NALA Code
of Ethics

NALA Code of Ethics and Professional Responsibility

Each NALA member agrees to follow the canons of the NALA Code of Ethics and Professional Responsibility Violations of the Code may result in cancellation of membership. First adopted by the NALA membership in May of 1975, the Code of Ethics and Professional Responsibility is the foundation of ethical practices of paralegals in the legal community.

A paralegal must adhere strictly to the accepted standards of legal ethics and to the general principles of proper conduct. The performance of the duties of the paralegal shall be governed by specific canons as defined herein so that justice will be served and goals of the profession attained. (See Model Standards and Guidelines for Utilization of Legal Assistants, Section II.)

The canons of ethics set forth hereafter are adopted by the National Association of Legal Assistants, Inc., as a general guide intended to aid paralegals and attorneys. The enumeration of these rules does not mean there are not others of equal importance although not specifically mentioned. Court rules, agency rules and statutes must be taken into consideration when interpreting the canons.

Definition: Legal assistants, also known as paralegals, are a distinguishable group of persons who assist attorneys in the delivery of legal services. Through formal education, training and experience, legal assistants have knowledge and expertise regarding the legal system and substantive and procedural law which qualify them to do work of a legal nature under the supervision of an attorney.

In **2001**, NALA members also adopted the ABA definition of a legal assistant/paralegal, as follows:

A legal assistant or paralegal is a person qualified by education, training or work experience who is employed or retained by a lawyer, law office, corporation, governmental agency or other entity who performs specifically delegated substantive legal work for which a lawyer is responsible. (Adopted by the ABA in 1997)

Canon 1.
A paralegal must not perform any of the duties that attorneys only may perform nor take any actions that attorneys may not take.

Canon 2.
A paralegal may perform any task which is properly delegated and supervised by an attorney, as long as the attorney is ultimately responsible to the client, maintains a direct relationship with the client, and assumes professional responsibility for the work product.

Canon 3.
A paralegal must not: (a) engage in, encourage, or contribute to any act which could constitute the unauthorized practice of law; and (b) establish attorney-client relationships, set fees, give legal opinions or advice or represent a client before a court or agency unless so authorized by that court or agency; and (c) engage in conduct or take any action which would assist or involve the attorney in a violation of professional ethics or give the appearance of professional impropriety.

Canon 4.
A paralegal must use discretion and professional judgment commensurate with knowledge and experience but must not render independent legal judgment in place of an attorney. The services of an attorney are essential in the public interest whenever such legal judgment is required.

Canon 5.
A paralegal must disclose his or her status as a paralegal at the outset of any professional relationship with a client, attorney, a court or administrative agency or personnel thereof, or a member of the general public. A paralegal must act prudently in determining the extent to which a client may be assisted without the presence of an attorney.

Canon 6.
A paralegal must strive to maintain integrity and a high degree of competency through education and training with respect to professional responsibility, local rules and practice, and through continuing education in substantive areas of law to better assist the legal profession in fulfilling its duty to provide legal service.

Canon 7.
A paralegal must protect the confidences of a client and must not violate any rule or statute now in effect or hereafter enacted controlling the doctrine of privileged communications between a client and an attorney.

Canon 8.
A paralegal must disclose to his or her employer or prospective employer any pre-existing client or personal relationship that may conflict with the interests of the employer or prospective employer and/or their clients.

Canon 9.
A paralegal must do all other things incidental, necessary, or expedient for the attainment of the ethics and responsibilities as defined by statute or rule of court.

Canon 10.
A paralegal's conduct is guided by bar associations' codes of professional responsibility and rules of professional conduct.

Appendix B

MODEL CODE OF ETHICS AND PROFESSIONAL RESPONSIBILITY AND GUIDELINES FOR ENFORCEMENT

PREAMBLE

The National Federation of Paralegal Associations, Inc. ("NFPA") is a professional organization comprised of paralegal associations and individual paralegals throughout the United States and Canada. Members of NFPA have varying backgrounds, experiences, education and job responsibilities that reflect the diversity of the paralegal profession. NFPA promotes the growth, development and recognition of the paralegal profession as an integral partner in the delivery of legal services.

In May 1993 NFPA adopted its Model Code of Ethics and Professional Responsibility ("Model Code") to delineate the principles for ethics and conduct to which every paralegal should aspire.

Many paralegal associations throughout the United States have endorsed the concept and content of NFPA's Model Code through the adoption of their own ethical codes. In doing so, paralegals have confirmed the profession's commitment to increase the quality and efficiency of legal services, as well as recognized its responsibilities to the public, the legal community, and colleagues.

Paralegals have recognized, and will continue to recognize, that the profession must continue to evolve to enhance their roles in the delivery of legal services. With increased levels of responsibility comes the need to define and enforce mandatory rules of professional conduct. Enforcement of codes of paralegal conduct is a logical and necessary step to enhance and ensure the confidence of the legal community and the public in the integrity and professional responsibility of paralegals.

In April 1997 NFPA adopted the Model Disciplinary Rules ("Model Rules") to make possible the enforcement of the Canons and Ethical Considerations contained in the NFPA Model Code. A concurrent determination was made that the Model Code of Ethics and Professional Responsibility, formerly aspirational in nature, should be recognized as setting forth the enforceable obligations of all paralegals.

The Model Code and Model Rules offer a framework for professional discipline, either voluntarily or through formal regulatory programs.

§1. NFPA MODEL DISCIPLINARY RULES AND ETHICAL CONSIDERATIONS

1.1 A PARALEGAL SHALL ACHIEVE AND MAINTAIN A HIGH LEVEL OF COMPETENCE.

Ethical Considerations

EC-1.1 (a) A paralegal shall achieve competency through education, training, and work experience.

EC-1.1 (b) A paralegal shall aspire to participate in a minimum of twelve (12) hours of continuing legal education, to include at least one (1) hour of ethics education, every two (2) years in order to remain current on developments in the law.

EC-1.1 (c) A paralegal shall perform all assignments promptly and efficiently.

1.2 A PARALEGAL SHALL MAINTAIN A HIGH LEVEL OF PERSONAL AND PROFESSIONAL INTEGRITY.

Ethical Considerations

EC-1.2 (a) A paralegal shall not engage in any ex parte communications involving the courts or any other adjudicatory body in an attempt to exert undue influence or to obtain advantage or the benefit of only one party.

EC-1.2 (b) A paralegal shall not communicate, or cause another to communicate, with a party the paralegal knows to be represented by a lawyer in a pending matter without the prior consent of the lawyer representing such other party.

EC-1.2 (c) A paralegal shall ensure that all timekeeping and billing records prepared by the paralegal are thorough, accurate, honest, and complete.

EC-1.2 (d) A paralegal shall not knowingly engage in fraudulent billing practices. Such practices may include, but are not limited to: inflation of hours billed to a client or employer; misrepresentation of the nature of tasks performed; and/or submission of fraudulent expense and disbursement documentation.

EC-1.2 (e) A paralegal shall be scrupulous, thorough and honest in the identification and maintenance of all funds, securities, and other assets of a client and shall provide accurate accounting as appropriate.

EC-1.2 (f) A paralegal shall advise the proper authority of non-confidential knowledge of any dishonest or fraudulent acts by any person pertaining to the handling of the funds, securities or other assets of a client. The authority to whom the report is made shall depend on the nature and circumstances of the possible misconduct, (e.g., ethics committees of law firms, corporations and/or paralegal associations, local or state bar associations, local prosecutors, administrative agencies, etc.). Failure to report such knowledge is in itself misconduct and shall be treated as such under these rules.

1.3   A PARALEGAL SHALL MAINTAIN A HIGH STANDARD OF PROFESSIONAL CONDUCT.

Ethical Considerations

EC-1.3 (a)   A paralegal shall refrain from engaging in any conduct that offends the dignity and decorum of proceedings before a court or other adjudicatory body and shall be respectful of all rules and procedures.

EC-1.3 (b)   A paralegal shall avoid impropriety and the appearance of impropriety and shall not engage in any conduct that would adversely affect his/her fitness to practice. Such conduct may include, but is not limited to: violence, dishonesty, interference with the administration of justice, and/or abuse of a professional position or public office.

EC-1.3 (c)   Should a paralegal's fitness to practice be compromised by physical or mental illness, causing that paralegal to commit an act that is in direct violation of the Model Code/Model Rules and/or the rules and/or laws governing the jurisdiction in which the paralegal practices, that paralegal may be protected from sanction upon review of the nature and circumstances of that illness.

EC-1.3 (d)   A paralegal shall advise the proper authority of non-confidential knowledge of any action of another legal professional that clearly demonstrates fraud, deceit, dishonesty, or misrepresentation. The authority to whom the report is made shall depend on the nature and circumstances of the possible misconduct, (e.g., ethics committees of law firms, corporations and/or paralegal associations, local or state bar associations, local prosecutors, administrative agencies, etc.). Failure to report such knowledge is in itself misconduct and shall be treated as such under these rules.

EC-1.3 (e)   A paralegal shall not knowingly assist any individual with the commission of an act that is in direct violation of the Model Code/Model Rules and/or the rules and/or laws governing the jurisdiction in which the paralegal practices.

EC-1.3 (f)   If a paralegal possesses knowledge of future criminal activity, that knowledge must be reported to the appropriate authority immediately.

1.4   A PARALEGAL SHALL SERVE THE PUBLIC INTEREST BY CONTRIBUTING TO THE IMPROVEMENT OF THE LEGAL SYSTEM AND DELIVERY OF QUALITY LEGAL SERVICES, INCLUDING PRO BONO PUBLICO SERVICES.

Ethical Considerations

EC-1.4 (a)   A paralegal shall be sensitive to the legal needs of the public and shall promote the development and implementation of programs that address those needs.

EC-1.4 (b)   A paralegal shall support efforts to improve the legal system and access thereto and shall assist in making changes.

EC-1.4   A paralegal shall support and participate in the delivery of Pro Bono Publico

(c)   services directed toward implementing and improving access to justice, the law, the legal system or the paralegal and legal professions.

EC-1.4
(d)   A paralegal should aspire annually to contribute twenty-four (24) hours of Pro Bono Publico services under the supervision of an attorney or as authorized by administrative, statutory or court authority to:

1. persons of limited means; or
2. charitable, religious, civic, community, governmental and educational organizations in matters that are designed primarily to address the legal needs of persons with limited means; or
3. individuals, groups or organizations seeking to secure or protect civil rights, civil liberties or public rights.

The twenty-four (24) hours of Pro Bono Publico services contributed annually by a paralegal may consist of such services as detailed in this EC-1.4(d), and/or administrative matters designed to develop and implement the attainment of this aspiration as detailed above in EC-1.4(a) or (c), or any combination of the two.

1.5   **A PARALEGAL SHALL PRESERVE ALL CONFIDENTIAL INFORMATION PROVIDED BY THE CLIENT OR ACQUIRED FROM OTHER SOURCES BEFORE, DURING, AND AFTER THE COURSE OF THE PROFESSIONAL RELATIONSHIP.**

Ethical Considerations

EC-1.5
(a)   A paralegal shall be aware of and abide by all legal authority governing confidential information in the jurisdiction in which the paralegal practices.

EC-1.5
(b)   A paralegal shall not use confidential information to the disadvantage of the client.

EC-1.5
(c)   A paralegal shall not use confidential information to the advantage of the paralegal or of a third person.

EC-1.5
(d)   A paralegal may reveal confidential information only after full disclosure and with the client's written consent; or, when required by law or court order; or, when necessary to prevent the client from committing an act that could result in death or serious bodily harm.

EC-1.5
(e)   A paralegal shall keep those individuals responsible for the legal representation of a client fully informed of any confidential information the paralegal may have pertaining to that client.

EC-1.5
(f)   A paralegal shall not engage in any indiscreet communications concerning clients.

1.6   A PARALEGAL SHALL AVOID CONFLICTS OF INTEREST AND SHALL DISCLOSE ANY POSSIBLE CONFLICT TO THE EMPLOYER OR CLIENT, AS WELL AS TO THE PROSPECTIVE EMPLOYERS OR CLIENTS.

Ethical Considerations

EC-1.6 (a)   A paralegal shall act within the bounds of the law, solely for the benefit of the client, and shall be free of compromising influences and loyalties. Neither the paralegal's personal or business interest, nor those of other clients or third persons, should compromise the paralegal's professional judgment and loyalty to the client.

EC-1.6 (b)   A paralegal shall avoid conflicts of interest that may arise from previous assignments, whether for a present or past employer or client.

EC-1.6 (c)   A paralegal shall avoid conflicts of interest that may arise from family relationships and from personal and business interests.

EC-1.6 (d)   In order to be able to determine whether an actual or potential conflict of interest exists a paralegal shall create and maintain an effective recordkeeping system that identifies clients, matters, and parties with which the paralegal has worked.

EC-1.6 (e)   A paralegal shall reveal sufficient non-confidential information about a client or former client to reasonably ascertain if an actual or potential conflict of interest exists.

EC-1.6 (f)   A paralegal shall not participate in or conduct work on any matter where a conflict of interest has been identified.

EC-1.6 (g)   In matters where a conflict of interest has been identified and the client consents to continued representation, a paralegal shall comply fully with the implementation and maintenance of an Ethical Wall.

1.7   A PARALEGAL'S TITLE SHALL BE FULLY DISCLOSED.

Ethical Considerations

EC-1.7 (a)   A paralegal's title shall clearly indicate the individual's status and shall be disclosed in all business and professional communications to avoid misunderstandings and misconceptions about the paralegal's role and responsibilities.

EC-1.7 (b)   A paralegal's title shall be included if the paralegal's name appears on business cards, letterhead, brochures, directories, and advertisements.

EC-1.7 (c)   A paralegal shall not use letterhead, business cards or other promotional materials to create a fraudulent impression of his/her status or ability to practice in the jurisdiction in which the paralegal practices.

EC-1.7 (d)   A paralegal shall not practice under color of any record, diploma, or certificate that has been illegally or fraudulently obtained or issued or which is misrepresentative in any way.

EC1.7 (e)   A paralegal shall not participate in the creation, issuance, or dissemination of fraudulent records, diplomas, or certificates.

1.8   A PARALEGAL SHALL NOT ENGAGE IN THE UNAUTHORIZED PRACTICE OF LAW.

Ethical Considerations

EC-1.8
(a)   A paralegal shall comply with the applicable legal authority governing the unauthorized practice of law in the jurisdiction in which the paralegal practices.

§2.   NFPA GUIDELINES FOR THE ENFORCEMENT OF THE MODEL CODE OF ETHICS AND PROFESSIONAL RESPONSIBILITY

2.1   BASIS FOR DISCIPLINE

2.1(a)   Disciplinary investigations and proceedings brought under authority of the Rules shall be conducted in accord with obligations imposed on the paralegal professional by the Model Code of Ethics and Professional Responsibility.

2.2   STRUCTURE OF DISCIPLINARY COMMITTEE

2.2(a)   The Disciplinary Committee ("Committee") shall be made up of nine (9) members including the Chair.

2.2(b)   Each member of the Committee, including any temporary replacement members, shall have demonstrated working knowledge of ethics/professional responsibility-related issues and activities.

2.2(c)   The Committee shall represent a cross-section of practice areas and work experience. The following recommendations are made regarding the members of the Committee.

> 1) At least one paralegal with one to three years of law-related work experience.
> 2) At least one paralegal with five to seven years of law related work experience.
> 3) At least one paralegal with over ten years of law related work experience.
> 4) One paralegal educator with five to seven years of work experience; preferably in the area of ethics/professional responsibility.
> 5) One paralegal manager.
> 6) One lawyer with five to seven years of law-related work experience.
> 7) One lay member.

2.2(d)   The Chair of the Committee shall be appointed within thirty (30) days of its members' induction. The Chair shall have no fewer than ten (10) years of law-related work experience.

2.2(e)   The terms of all members of the Committee shall be staggered. Of those members initially appointed, a simple majority plus one shall be appointed to a term of one year, and the remaining members shall be appointed to a term of two years. Thereafter, all members of the Committee shall be appointed to terms of two years.

2.2(f)   If for any reason the terms of a majority of the Committee will expire at the same time, members may be appointed to terms of one year to maintain continuity of the Committee.

2.2(g)   The Committee shall organize from its members a three-tiered structure to investigate, prosecute and/or adjudicate charges of misconduct. The members shall be rotated among the tiers.

2.3   OPERATION OF COMMITTEE

2.3(a)   The Committee shall meet on an as-needed basis to discuss, investigate, and/or adjudicate alleged violations of the Model Code/Model Rules.

2.3(b)   A majority of the members of the Committee present at a meeting shall constitute a quorum.

2.3(c)   A Recording Secretary shall be designated to maintain complete and accurate minutes of all Committee meetings. All such minutes shall be kept confidential until a decision has been made that the matter will be set for hearing as set forth in Section 6.1 below.

2.3(d)   If any member of the Committee has a conflict of interest with the Charging Party, the Responding Party, or the allegations of misconduct, that member shall not take part in any hearing or deliberations concerning those allegations. If the absence of that member creates a lack of a quorum for the Committee, then a temporary replacement for the member shall be appointed.

2.3(e)   Either the Charging Party or the Responding Party may request that, for good cause shown, any member of the Committee not participate in a hearing or deliberation. All such requests shall be honored. If the absence of a Committee member under those circumstances creates a lack of a quorum for the Committee, then a temporary replacement for that member shall be appointed.

2.3(f)   All discussions and correspondence of the Committee shall be kept confidential until a decision has been made that the matter will be set for hearing as set forth in Section 6.1 below.

2.3(g)   All correspondence from the Committee to the Responding Party regarding any charge of misconduct and any decisions made regarding the charge shall be mailed certified mail, return receipt requested, to the Responding Party's last known address and shall be clearly marked with a "Confidential" designation.

2.4 PROCEDURE FOR THE REPORTING OF ALLEGED VIOLATIONS OF THE MODEL CODE/DISCIPLINARY RULES

2.4(a)　An individual or entity in possession of non-confidential knowledge or information concerning possible instances of misconduct shall make a confidential written report to the Committee within thirty (30) days of obtaining same. This report shall include all details of the alleged misconduct.

2.4(b)　The Committee so notified shall inform the Responding Party of the allegation(s) of misconduct no later than ten (10) business days after receiving the confidential written report from the Charging Party.

2.4(c)　Notification to the Responding Party shall include the identity of the Charging Party, unless, for good cause shown, the Charging Party requests anonymity.

2.4(d)　The Responding Party shall reply to the allegations within ten (10) business days of notification.

2.5 PROCEDURE FOR THE INVESTIGATION OF A CHARGE OF MISCONDUCT

2.5(a)　Upon receipt of a Charge of Misconduct ("Charge"), or on its own initiative, the Committee shall initiate an investigation.

2.5(b)　If, upon initial or preliminary review, the Committee makes a determination that the charges are either without basis in fact or, if proven, would not constitute professional misconduct, the Committee shall dismiss the allegations of misconduct. If such determination of dismissal cannot be made, a formal investigation shall be initiated.

2.5(c)　Upon the decision to conduct a formal investigation, the Committee shall:
　　　　1) mail to the Charging and Responding Parties within three (3) business days of that decision notice of the commencement of a formal investigation. That notification shall be in writing and shall contain a complete explanation of all Charge(s), as well as the reasons for a formal investigation and shall cite the applicable codes and rules;

　　　　2) allow the Responding Party thirty (30) days to prepare and submit a confidential response to the Committee, which response shall address each charge specifically and shall be in writing; and

　　　　3) upon receipt of the response to the notification, have thirty (30) days to investigate the Charge(s). If an extension of time is deemed necessary, that extension shall not exceed ninety (90) days.

2.5(d)　Upon conclusion of the investigation, the Committee may:
　　　　1) dismiss the Charge upon the finding that it has no basis in fact;
　　　　2) dismiss the Charge upon the finding that, if proven, the Charge would not constitute Misconduct;
　　　　3) refer the matter for hearing by the Tribunal; or
　　　　4) in the case of criminal activity, refer the Charge(s) and all investigation results to the appropriate authority.

2.6   PROCEDURE FOR A MISCONDUCT HEARING BEFORE A TRIBUNAL

2.6(a)   Upon the decision by the Committee that a matter should be heard, all parties shall be notified and a hearing date shall be set. The hearing shall take place no more than thirty (30) days from the conclusion of the formal investigation.

2.6(b)   The Responding Party shall have the right to counsel. The parties and the Tribunal shall have the right to call any witnesses and introduce any documentation that they believe will lead to the fair and reasonable resolution of the matter.

2.6(c)   Upon completion of the hearing, the Tribunal shall deliberate and present a written decision to the parties in accordance with procedures as set forth by the Tribunal.

2.6(d)   Notice of the decision of the Tribunal shall be appropriately published.

2.7   SANCTIONS

2.7(a)   Upon a finding of the Tribunal that misconduct has occurred, any of the following sanctions, or others as may be deemed appropriate, may be imposed upon the Responding Party, either singularly or in combination:
   1) letter of reprimand to the Responding Party; counseling;
   2) attendance at an ethics course approved by the Tribunal; probation;
   3) suspension of license/authority to practice; revocation of license/authority to practice;
   4) imposition of a fine; assessment of costs; or
   5) in the instance of criminal activity, referral to the appropriate authority.

2.7(b)   Upon the expiration of any period of probation, suspension, or revocation, the Responding Party may make application for reinstatement. With the application for reinstatement, the Responding Party must show proof of having complied with all aspects of the sanctions imposed by the Tribunal.

2.8   APPELLATE PROCEDURES

2.8(a)   The parties shall have the right to appeal the decision of the Tribunal in accordance with the procedure as set forth by the Tribunal.

DEFINITIONS

"Appellate Body" means a body established to adjudicate an appeal to any decision made by a Tribunal or other decision-making body with respect to formally-heard Charges of Misconduct.

"Charge of Misconduct" means a written submission by any individual or entity to an ethics committee, paralegal association, bar association, law enforcement agency, judicial body, government agency, or other appropriate body or entity, that sets forth non-confidential information regarding any instance of alleged misconduct by an individual paralegal or paralegal entity.

"Charging Party" means any individual or entity who submits a Charge of Misconduct against an individual paralegal or paralegal entity.

"Competency" means the demonstration of: diligence, education, skill, and mental, emotional, and physical fitness reasonably necessary for the performance of paralegal services.

"Confidential Information" means information relating to a client, whatever its source, that is not public knowledge nor available to the public. ("Non-Confidential Information" would generally include the name of the client and the identity of the matter for which the paralegal provided services.)

"Disciplinary Hearing" means the confidential proceeding conducted by a committee or other designated body or entity concerning any instance of alleged misconduct by an individual paralegal or paralegal entity.

"Disciplinary Committee" means any committee that has been established by an entity such as a paralegal association, bar association, judicial body, or government agency to: (a) identify, define and investigate general ethical considerations and concerns with respect to paralegal practice; (b) administer and enforce the Model Code and Model Rules and; (c) discipline any individual paralegal or paralegal entity found to be in violation of same.

"Disclose" means communication of information reasonably sufficient to permit identification of the significance of the matter in question.

"Ethical Wall" means the screening method implemented in order to protect a client from a conflict of interest. An Ethical Wall generally includes, but is not limited to, the following elements: (1) prohibit the paralegal from having any connection with the matter; (2) ban discussions with or the transfer of documents to or from the paralegal; (3) restrict access to files; and (4) educate all members of the firm, corporation, or entity as to the separation of the paralegal (both organizationally and physically) from the pending matter. For more information regarding the Ethical Wall, see the NFPA publication entitled "The Ethical Wall - Its Application to Paralegals."

"Ex parte" means actions or communications conducted at the instance and for the benefit of one party only, and without notice to, or contestation by, any person adversely interested.

"Investigation" means the investigation of any charge(s) of misconduct filed against an individual paralegal or paralegal entity by a Committee.

"Letter of Reprimand" means a written notice of formal censure or severe reproof administered to an individual paralegal or paralegal entity for unethical or improper conduct.

"Misconduct" means the knowing or unknowing commission of an act that is in direct violation of those Canons and Ethical Considerations of any and all applicable codes and/or rules of conduct.

"Paralegal" is synonymous with "Legal Assistant" and is defined as a person qualified through education, training, or work experience to perform substantive legal work that requires knowledge of legal concepts and is customarily, but not exclusively performed by a lawyer. This person may be retained or employed by a lawyer, law office, governmental agency, or other entity or may be authorized by administrative, statutory, or court authority to perform this work.

"Pro Bono Publico" means providing or assisting to provide quality legal services in order to enhance access to justice for persons of limited means; charitable, religious, civic, community, governmental and educational organizations in matters that are designed primarily to address the legal needs of persons with limited means; or individuals, groups or organizations seeking to secure or protect civil rights, civil liberties or public rights.

"Proper Authority" means the local paralegal association, the local or state bar association, Committee(s) of the local paralegal or bar association(s), local prosecutor, administrative agency, or other tribunal empowered to investigate or act upon an instance of alleged misconduct.

"Responding Party" means an individual paralegal or paralegal entity against whom a Charge of Misconduct has been submitted.

"Revocation" means the recision of the license, certificate or other authority to practice of an individual paralegal or paralegal entity found in violation of those Canons and Ethical Considerations of any and all applicable codes and/or rules of conduct.

"Suspension" means the suspension of the license, certificate or other authority to practice of an individual paralegal or paralegal entity found in violation of those Canons and Ethical Considerations of any and all applicable codes and/or rules of conduct.

"Tribunal" means the body designated to adjudicate allegations of misconduct.

Glossary

Abuse of process   The improper use of a civil or criminal process.

Administrative agency   A government body responsible for the control and supervision of a particular activity or area of public interest.

Advanced fee   A fee paid by a client to a lawyer in advance of the work being done that is earned by the lawyer as the work is done.

Associate   A lawyer in a law firm who is not a partner but is an employee.

Attorney-client privilege   The rule of evidence that protects confidential communications between a lawyer and client made in the course of the professional relationship.

Barratry   The common law crime of stirring up lawsuits and disputes.

Bribery   The crime of giving or receiving something of value as payment for an official act.

Certification   A form of recognition of an occupation based on a person's having met specified qualifications.

Champerty   An old common law agreement between a lawyer and client under which the lawyer undertakes representation and pays costs and is reimbursed and paid a fee out of the recovery; such agreements were outlawed in most states.

Chat   Discussion carried on electronically over the Internet, which can be live or asynchronous.

Chinese wall   An antiquated term for a screen. See **Screen/ screening.**

Class action suit   A lawsuit brought by a representative of a group of persons on behalf of the group.

Client security fund   A fund set aside to reimburse clients whose funds have been converted or misappropriated by lawyers.

Client trust account   A bank account set up by a lawyer in which funds are kept that belong in whole or in part to the client.

Commingling   The mixing of the funds of a fiduciary, including a lawyer, with those of a client.

Cone of silence   The silence imposed on a person with a conflict of interest when a screen is erected to protect against breaches of confidentiality.

Confidentiality agreement   An agreement entered into between a law firm and an employee or other agent in which the employee or agent agrees to keep client information confidential.

Contempt An act that obstructs the administration of justice, impairs the dignity of the court, or shows disrespect for the authority of the court.

Contingency fee A fee that is contingent on the successful outcome of a case and based on a percentage of the recovery.

Control group test The test applied by some courts to determine whether communications in a corporate setting are covered by the attorney-client privilege; under this test, communications are privileged only if they are made with the management and board members.

Conversion The tortious deprivation of another's property without justification or authorization.

Court facilitators Persons employed by the courts to assist lay persons who are representing themselves in their own court matters. Typically employed in family law courts.

Deposition A method of pretrial discovery that consists of a witness statement taken under oath in a question-and-answer format and recorded.

Disbarment The rescinding of a lawyer's license to practice law.

Discovery Pretrial procedures designed for the parties to gain information to narrow the issues of fact and law.

Document production A form of discovery under which one party must provide copies of specified documents to the other side.

Ethics advisory opinions Written opinions promulgated by bar associations in which the association interprets the relevant ethical precedents in the context of a specific ethical dilemma posed to it.

Ex parte An action taken by or on behalf of a party without the presence of the opposing party.

Extrajudicial An act that takes place outside the presence of the judge or jury.

Fee-shifting statute Legislation that permits the award of attorney's fees to the prevailing party.

Fixed fees A fee for legal services based on a set amount, usually used for standardized routine work.

Forwarding fee A fee paid by a lawyer to another lawyer for referring a case.

Freelance paralegals Legal assistants who work as independent contractors providing services to lawyers on an as-needed basis.

Gag order A court-imposed order that restricts information or comment about a case.

Hourly fees   Fees for legal services based on hourly rates and the amount of time actually expended in rendering the services.

Imputed conflict/disqualification   A conflict of interest involving one person that is attributed vicariously to the entire law firm, which is disqualified from representing the party at issue.

In camera   Proceedings held in the judge's chambers without the jury or public present; the examination of documents to determine if there is privileged information is conducted "in camera."

Independent paralegals   A term sometimes used by nonlawyer legal service providers and sometimes used by freelance paralegals. See both these terms in this glossary.

Integrated bar   A bar association in which the mandatory and voluntary aspects of bar activities are combined and membership is required.

Inter vivos   During life.

IOLTA   Interest on Lawyers' Trust Accounts. A program under which the interest from lawyers' client trust accounts, which is too small to pay to clients, is collected by banks and used by bar associations and/or courts to fund law-related programs.

Issue conflict   The situation that arises when a lawyer argues opposing sides of a legal issue, the result of which may be that one client's interests are harmed, even though that client is not a party to the matter.

Jailhouse lawyers   Prison inmates who assist other prisoners in preparing writs and lawsuits.

Legal document assistants   Nonlawyer legal service providers who assist persons in preparing legal documents without giving legal advice under California statutes.

Legal malpractice   Improper conduct in the performance of duties by a legal professional, either intentionally or through negligence.

Legal technicians   A term used by some nonlawyer legal service providers.

Licensing   Mandatory governmental regulation of a profession requiring that the members meet specified qualifications.

Lien   An encumbrance or claim on the property of another as security for a debt or charge.

Malicious prosecution   An action to recover damages resulting from an unsuccessful criminal or civil action that was instituted without probable cause and with malice.

Malpractice   Improper conduct in the performance of duties by a professional, either intentionally or through negligence.

Mistrial   A trial terminated and declared void prior to the return of a verdict, often because of a jury deadlock.

Multidisciplinary practice   A business model under which law firms and other professionals form partnerships to deliver legal and other related services to clients.

Multijurisdictional practice   Engaging in the practice of law in more than one state.

Nonlawyer legal service providers   Laypersons who provide legal services directly to the public.

Paraprofessional   A person who works within a profession in a subordinate position but with special training and a degree of independence in carrying out duties.

Perjury   A criminal offense of making false statements under oath.

Pleading   Statements in written legal form that set forth the plaintiff's cause of action and the defendant's grounds of defense.

Probation   A procedure under which someone found guilty of an offense is subjected to certain conditions and oversight by the entity involved and is released from a more serious sanction.

Pro bono   For free.

Professional negligence   Improper conduct in the performance of duties by a professional, either intentionally or through negligence.

Pro hac vice   The permission granted by a court to an out-of-state lawyer to appear in a particular case as though admitted to practice in that jurisdiction.

Pro per   A nonlawyer representing himself or herself in a legal matter.

Pro se   A nonlawyer representing himself or herself in a legal matter.

Real estate closing   The consummation of the sale of real estate by payment of the purchase price, delivery of the deed, and finalizing collateral matters, such as mortgage, insurance, and taxes.

Reprimand   The least serious of the sanctions that can be placed on a lawyer for unethical conduct; it may be public or private.

Reproval   Another word for reprimand, used in some states.

Retainer fee   A fee for legal services paid to assure the availability of the lawyer to handle specified matters whether or not any such matters arise during the retainer period.

Screen/screening   The isolation of a person from participation in a matter through the timely imposition of procedures within a firm that are reasonably adequate under the circumstances to protect information that the person is obligated to protect under the ethics rules or the attorney-client privilege.

Self-representation   The act of representing oneself in legal proceedings before a tribunal.

Simultaneous representation The representation of clients in current legal matters that involve a conflict of interest.

Spoilation Destruction of evidence that may result in a civil cause of action for damages for interference with the ability to prove a claim or defense.

Subject matter test The test applied by some courts to determine whether communications in a corporate setting are covered by the attorney-client privilege; under this test, communications with corporate employees are privileged if they related to the legal matter being discussed.

Subornation of perjury The criminal offense of encouraging another to commit perjury.

Successive representation The representation of clients in a conflict of interest situation involving a current matter and a former client whose interests conflict.

Suspension The temporary removal of a lawyer's license to practice law for a stated period.

Testamentary Through a will.

Unconscionable So unreasonable as to render a contract unenforceable, usually because the terms are so favorable to one party.

Unlawful detainer assistant Title granted by the California legislature for persons who provide legal-clerical services to persons representing themselves in matters relating to evictions.

Vicarious disqualification The imputation of a conflict to others in a firm so that the entire firm is disqualified from undertaking the representation.

Whistleblower statutes Statutes that protect and/or reward persons who reveal unlawful practices.

Will execution The formal process of signing and witnessing of a will.

Work product rule The rule of evidence that protects the work done by a lawyer and his or her employees and agents in the process of representing a client in litigation.

Index

ABA. *See* American Bar Association (ABA)
Abuse of process, action for, 157
Access to legal services, limited, 10, 19–20, 190
Accident victims
  direct-mail advertising targeted to, 90–92
  solicitation of, 98–100
Administrative agencies
  defined, 26, 27
  examples of, 28
  nonlawyer practice before, 27–28
Administrative Procedure Act, 27
Advanced fees, 113
Adverse controlling authority, disclosure of, 159
Advertising, 89–102. *See also* Solicitation
  advent and evolution of lawyer, 90–91
  areas of law, 90
  certification, 91, 93
  comparison, 92
  creating unjustified expectations, 92
  current ethics rules, 92–94
  current issues and trends in, 94–98
  direct-mail, 91
    targeted to accident and disaster victims, 91
  disclaimers, 93
  dramatizations, 92
  false or misleading, 92
  of fee information, 92
  Internet, 94, 96–97
  media, 94
  of past performance, 95
  testimonials, 92
  trade names in, 93

Agents
  attorney's
    attorney-client privilege and, 45
    define, 45
    contact with unrepresented persons through, 164
  solicitation and, 99
Aggravating and mitigating factors, sanctions decisions and, 4
Alcohol dependency, 141, 147, 181
"Ambulance chasers," 98
American Association for Paralegal Education (AAfPE), 6, 135, 186
American Bar Association (ABA), 2, 164
  Canons of Professional Ethics (1908), 3
  curriculum for paralegals, guidelines for, 6
  Ethics 2000. *See* Ethics 2000
  ethics advisory opinions, 3
    Ethics Opinion 88–1521, 81
    Formal Opinion 95–396 (1995), 164
    Formal Opinion 331 (1974), 166
    on inadvertent disclosure, 47–48
  House of Delegates 117
  licensing of paralegals, stance on, 8
  membership of, 2–3
  Model Code of Professional Ethics. *See* Model Code of Professional Responsibility, ABA (1969)
  Model Guidelines for the Utilization of Paralegal Services. *See* Model Guidelines for the Utilization of Paralegal Services, ABA
  Model Rules of Professional Conduct. *See* Model Rules of Professional Conduct, ABA (1983)

American Bar Association (*Continued*)
 paralegal programs approved by, 135
 regulation of lawyers by, 2–3
 Standards for Criminal Justice, 168
 Standing Committee on Paralegals, 6
American Civil Liberties Union (ACLU), 99
Anti-virus software, 56
Appearance in court. *See* Court appearances
Appearance of impropriety, conflicts of interest
  and, 70
Arbitration, 70
Arizona, 8, 10, 19
Associations, paralegal, 6–7. *See also individual
  associations*
 codes of ethics. *See Codes of ethics*
Attorney-client privilege, 28, 29, 44–49
 corporate client and, 49
 court-ordered disclosure, 50
 defined, 44
 disclosure to parties other than client's lawyer, 45
 exceptions and waivers, 45, 48
 inadvertent disclosure, 46–48
 matters not covered by, 45–46
Attorney-client relationships
 as fiduciary relationship, 28–29, 44
 scope of representation, 29
 unauthorized practice of law and
  establishing, 28–29
Attorney review of paralegal work, 145
Audits
 corporate internal, and attorney-client
  privilege, 49
 of legal bills, 111, 122

Bankruptcy filings by nonlawyer legal service
  providers, 20
 Court Rules, 117
Bar associations
 American Bar Association. *See* American Bar
  Association (ABA)
 efforts to improve image of lawyers, 180
 pro bono work encouraged by, 189
 state, 2
 unauthorized practice of law and, 19
Barratry, 73
Bates v. State Bar of Arizona, 35, 90
Billable hours, 110, 179
Billing practices, 110, 143
 ethics rules about, 110–112
Board of directors of corporate client, serving
  on, 69
Bonuses, 118
Bookkeeping for client funds and property,
  122–124
Borrowing from client, 72
Branding, 95
Bribery
 of judges, 161–162
 of jurors, 162

Brochures, law firm, 95
Burnout, 181
Business cards, 35, 94
Business transactions with clients, conflicts of
  interest and, 72, 115, 143
 code of professional ethics for lawyers, 3
 fee arrangements and, 109
 inadvertent disclosure in, 47
 nonlawyer legal service providers, regulation
  of, 10
 regulation of lawyers in, 2
 regulation of paralegals in, 8–9
 representation by counsel related to
  opposing counsel, 76–77
 screening of paralegals, 80
 solicitation of accident victims, 98–99
 testamentary gifts from clients, 74

California Alliance of Paralegal Associations, 8,
  12
California Business and Professions Code, 107
Canada, fee shifting in, 115
Candor to the court, lawyer's duty of,
  159–161
Canons of Professional Ethics, ABA (1908), 3
Cappers and runners, 98
Cellular telephones, confidentiality issues for, 55
Certification, 7
 advertising of lawyer, 91, 93
 programs for paralegals, 6, 7, 8, 93–94, 136
Certified Legal Assistant (CLA) program, 6, 7,
  8, 12, 13, 41
Champerty, 73
Chat groups, 199
Child support proceedings,
  contingency fees and, 107
Chinese wall (screen), 80
Claim or defense
 bringing unmeritorious or frivolous, 155, 157
 revealing confidential information to
  establish, 51
Class action suits
 conflicts of interest in representation, 67
 solicitation exception for, 99
Client contact, 29
Client files, policy for handling, 123
Client funds and property, 122–123
 client security funds, 122
 client trust accounts, 120–121
 Interest on Lawyers' Trust Accounts
  (IOLTA), 122
 other client property and files, 122–123
Client perjury, 160
Client security funds, 122
Client selection, 143
Client surveys, 95
Client trust accounts, 114, 120–121, 143
Code of Ethics and Professional Responsibility,
  NALA, 12, (Appendix B)

Canon 3(b), 113
Canon 3(c), 65, 100
Canon 5, 35
Canon 6, 136
Canon 7, 53, 65
Codes of ethics
American Bar Association
Canons of Professional Ethics, 3
Ethics 2000. *See* Ethics 2000
Model Code of Professional
Responsibility. *See* Model Code of
Professional Responsibility, ABA
(1969)
Model Rules of Professional
Conduct. *See* Model Rules of
Professional Conduct, ABA (1983)
for Paralegals
Code of Ethics and Professional
Responsibility, NALA. *See* Code of
Ethics and Professional Responsibility,
NALA
of local and regional associations, 12
Model Code of Ethics and Professional
Responsibility, NFPA. *See* Model
Code of Ethics and Professional
Responsibility, NFPA
Model Disciplinary Rules, NFPA, 11
Commingling of funds, 120
Communications
with clients, competence and, 139–140
with judges, 161–162
with jurors, 162–163
with parties and represented persons, 163
with unrepresented persons, 164
with witnesses, 164–165
Competence, 137–140
definition of, 137
communication with clients, 139
diligence and promptness, 139
knowledge and, 137–138
skills and, 138
thoroughness and preparation, 139
incompetence, 156
sanctions for, 140, 156
knowing limits of one's, 143
legal education
of lawyers, 134–135
of paralegals, 135–136
overview, 137
paralegal, 137, 144
sanctions for incompetence, 140
Computerized litigation support systems, work
product doctrine and, 47
Computer programs
anti-virus, 56
for conflicts checks, 81
for form preparation, 32
unauthorized practice of law
considerations, 33
Computers, measures to protect confidentiality
of, 56

Concurrent representation. *See* Simultaneous
representation, conflicts of interest and
Cone of silence (screen), 80
Confidences and secrets, 51
Confidentiality, 43–62, 64, 143
agreements, 54
attorney-client privilege. *See* Attorney-client
privilege
conflicts of interest and duty of, 64
ethics rules of, 51–52
information becoming public and, 51
paralegal and, 52–54, 78
application of rules, 52–53
in daily practice, 52–54
technology, special issues relating to,
55–57
principle of, 44
work product rule, 50
Conflicts of interest, 63–89
business transactions with clients,
72–74, 143
conflicts checks, 82–84
duty of confidentiality and, 64
financial assistance to clients, 73
gifts from clients, 74–75
imputed or vicarious. *See* Imputed or
vicarious conflicts of interest
literary rights, 73
malpractice liability, contact with clients
limiting lawyer's, 75–76
media rights, 73
motions to disqualify counsel, 5
overview, 64–65
proprietary interest in litigation, 74
publication rights, 73
relatives of lawyers, 76–77
sexual relations with clients, 77–78
simultaneous representation. *See*
Simultaneous representation, conflicts
of interest and
statutory fees and, 115–117
successive representation, 70–72
defining "substantial relationship," 71
general rules, 70–72
third party payments of attorneys' fees, 76
Consent
to business transactions with client, 72
to representation by counsel related to
opposing counsel, 78
for simultaneous representation, 65, 66
Constitutional rights, prosecutorial violation
of, 170
Consumer fraud suits against lawyers, 141
Contempt power of courts, 5, 157, 158, 161
Contingency fees, 106–107
limitations on, 107
sliding scale, 107
written agreements, 107, 112
Continuing education programs, 136
Control group test for determining the
corporate client, 49

Conversion of client funds, 121, 123
Co-parties to litigation, simultaneous
    representation of, 68
Cordless telephones, confidentiality issues
    for, 55
Corporate clients
    attorney-client privilege and, 48
    billing practices, steps to prevent
        unscrupulous, 112
    conflicts of interest arising with, 68–70
    internal audits and attorney-client
        privilege, 49
    securities work for, 142
Corporate setting, contact with unrepresented
    persons in, 164
Costs of litigation. *See* Expenses
Counseling programs, 181
Court appearances, 154
    unauthorized practice of law and, 24–28
Court facilitators, 10
Court-ordered disclosure and attorney-client
    privilege, 49–50
Credit card, payment of legal fees by, 114
Crime, future. *See* Future crime or fraud
Criminal charges, prosecutor's duty not to
    institute unsupported, 168
Criminal defendants
    communication with represented
        persons, 163
    contingency fees and, 107
    third party payment of attorneys' fees for, 76
Criminal prosecution for violation of statutes
    regulating lawyer conduct, 5
Criticism of judges, inappropriate, 161

Databases, work product rule and protection of
    information in, 54
Defense or claim
    bringing unmeritorious or frivolous,
        155–157
    revealing confidential information to
        establish, 52
Delaying litigation, unethically, 158–159
Depositions
    attendance by paralegals, 24–25
    defined, 24
Destruction of evidence, 161
Direct-mail advertising, 91, 93, 95
    targeted, to accident and disaster victims, 91
Disabilities, 188
Disaster victims, direct-mail advertising
    targeting, 91
Disbarment, 4
Disciplinary proceedings, 140, 167, 179
Disclaimers, advertising, 93, 97
Disclosure of information that tends to negate
    or mitigate guilt or reduce punishment,
    prosecutor's duty of, 167
Disclosure of status as legal assistant, 33–35

Discovery
    abuses of the process of, 157, 179
    streamlining, 156, 179
Dismissal of charges, 168
Disobeying a court order, 158
Disqualification of counsel, 64, 78–81, 163
    motions to disqualify. *See* Motions to
        disqualify counsel
Disruptive conduct in the courtroom,
    158–159
Divorce
    arbitration and mediation, 70
    contingency fees and, 109
    nonlawyer assistance to pro se defendants, 33
    simultaneous representation, 68, 70
Document production, inadvertent disclosure
    during, 47–48
Do-it-yourself legal kits, 32
Double-billing, 111
Drug dependency problems, 141, 147, 178, 181

Edenfield v. Fane, 98
Education of lawyers, 134–135
Education of paralegals. *See* Training programs
    for paralegals
800 telephone numbers, law firms with, 96
Electronic identification cards (smart cards), 56
Electronic mail (e-mail)
    advertising, 93
    prompt response to client, 143
    protecting confidentiality and, 56–57
    solicitation by, 93
Electronic records, confidentiality of, 56–57
E-mail. *See* Electronic mail (e-mail)
Encryption software, 56, 57
Engagement letters, 142
England, fee shifting in, 115
Estate of deceased lawyer, fees paid to, 119
Estate planning, 142
Ethics 2000, 3
Ethics, teaching, 180
Ethics advisory opinions, 3–4, 81
    ABA. *See* American Bar Association (ABA),
        ethics advisory opinions
Ethics or conflicts committees, law firm, 81
Executor, naming lawyer drafting a document
    as, 74
Exempt or nonexempt status of paralegals, 187
Ex parte communications
    with judges, 162
    with jurors, 162
    with unrepresented persons, 164
Expenses
    advancing or guaranteeing, of litigation, 73
    fee agreement stipulations about, 113
    witness, payment of, 166
Expert witnesses
    conflicts of interest involving, 67
    expenses, payment of, 166

fees, 166
Extra-judicial statements, preventing persons
    involved with the prosecution from
    making, 168

Facsimile communications, confidentiality
    issues of, 55
Fair Labor Standards Act, 187
Fair trial, right to a, 166
False evidence, offering, 159
False statements of fact or law, 159
False testimony, 160, 165, 166
Family relationships
    conflicts of interest based on, 77–78
    nonlawyer representation in court, 26
Faretta v. California, 26
Federal Electronic Communications Privacy
    Act, 55
Federal Rules of Civil Procedure
    Rule 11, 157
    work product doctrine, 50
Federal Torts Claims Act, 107
Fees, 105–131, 178
    advanced, 113
    advertising of, 92
    alternative arrangements, 108
    attorney-client privilege and fee
        arrangements, 46–47
    common fund for, 115
    contingency. *See* Contingency fees
    credit card payment of, 114
    disgorging, on disqualification of counsel, 78
    disputes, resolution of, 113
    ethics rules about, 109–113
    expert witness, 166
    fee-shifting statutes, 115
    fee-splitting, 118–119
    fixed, 106
    forwarding, 118
    hourly, 108, 113
    illegal, 109
    liens to secure, 73
    for paralegal time, 116
    partnerships of lawyer and nonlawyer and
        dividing, 119
    percentage of the worth of the matter, 107
    petitions to the court for paralegal fees,
        116–117
    property as payment of, 114
    referral, 100, 119
    retainers, 114
    screens and sharing of, 80
    seizure of fee paid with assets obtained
        through illegal activities, 46
    "setting" vs. "quoting," 28, 113
    splitting, 118
    statutory awards, 115–117
    terms and communication of fee
        arrangements with clients, 113

third parry payment of, 76
    unauthorized practice of law and setting
        of, 28
    unreasonable or excessive, 109
    written agreements, 107, 112, 143
        fee dispute resolution clause, 115
        language of, 115
        malpractice claim resolution clause, 114
        on payment of costs, 114
Fiduciary relationship of lawyer and client,
    28, 44
Financial assistance to clients, 73
Firewalls, 56
Fixed fees, 106
Flat fees, 106
Fleeing of jurisdiction, advising witness on, 164
Florida, 9, 19, 91
Florida Bar v. Went For It, Inc., 91
Florida Legal Assistants, Inc., 8
Forwarding fees, 118
Fraud, future. *See* Future crime or fraud
Free expression, right of, 166
Freelance paralegals, 35
    conflicts checks, 82
    screening of, 82
Frivolous claims or defenses, asserting, 155
Future crime or fraud
    attorney-client privilege and, 48

Gag order, 166
Gender-related issues far paralegals, 188
Gifts from clients, 74–75
Government lawyers
    screens to overcome imputed disqualification
        of law firm, 80
    successive representation, 71
Grant v. Thirteenth Court of Appeals, 82

Habeas corpus writs, prisoner preparation
    of, 32
Hickman v. Taylor, 50
History of paralegal profession, 5–7
Honesty, 159
    special rules for prosecutors, 167
Hourly fees, 108, 113

*Ibanez v. Florida Dept. of Business and Professional
    Regulations*, 91
Idaho
    fee-shifting statute, 116
Identity of client, attorney-client privilege
    and, 45
Immigration "consultants," 20
Imputed disqualification
    simultaneous representation, 67

Imputed or vicarious conflicts of interest, 64, 67, 78–82
  defined, 79
  general rules, 79–80
  use of screens, 79–81
Inadvertent disclosure and attorney-client privilege, 46–48
In camera examination, 49
Incompetence. *See* Competence
Independent contractor paralegals, 36
Independent counsel, 72
Independent professional judgment, 76
Influencing judges, attempts at, 161
Informational material and work product rule, 50
Injunctive relief for unauthorized practice of Law, 22
In propria persona, 26
In re Complex Asbestos Litigation, 81
In re Primus, 99
In re R.M.J., 90
Insider Trading and Securities Fraud Enforcement Act of 1988, 55
Insider trading rules, 55
Insurance
  legal fees paid by, 111
  malpractice, 140, 142
  paralegal misconduct, lawyer coverage for, 13
Integrated bar associations, 2
Interest on Lawyers, Trust Accounts (IOLTA), 122
Intermediary, conflicts of interest when serving as, 68
Internal Revenue Service, 46
International Paralegal Management Association (IPMA), 6, 7, 9, 186
Internet
  advertising, 96–97
  e-mail. *See* Electronic mail (e-mail)
  legal information or legal advice on unauthorized practice of law, 33
Inter vivos gifts from clients, 74
IOLTA (Interest on Lawyers, Trust Accounts), 122
Issue conflicts, 67–68

Jailhouse lawyers, 31
Job opportunities for paralegals, 6
Johnson v. Avery, 31
Judges, relationships and communications with, 161
Judiciary
  state courts. *See* State courts
  Supreme Court. *See* Supreme Court
Jurors
  ex parte communications with, 162
  improper conduct toward or among, duty to reveal, 162

jury tampering, 162, 164
post-trial communications with, 162

Laptop computers, confidentiality measures for, 56
Law school education, 134–135
Law students, representation in court by, 26
Lawyer referral services, fees to, 119
Legal advice
  prohibition of nonlawyers from giving, 29–33
    examples, 30–31
    exceptions, 31
    nonlawyer legal service providers and related trends, 32–33
  securing of, revealing of confidential information for, 51
  to unrepresented persons, 164
  on Web sites, 96
Legal aid organizations, 6, 90
Legal assistant. *See* Paralegals
Legal Assistant Management Association, *See* International Paralegal Management Association
  licensing of paralegals, stance on, 9
  membership of, 7
Legal document assistants, 10, 19
Legal document preparers, 10, 19
Legal marketing, 94
Legal Services Corporation, funding of, 19
Leibowitz v. Eigth Jud. *D.,* 81
Letterhead, 94
  paralegals listed on, 35, 94
Licensing
  of attorneys, 1, 7
  defined, 7
  of paralegals, 7
    arguments against, 9–10
    arguments favoring, 9
    stance of paralegal associations, 9
Liens to secure fees or expenses, 73
Literary rights, 73
Litigiousness of society, 154, 178
Living costs, advancing a client, 73
Living trusts, 20
Location of client, attorney-client privilege and, 44
Louisiana State Paralegal Association, 8
Loyalty, duty of, 64, 77

Maine, regulation of paralegals, 8
Malicious prosecution, action for, 157
Malpractice insurance, 140, 142
Malpractice suits, civil, 5, 141–143
  advice for lawyers and paralegals, 143
  agreements with clients limiting lawyer's liability, 75–76

fee agreement clause regarding, 113
trends in, 141–143
Marital relationship, *See* spouse
Medical malpractice cases, contingency fees
    in, 107
Mental impressions and work product rule, 50
Michigan fee-shifting statute, 116
Missouri v. Jenkins, 109, 116
Mistrial, 162
Model Code of Ethics and Professional
    Responsibility NFPA, 12,
    (Appendix C)
  DR 1.1, 136
  DR 1.2, 112
  DR 1.3, 12, 179
  DR 1.5, 53
  DR 1.6, 65
  DR 1.7, 35, 93
  EC 1.2, 14, 162
  EC 1.2(e), 124
  EC 1.3, 159
  EC 1.4(d), 190
  reporting of ethical of legal violations, 179
Model Code of Professional Responsibility,
    ABA, 3
  advertising by lawyers, 90
  Canon 2, 190
  Canon 4, 51
  Canon 7, 155
  Canon 9, 70
  DR 2-101 to 2-105, 92
  DR 2-106, 109
  DR 2-107, 118
  DR 3-102, 118
  DR 3-103, 120
  DR 4-101, 51
  DR 5-101, 72
  DR 5-103(A), 73
  DR 5-103(B), 73
  DR 5-104(B), 73
  DR 5-105, 79
  DR 5-106, 68
  DR 5-107(A), 76
  DR 6-102, 75
  DR 7-102, 155, 159
  DR 7-102(A), 156
  DR 7-102(A)(l), 156, 165
  DR 7-102(A)(4), 166
  DR 7-103(A), 168
  DR 7-103(B), 168
  DR 7-104(A)(l), 163
  DR 7-106, 159
  DR 7-106(A), 158
  DR 7-106(C)(2), 165
  DR 7-106(C)(6), 158
  DR 7-108(A), 162
  DR 7-108(D), 163
  DR 7-108(G), 163
  DR 7-108(J), 167
  DR 7-109, 159
  DR 7-109(A), 165

  DR 7-109(B), 164
  DR 7-109(C), 166
  DR 7-110(B), 162
  DR 8-102(A), 161
  DR 9-101, 71
  DR 9-101(C), 162
  DR 9-102(A), 120
  EC 3-5, 22
  EC 5-5, 74
  states with codes based on, 3
Model Disciplinary Rules, NPPA, 12
Model Guidelines for the Utilization of
    Paralegal Services, ABA,
    (Appendix A), 11
  Guideline 1, 24, 100, 145
  Guideline 2, 24
  Guideline 3(b), 113
  Guideline 4, 34
  Guideline 6, 53
  Guideline 7, 64, 81
  Guideline 8, 109
  Guideline 9, 118
  Guideline 10, 190
  Purpose of, 11
Model Rules of Professional Conduct,
    ABA 3, 69
  Rule 1.2(C), 76
  Rule 1.3, 155
  Rule 1.5, 109
  Rule 1.5(b), 112
  Rule 1.5(c), 112
  Rule 1.5(d)(l), 107
  Rule 1.5(d)(2), 107
  Rule 1.5(e), 118
  Rule 1.6, 51
  Rule 1.7, 65, 77
  Rule 1.8, 68
  Rule 1.8(a), 72
  Rule 1.8(c), 74
  Rule 1.8(d), 73
  Rule 1.8(e), 73
  Rule 1.8(f), 76
  Rule 1.8(h), 76
  Rule 1.8(i), 73
  Rule 1.8(j), 77
  Rule 1.9, 71
  Rule 1.10, 79
  Rule 1.11, 71
  Rule 1.15(a), 120
  Rule 1.15(d), 123
  Rule 1.15(a), 120
  Rule 3.1, 155
  Rule 3.2, 156
  Rule 3.3(a), 159, 160
  Rule 3.3(b), 160
  Rule 3.4(a), 159
  Rule 3.4(b), 165, 166
  Rule 3.4(c), 158
  Rule 3.4(d), 156
  Rule 3.4(f), 164
  Rule 3.5(a), 162

Model Rules of Professional
Conduct (*Continued*)
  Rule 3.5(b), 162
  Rule 3.5(c), 158, 165
  Rule 3.6, 167
  Rule 3.8(a), 168
  Rule 3.8(b), 168
  Rule 3.8(c), 168
  Rule 3.8(d), 168
  Rule 3.8(e), 168
  Rule 3.8(f), 167
  Rule 4.2, 163
  Rule 4.3, 164
  Rule 4.4, 168
  Rule 4.4(a), 163, 165
  Rule 5.3, 13, 23, 167
  Rule 5.4, 118
  Rule 5.4(a), 118
  Rule 5.4(b), 120
  Rule 5.4(c), 76
  Rule 5.5, 21
  Rule 6.1, 190
  Rule 8.2(a), 161
  Rule 8.3(a), 179
  Rule 8.4(e), 162
  Rule 8.4(f), 162
  Rule 7.1 to 7.5, 92
  states adopting, 3
Monetary sanctions, 157
Motions to disqualify counsel, 64, 78–81
  as strategy to delay or harass the
    opposition, 79
Multidisciplinary practice, 120
Multijurisdictional practice and unauthorized
  practice of law, 21

NAACP v. Button, 99
NALS, 6
National Association for the Advancement of
  Colored people (NAACP), 99
National Association of Law Firm Marketing
  Administrators, 94
National Association of Legal Assistants
  (NALA), 6–7
  Certified legal Assistant (CLA) program, 6,
    7, 8, 93, 136, 182
  CLA Specialist examination, 136
  CP, *See* CLA
  code of ethics. *See* Code of Ethics and
    Professional Responsibility, NALA
  contacting, 12
  Guideline V, 109
  Guideline IV, 53
  licensing of paralegals, stance on, 9
  membership of, 6–7
National Federation of Paralegal Associations
  (NFPA), 6, 7, 8, 190
  contacting, 12
  membership of, 6–7

Paralegal Advanced Competency
  Examination (PACE), 6, 7, 8, 136, 185
Network administration, 56
Newsletters, law firm, 95
New York
  regulation of lawyers in, 2
  titles that may be used by paralegals in, 35
Nix v. Whiteside, 160
Nonexempt status of paralegals, 187
Nonlawyer legal service providers, *See also*
  Unauthorized practice of law
  areas for practice, 19
  need for, 19–20
  regulation of, 10
  right to self-representation and, 26
North Carolina regulation, 8

Obstruction of justice statutes, 161, 165
Ohralik v. Ohio State Bar Association, 98
On-the-job training, 138
Oregon, voluntary certification program for
  paralegals, 8
Over-coaching witnesses, 165

Paralegal Advanced Competency Examination
  (PACE), 6, 7, 8, 136
Paralegals
  advertising by lawyers, paralegals names used
    in, 93
  billable hours, 110
  billing abuses and, 110
  billing time of, 109, 116–117
  bonuses, 119
  certification of, 6, 7, 8
  codes of ethics. *See* Codes of ethics, for paralegals
  competence, 135–141
  confidentiality and, *See* Confidentiality,
    paralegal and
  conflicts of interest, 75, 77, 82–84
  court appearances in uncontested matters, 26
  definition of, 7
  exempt or nonexempt status of, 187
  fee splitting with, 118–119
  gender issues, 188
  history of the professional, 5–7
  marketing role of, 95
  other terms for, 7
  pro bono work by, 189–190
  professionalization of the occupation, 181–185
    acting with integrity and honor, 184
    commitment to excellence, 184
    commitment to paralegal profession, 184
    development of the whole person, 185
    education, 183–184
    exercising good judgment, common
      sense, and communication skills, 185
    highest standards of ethical conduct, 184

public service, 183
strong work ethic, 184
profit-based compensation for, 119
referral fees, 119
regulation of. *See* Regulation of paralegals
represented persons, communication
with, 163
screening of, 79–80
titles that may be used by, 35, 94
treatment of, 186–187
trial publicity and, 167
unauthorized practice of law. *See*
Unauthorized practice of law
unrepresented persons, communication
with, 164
utilization of, 186–187
Paraprofessionals, classification of paralegals as,
183
Partnerships with nonlawyers, 119
dividing legal fees and, 119–120
Partners in law firms, disciplinary action
and, 5
Passwords, computer, 56
*Peel v. Attorney Registration and Disciplinary
Commission of Illinois*, 91
Perception of lawyers, public, 178
Perjury
by client or witness, 160, 165
subornation of, 165
Personal problems, 141
Phoenix Founders, Inc. v. Marshall, 81
Pleadings
defined, 25–26
unauthorized practice of law, 25–26
Pleas, collective, 68
Post-trial communications with jurors,
162–163
Practice of law
definitions of, 22
unauthorized. *See* unauthorized practice
of law
Preexisting documents, attorney-client
privilege and, 46
Preparing witnesses, 166
Prerecorded telephone messages, 99
Probable cause for criminal charges, 168
Probate matters, percentage of worth fees for,
106
Probation, 4
Pro bono work, 189–190
Procrastination, 140
Professionalism of lawyers, 178–179
Profit-based compensation, 118
Pro hac vice, 21
Propria persona. *See* Pro se
Prosecutors, special rules for, 167–168
Pro se, 26
nonlawyer legal service providers, advice
from, 33
Publication rights, 73
Public defender's office, 77

Public interest work, 189–190
Publicity, trial, 166–167
Public opinion, trial publicity to influence, 167

Racial bias, 188
Rainmakers, 95
Real estate transactions
closings, 30
conflicts of interest, 69–70, 72–73
Record keeping for client funds and property,
122–124
Referral fees, 100, 119
Registered Paralegal designation, 6, 136
Regulation of lawyers, 1–5
by American Bar Association codes of ethics
of, 2–3
by case law, 4
by ethics advisory opinions, 4
by integrated state bar associations, 2
sanctions and remedies used in, 4–5
by state courts, 2
by state statutes, 3–4
Regulation of paralegals, 5–12, 183,
185–186
codes of ethics and guidelines of paralegal
associations, 11–12
direct, 7–11
responsibility of lawyers and paralegals for
paralegal conduct. *See* Supervisory or
managerial authority of lawyers
state guidelines for the utilization of
paralegals, 11
Relatives. *See* Family relationships
Represented persons, communication with,
163
Reprimand, 4
Retainer fees, 114
Retirement plans, 118
Review of legal bills, 112
Right to counsel, informing accused of, 168
Runners and cappers, 98

Safe deposit boxes, 122
Safe harbors, multijurisdictional issues and, 21
Salaries of lawyers, 180
Sanctions and remedies
for ethical misconduct of lawyers, 4–5, 157
for incompetence, 140–141
Sarbanes-Oxley Act, 49
Savings and loan crisis, 142
Scope of representation, limiting, 76
Screens to overcome imputed disqualification,
79–82
Securities law, 141
Self-assessment, 146
Self-help legal kits, 32
Self-representation, right of, 26

Settlements
  aggregate, for lawyer representing multiple clients, 66
  negotiations, unauthorized practice of law and, 31
Sex discrimination, 188
Sexual harassment, 188
Sexual orientation, discrimination based on, 188
Sexual relations with clients, 77–78, 188
Shapero v. Kentucky Bar Association, 91
Sherman Antitrust Act, 8
Signing of correspondence by paralegals, 35
Simultaneous representation, conflicts of interest and, 65–70
  consents, 66
  examples
    in litigated matters, 68
    in non-litigated matters, 68–69
  general rules, 66
  imputed disqualification, 67
  issue conflicts and other indirect simultaneous conflicts, 67
  withdrawal to avoid conflicts, 67
Sliding scale for contingency fees, 107
Smart cards (electronic identification cards), 56
Smart Industries Corp. v. Superior Court, 81
Snitch rules, 179
Solicitation, 98–101. *See also* Advertising
South Dakota
  regulation of paralegals, 8
Spam, 97
Spoliation, cause of action for, 161
Spouse
  conflicts of interest involving, 76
  representation by nonlawyer in court, 26
State bar associations, ethics advisory opinions, 3
State bar associations, regulation of lawyers by, 2
State courts, regulation of lawyers by, 2
Stress, 181
Subject matter test for determining the corporate client, 49
Subornation of perjury, 165
Substance abuse. *See* Alcohol dependency; Drug dependency problems
Substantial likelihood of materially prejudicing an adjudicative proceeding, 166
"Substantial relationship" successive representation and, 71
Successive representation, conflicts of interest and, 70–72
  defining "substantial relationship," 71
  general rules, 70–71
Supervisory or managerial authority of lawyers 12–13
  inadequate exercise of, 20–21, 145–146
  independent contractor paralegals and, 36
Suppression of evidence, 163, 165
Supreme Court, U.S.

attorney-client privilege and, 46–47
Bates v. State Bar Arizona, 35, 90
Edenfield v. Fane, 98
Florida Bar v. Went For It, Inc., 91
Hickman v. Taylor, 50
Ibanez v. Florida Dept. of Business and Professional Regulations, 91
Johnson v. Avery, 31
Missouri v. Jenkins, 109, 116
Nix v. Whiteside, 160
Peel v. Attorney Registration and Disciplinary Commission of Illinois, 91
In re R. M. J., 90
Shapero v. Kentucky Bar Association, 91
Zauderer v. Office of Disciplinary Counsel of Supreme Court of Ohio, 91
Surcharges, 111
Suspension, 4

Tampering with a jury, 162
Tape recording of a person without permission, 165
Technological advances, keeping abreast of, 137
Termination of representation, letters for, 142
Testamentary gifts from clients, 74
Third parties
  malpractice claims of, 140
  payment of attorneys' fees by, 76
Threaded discussions, 97
Titles that paralegals may use, 34–35, 94
Tort liability for professional negligence, 134
Trade names in advertising, 93
Training programs for paralegals, 6, 138, 186
  ABA approved, 135
  ABA curriculum guidelines, 6
Treatment of paralegals, 186–187
Trial publicity, 166–167
Trustee, naming lawyer drafting a document as, 75
Typing services for legal documents, 32

Unauthorized practice of law, 17–36
  administrative agencies, nonlawyer practice before, 26–27
  conduct that constitutes, 24–33
  court appearances, 24–28
  disclosure of status as paralegal and job titles, 33–35
  establishing the attorney-client relationship, 28–29
  giving legal advice, 29–33
  history of, 18–19
  independent contractors, paralegals as, 36
  as misdemeanor, 23
  multijurisdictional practice issues, nonlawyer legal service providers, 19–22

practice of law. *See* Practice of law
  remedies, 23
  responsibility of lawyer to prevent, 23
  trends in, 19–21
U.S. Department of Labor, 187
Unlawful detainer assistants, 10, 19
Unlawful detainer/summary ejection
    proceedings, 19, 31
Unmeritorious claims or defenses, bringing,
    155–158
Unrepresented persons, contact with, 164
Unwarranted actions, bringing, 155
Utilization of paralegals, 52–53

Virginia Alliance of Legal Assistant
    Associations, 12
Viruses, computer, 56
Visa consultants, 20

Waivers of conflicts, 66
  of attorney-client privilege, 45–46
Washington, regulation of nonlawyer legal
    service providers in, 11
Web sites
  advertising on, 96–97
  providing legal information, 96

Whereabouts of client, attorney-client privilege
    and, 45, 46
Whistleblower statutes, 179
Wills
  drafting of, simultaneous representation
    and, 69
  execution of, 30
Withdrawal from representation, 67
Witnesses
  advising or causing flight of the
    jurisdiction, 164
  advising to hide or avoid testifying, 164
  advising to testify falsely, 165
  contact of lawyers with, 159–166
  expert. *See* Expert witnesses
  false testimony, 160, 165–166
  harassing, 165
  interviewing, 165
  over-coaching, 165
  payment for expenses, 166
  perjury by, 160, 165
  preparing, 165
Witnessing a will, 30
Work product rule, 50

Zauderer v. Office of Disciplinary Counsel of
    Supreme Court of Ohio, 91
Zealous representation, 77, 155, 178